Introducing Archaeology

Introducing Archaeology

ROBERT J. MUCKLE

broadview press

Library and Archives Canada Cataloguing in Publication

Muckle, Robert James

Introducing archaeology / Robert J. Muckle.

Includes bibliographical references and index.
ISBN-13: 978-1-55111-505-4
ISBN-10: 1-55111-505-0

1. Archaeology—Textbooks. I. Title.

CC165.M83 2006 930.1 C2006-903842-2

Broadview Press is an independent, international publishing house, incorporated in 1985. Broadview believes in shared ownership, both with its employees and with the general public; since the year 2000 Broadview shares have traded publicly on the Toronto Venture Exchange under the symbol BDP.

We welcome comments and suggestions regarding any aspect of our publications–please feel free to contact us at the addresses below or at broadview@broadviewpress.com / www.broadviewpress.com

North America
PO Box 1243, Peterborough, Ontario, Canada K9J 7H5
Tel: (705) 743-8990; Fax: (705) 743-8353
email: customerservice@broadviewpress.com
3576 California Road, PO Box 1015, Orchard Park, NY, USA 14127

UK, Ireland, and continental Europe
NBN International
Estover Road
Plymouth PL6 7PY UK
Tel: 44 (0) 1752 202 300
Fax: 44 (0) 1752 202 330
email: enquiries@nbninternational.com

Australia and New Zealand
UNIREPS, University of New South Wales
Sydney, NSW, 2052
Australia
Tel: 61 2 9664 0999; Fax: 61 2 9664 5420
email: info.press@unsw.edu.au

Broadview Press gratefully acknowledges the financial support of the Government of Canada through the Book Publishing Industry Development Program for our publishing activities.

PRINTED IN CANADA

Contents

List of Figures

List of Tables

Note to Instructors

This book is designed as a textbook for introductory archaeology courses as they are taught in most colleges and universities in North America: with the focus on methods. It is deliberately concise, offering the option of combining it with a package of readings or a case study. The concise nature of this text also makes it suitable to be used as one of multiple books in introductory courses that combine methods with world prehistory, archaeology with biological anthropology, or all four branches of anthropology together (archaeology, biological anthropology, cultural anthropology, and linguistics). But the coverage is broad enough that some instructors may wish to use it as the sole required reading for a course.

The development of the book has been guided by the principles of curriculum reform articulated in the early twenty-first century by the Society for American Archaeology (SAA). In the late 1990s, the SAA concluded that the archaeology curriculum at colleges and universities needed serious revision. This conclusion was supported by the American Anthropological Association, the Archaeological Institute of America, the Canadian Archaeological Association, the National Association of State Archaeologists, and the Society for Historical Archaeology.

To bring the teaching of archaeology more into line with the reality of archaeology in the real world today, the SAA promotes seven principles for curriculum reform at all levels of college and university education, which revolve around making students explicitly aware of (i) the nonrenewable nature of the archaeological record, (ii) the fact that many other groups besides archaeologists have vested interests in the archaeological record, (iii) the socially relevant contributions of archaeology in the present and future, (iv) the ethical principles that guide archaeologists, (v) the importance that archaeologists be effective communicators, (vi) the basic cognitive and methodological skills used by archaeologists, and (vii) real-world problem solving by archaeologists.

I don't think it was the intention of the SAA that each principle necessarily guide the formation of each course or text used in archaeology education, but I have incorporated each into this book. The nonrenewable nature of the archaeological record is emphasized through such topics as the rise of cultural resource management, heritage legislation, and the destruction of sites through looting and warfare. The vested interests in the archaeological record by non-archaeologists is covered by examining indigenous archaeology and the many parts of the heritage industry, including tourism. Making archaeology socially relevant is included in many areas, such as studies of contemporary garbage. Archaeological ethics is made explicit, as is communication, with the sharing of information built into research designs. Real-world problem solving is explored in such topics as forensics and the use of archaeologists in designing markers for nuclear waste sites.

Besides being guided by the SAA principles of curriculum reform, many characteristics of this book set it apart from competitors. It situates archaeology in the contemporary world much more than others. This includes contextualizing archaeology in academia, industry, global social movements, politics, and popular culture. It places more emphasis on the management of heritage resources and includes sections on legislation and international agreements concerning archaeology. Unlike most textbooks for courses focusing on methods, this book includes a brief section outlining world prehistory and ancient civilizations, providing a frame of reference for students. Most books avoid the disagreements, ambiguities, and gray areas within the discipline, instead presenting information as if there were consensus among archaeologists. This book explicitly identifies these areas, ranging from differences in definitions of archaeology to explanations of the collapse of civilizations.

Supplements for this text include an instructor's manual, test bank, and a chapter-by-chapter series of Powerpoint presentations, all on a CD-Rom. The Powerpoint presentations include many of the figures (in color) and tables in the text.

For those who wish to supplement the text with a reader, *Reading Archaeology: An Introduction* (Robert Muckle, forthcoming) is a good fit. Many of the key resources and suggested readings mentioned in *Introducing Archaeology* are included in the reader.

Comments and suggestions for future editions from instructors are welcome and can be directed to the author at bmuckle@capcollege.bc.ca

Note to Students

Welcome to the world of archaeology. This text provides a broad introduction to archaeology as it is practiced in the twenty-first century. It focuses on the practical aspects of research, such as how projects are designed, what methods are used in field and laboratory work, and how archaeologists make interpretations. It is also about how archaeology is situated in the contemporary world outside colleges and universities, such as in industry, and how it is related to global social movements, politics, popular culture, and real-world problem solving.

One of the purposes of an introductory course is to familiarize students with vocabulary common to the subject. Even though this text is relatively short, you will undoubtedly come across many words you have never seen before or see other words being used in a new way. Such words are included in the Glossary and are identified in bold type the first time they appear in the text.

Acknowledgments

Many people deserve thanks for their ideas, comments, and support. I am indebted to Broadview Press, especially company founder and director of special projects Don LePan, president Michael Harrison, and anthropology editor Anne Brackenbury. I initially identified the niche for this book, but did not want to be the one to write it. They confirmed the niche, and convinced me that I was the one to do it. Most of my work on the book was done under the guidance of Anne Brackenbury, and I have appreciated her advice and patience. Keely Winnitoy filled in as my editor for a time and did an admirable job. Catherine Dorton did a masterful job on the copy edit and made many practical suggestions. I also thank the several anonymous reviewers of the book proposal who supported my vision for it.

I appreciate the work of those who read the almost-complete manuscript with a critical eye, including teaching archaeologists recruited by Broadview Press. Pamela Ford of Mt. San Jacinto College in California, Patricia Hamlen of Harper College in Illinois, and an anonymous reviewer from Canada all provided thorough reviews with numerous comments and constructive criticisms, which have led to a better book. Two of my colleagues at Capilano College also deserve recognition for their review of the manuscript. Archaeologist Suzanne Villeneuve made many useful comments and geographer Cheryl Schreader offered constructive criticism on the areas relating to geography and geology. I did not act on all of the suggestions of the reviewers, however, and remain entirely responsible for the book's content.

I am grateful for the overall supportive environment at Capilano College. In particular, I wish to acknowledge the support of members of the department of anthropology, past and present. This includes former colleagues Karin Lind, Cassandra Bill, and Tad McIlwraith, and current colleagues Gillian Crowther, Maureen Bracewell, and Suzanne Villeneuve. I am especially grateful for their support of my annual archaeological field projects and frequent discussions on matters relating to archaeology and pedagogy, all of which have made me a better archaeologist and teacher.

I am also grateful for the infectious passion for teaching, research, and writing that my friends and colleagues in several archaeological and anthropological organizations have demonstrated—none more so than those in the Society for Anthropology in Community Colleges. I have learned from and been inspired by many in this fine group, especially Mark Lewine of Cuyahoga Community College in Ohio, Lloyd Miller of Des Moines Areas Community College in Iowa, Barry Kass from SUNY/Orange County Community College in New York, Rob Edwards of Cabrillo College in California, Tony Balzano of Sussex Community College in New Jersey, Phil Stein of Pierce College in California, and Becky Stein of Los Angeles Valley College in California, and Jo Rainie Rodgers and George Rodgers, both of Ohlone College in California.

Of course none of this would have been possible without the support of my wife, Victoria, and our four children still living at home: Cody, Jonathan, Tomas, and Anna. I have written this book during what was supposed to be my leisure time, mostly on evenings and weekends at home and during vacation time. Consequently, I had less family time, did fewer chores, and hogged the computer more than if I wasn't writing the book. They never complained.

About the Author

Robert Muckle, or Bob, as he prefers to be called, has been doing archaeology for more than 20 years. He discovered archaeology while a student at a community college and remains passionate about both archaeology and undergraduate education. He has done fieldwork in Alaska, Alberta, British Columbia, Egypt, and Kenya and has taught archaeology at several different colleges and universities. Currently, he is a professor at Capilano College, where he has been teaching full time since 1995. In addition to teaching and since his university days as a student, Bob has been active doing contract archaeology under the auspices of his own cultural resource management firm; he has spent long periods in the realm of indigenous archaeology, working with and for First Nations, and he has directed multiyear historical and community-oriented field projects. He continues to direct field projects during the summer months. Bob has been on the executive of the Society for Anthropology in Community Colleges (a section of the American Anthropological Association) for several years, including a term as president. He is also a member of the Canadian Archaeological Association, the Society for American Archaeology, the Society for Historical Archaeology, and the World Archaeological Congress. Additionally, he is listed on the Register of Professional Archaeologists, which may have the highest standards for membership of any archaeological association in North America, and perhaps the world.

Bob's other professional activities include presentations and writing. He makes multiple presentations on his archaeological research each year to community groups, and he has made formal presentations at several academic conferences. His publications include one book on the archaeology and anthropology of First Nations and several articles on such topics as community archaeology, the archaeology of logging camps, and the taphonomy of shells in archaeological sites. He also writes a regular column called "Archaeology Matters" for the journal *Teaching Anthropology*.

Bob lives with his wife, kids, and a menagerie of animals. He is fairly clean living, although he does have a penchant for pickup trucks and the occasional drink of honey-brown lager. He has also been known to have the occasional sip of brandy and puff of a cigar. Since January 1, 2006, when he went for a dip in the chilly waters of the northern Pacific Ocean, Bob has been a proud member of the Vancouver Polar Bear Swim Club.

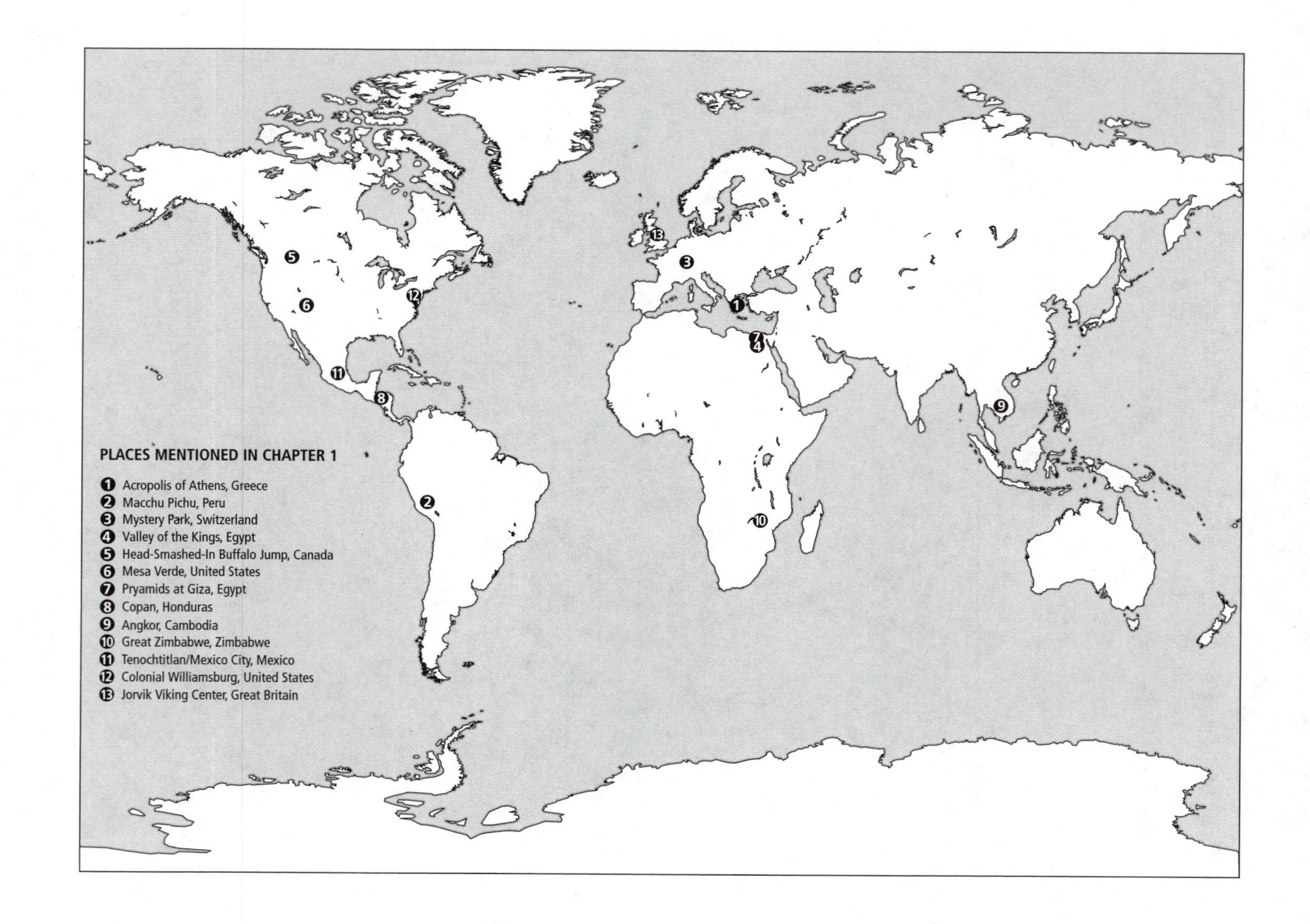
PLACES MENTIONED IN CHAPTER 1
1 Acropolis of Athens, Greece
2 Macchu Pichu, Peru
3 Mystery Park, Switzerland
4 Valley of the Kings, Egypt
5 Head-Smashed-In Buffalo Jump, Canada
6 Mesa Verde, United States
7 Pryamids at Giza, Egypt
8 Copan, Honduras
9 Angkor, Cambodia
10 Great Zimbabwe, Zimbabwe
11 Tenochtitlan/Mexico City, Mexico
12 Colonial Williamsburg, United States
13 Jorvik Viking Center, Great Britain

CHAPTER 1

Situating Archaeology

Introduction

Archaeology is everywhere in the early twenty-first century. It is part of the multibillion-dollar **heritage industry**; taught as a scholarly discipline in colleges and universities throughout the world; and firmly embedded in politics, global social movements, and popular culture. It has been defined in dozens of ways and is commonly referred to as a scholarly or intellectual endeavor, a profession, a practice, a craft, and a hobby. It is rationalized in many different ways and relies on several basic concepts.

This chapter introduces archaeology by clarifying these definitions, contexts, rationalizations, and concepts. It begins with a brief description of two of the many **archaeological sites** that have come to symbolize archaeology—the Acropolis of Athens in Greece and the **Inka** site of Machu Picchu in Peru.

Images of Archaeology

In many people's minds, archaeology is correlated with architectural ruins in fabulous settings. In addition to the Acropolis and Machu Picchu, these sites include the pyramids from Egypt and Central America, the Great Wall of China, cliff dwellings of the American Southwest, and Britain's Stonehenge.

The Acropolis and Machu Picchu are excellent starting points for the study of archaeology because they represent so many of the things archaeologists in the early twenty-first century are interested in, such as politics and tourism. The Acropolis is certainly among the most famous archaeological sites in the world. Comprising the Parthenon and surrounding buildings, the Acropolis has come to symbolize Western civilization. Based primarily on its preservation of ancient Greek art and architecture, it has been designated a World Heritage Site by the United Nations. It also symbolizes the beginnings of archaeology, which, as outlined in Chapter 2, is rooted in the collection of antiquities from ancient Greece and Rome. The Acropolis further represents the increasingly explicit political nature of archaeology and archaeology sites (discussed later in

GILLIAN CROWTHER

FIGURE 1.1: THE PARTHENON on the Acropolis of Athens, Greece. A UNESCO designated World Heritage Site, the Acropolis symbolizes Western civilization, the beginnings of archaeology, the political nature of the discipline, Greek identity, and archaeotourism.

this chapter), insofar as the Acropolis is firmly tied to Greek identity, and because it receives hundreds of thousands of visitors annually, it is a heritage management concern (see Chapter 3).

Located high in the Peruvian Andes, the Inka site of Machu Picchu was abandoned in the early 1500s and rediscovered in 1911. Its population is estimated at several hundred, and its principal function was probably as a summer retreat for a ruling Inka family. Like the Acropolis, Machu Picchu has been designated a World Heritage Site by the United Nations. Insofar as it has become a national symbol of Peru, even having been used for the inauguration of the president in 2001, it is symbolic of the political nature of archaeology. And as one of the most popular heritage tourism destinations in South America, it is visited by close to 500,000 people annually.

Defining Archaeology

A rough translation of the term *archaeology* from ancient Greek and Latin is "the study of ancient things or stories." The term does not appear in English language dictionaries until the 1600s however, and since that time, has been defined and described in many ways (see Table 1.1).

FIGURE 1.2: MACHU PICCHU, Peru. Located high in the Andes, Machu Picchu was probably a summer retreat for a ruling Inca family. It is a UNESCO designated World Heritage Site, a national symbol of Peru, and one of the most popular heritage tourism destinations in South America.

One of the first and most important things a student of archaeology should learn is that there is no consensus definition of archaeology. Indeed, there are almost as many definitions of archaeology as there are books, dictionaries, encyclopedias, and websites that focus on the subject. Some definitions restrict archaeology to the study of the human past, while others include the present as well as the past as the periods of interest. Some definitions focus on the objects of interest, such as the study of **artifacts** or the study of ancient civilizations, yet most do not restrict archaeology to any particular subset of the **material remains** of human physical activity. Many definitions include the phrase "the scientific study of...." Yet others have rejected the scientific approach in archaeology, promoting more humanistic methods. Some definitions focus on the objectives of archaeology, such as describing the human past or explaining past events, while others make no mention whatsoever of the research goals.

While differences in definitions may lead to some initial confusion for those unfamiliar with archaeology, these differences do provide some indication of the breadth of the discipline. Also, even a cursory examination of the plethora of definitions shows that there are two constants in almost all of them. First, archaeology is focused on

TABLE 1.1: Defining Archaeology

Archaeolology is...	Source
The study of humans through their material remains	This text
The study of the human past using the surviving material remains of human behavior	Brian Fagan, 2004
The study of the social and cultural past through material remains with the aim of ordering and describing the events of the past and explaining the meaning of those events	Robert Sharer and Wendy Ashmore, 2003
The study of the physical remains to help understand the behavior of people in the past	Jim Grant, Sam Gorin, and Neil Fleming, 2002
The study of the past through the systematic recovery and analysis of material remains	David Hurst Thomas and Robert Kelly, 2006
A special form of anthropology that uses material remains to study extinct human societies	Brian Fagan, 2006
The study of the material remains of human behavior	Kenneth Feder, 2004
The scientific study of the human past	Mark Sutton and Robert Yohe II, 2003
A subdiscipline of anthropology involving the study of the human past through its material remains	Colin Renfrew and Paul Bahn, 2004
An inherently ridiculous and often futile profession	Paul Bahn, 1989

humans. Second, the essential database of archaeology is the remains of their physical activities, often referred to as material remains.

Considering these two constants, a good all-purpose definition of the discipline is this: *archaeology is the study of humans through their material remains.* This includes the identification, collection, analysis, interpretation, and management of those remains.

This definition does not restrict archaeology to a specific time period, a particular subset of material remains, or the use of the scientific method. It should be understood, however, that most archaeology as it is practiced in the early twenty-first century focuses on the human past and adheres to the fundamental principles and methods of **science**.

In order to more completely understand the definition, it is necessary to know in greater detail what archaeologists mean by the words *human* and *material remains*. There is no universal agreement about what it means to be human. Almost all archaeologists allow that at a minimum, human is taken to mean all members of the genus ***Homo***. As outlined more fully in chapter 7, the genus appears to have arisen about 2.5 million years ago and coincides with the undeniable evidence of human technology, primarily through the manufacture of stone tools. Many archaeologists are less restrictive and equate human with the biological family **hominidae**. This family includes multiple genera, including *Homo*, and appears to have arisen between about 7 and 5 million years ago. No undisputed evidence of material remains have been found for any genus other than *Homo*, so for many archaeologists, whether one equates human with *Homo* or hominidae is not all that important.

Material remains comprise all kinds of physical evidence of human activities, including, but certainly not restricted to, tools, houses, things buried deliberately or lost, refuse, and modifications to the landscape. The variety of material remains is discussed in greater detail in Chapter 4.

A Scholarly Endeavor, a Profession, and a Craft

Archaeology is at once a scholarly endeavor and a profession. There is no question of the scholarly nature of archaeology. It is embedded in colleges and universities throughout the world; it is funded by major research agencies; it makes extensive use of theory at all stages of research; and it produces scholarly, peer-reviewed publications.

There is also no question that archaeology is a profession. Many archaeologists, especially those serving clients in the heritage industry, are more likely to consider their work as a business rather than a scholarly pursuit. Professions are generally considered to require specialized knowledge, provide a service to the community, and have a high degree of autonomy, a system of licensing or a registry of qualified members, and self-organized associations. While there are no formal national systems of licensing for archaeologists in North America, registries exist at local, regional, and international levels. These registries typically have codes of ethics and minimum standards of qualification, including postgraduate university degrees and considerable experience in field archaeology. One such registry to which many archaeologists in North America belong is the **Register of Professional Archaeologists (ROPA)**.

Although in a clear minority, some archaeologists consider archaeology to be more a craft than either a scholarly endeavor or a profession. For example, some proponents of this view compare archaeology to the craft of **pottery**, suggesting that like making a pot, archaeology involves both abstract thought and physical labor; thereby they avoid a distinct separation of reasoning and execution, and unify theory and practice. Unlike other academic disciplines that are associated with well-defined subject matter, the essential craft of archaeology is in manufacturing knowledge and interpreting the past.

Archaeology versus Archeology

The variety of spellings of the word *archaeology* confuses many people. There are two common spellings in the English language: archaeology and archeology. Most archaeologists use the longer spelling, with the second *a* after the *h*, while much of the popular press, some professional organizations, and some governments prefer the shorter version. One is more inclined to see the shorter spelling in the United States than elsewhere in the world, but both spellings are considered valid.

Contextualizing Archaeology

How archaeology is perceived and practiced often depends on the framework in which it operates. Archaeology can be considered in many contexts, falling into the principal categories of academia, industry, politics, global social movements, and popular culture.

These categories should not be considered mutually exclusive, and any single project can be considered in multiple contexts. It is not uncommon for ongoing projects to be both scholarly and political; and research from purely academic projects is often used to further global social movements long after the fieldwork and analysis has been completed.

Archaeology in the Context of Academia

On a broad level, archaeology fits comfortably within the academic world of colleges, universities, and research institutes. Archaeology is an academic discipline that falls within the western intellectual tradition, with courses taught and research undertaken in academic settings.

Within these academic settings, however, the place of archaeology varies. Archaeology is situated in three basic models, both intellectually and administratively in colleges and universities. Archaeology as a branch of **anthropology** is one model; another is that of archaeology as a stand-alone department; and in the third model, archaeology is recognized as neither a department nor a branch, but rather as specialized courses situated within any of a number of departments.

Archaeology as a branch of anthropology is the most prevalent model in North America. With the other branches, archaeology shares evolutionary, **holistic**, and comparative perspectives of humankind, and depends on fieldwork for the acquisition of data. An overview of each of the major branches is summarized in Table 1.2.

Anthropology may be a distinct department in colleges or universities, or it may be associated with geography, history, sociology, classics, cultural studies, Near Eastern studies, or other disciplines to form combined departments. In some institutions, this is done for ease of administration, but some people view archaeology as intellectually embedded in these disciplines as well. In some colleges and universities, archaeology courses can be found in multiple departments.

A small percentage of colleges and universities in North America, and many colleges and universities elsewhere in the world, have stand-alone departments of archaeology. These departments sometimes also include courses in biological anthropology.

Archaeology is usually considered to be part of a liberal arts education, most often associated with the social sciences. However, in some institutions that have archaeological laboratories, use sophisticated technology, and explicitly consider the scientific method, archaeology is considered part of a science education. Other institutions situate archaeology and anthropology within the humanities. This particularly suits those archaeologists who view their role as being one primarily of storytelling, often drawing parallels with literature, visual arts, theater, and other kinds of performance.

TABLE 1.2: Branches of Anthropology

Branch Of Anthropology	Description
Archaeology	focuses on past human culture through the analysis of material remains.
Cultural anthropology	focuses on all aspects of contemporary human cultures, including language, economic systems, social systems, art, and ideology. Data is usually collected through long-term observation of people. Also known as social anthropology or socio-cultural anthropology.
Biological anthropology	focuses on human biology, past and present, including human biological evolution and contemporary biological diversity. Also known as physical anthropology.

As in most academic disciplines, students of archaeology may sequentially work towards a bachelor's degree, a master's degree, and a Ph.D. To meet increased demand for field and laboratory workers since the late 1900s, some colleges in the United States have developed two year archaeology programs intended for entry-level employment in the heritage industry.

The vast majority of pure scholarly research in archaeology is undertaken by those affiliated with universities, including professors who have usually received money from a funding agency, such as the National Endowment for the Humanities (NEH) or the National Science Foundation (NSF) in the United States, or the Social Sciences and Humanities Research Council (SSHRC) in Canada.

Archaeology in the Context of Industry

The vast majority of archaeologists make their careers in the heritage industry, often working alongside or in cooperation with historians, lawyers, law makers, indigenous groups, tourism operators, and educators.

As outlined in Table 1.3, the heritage industry has several functions. Archaeology is most prominent in the areas of documenting and assessing heritage sites, and archaeologists who perform these functions are generally considered to be working in the field of **cultural resource management** (CRM), which is described more fully in Chapter 3.

Although archaeologists have been active in the other areas of the heritage industry, historically they have tended to be secondary to indigenous advocacy groups, law makers, educators, and tourism professionals. In the early twenty-first century, however, archaeologists have been increasing their role in these other areas. They often lobby politicians

TABLE 1.3 Principal Functions of the Heritage Industry

The heritage industry is designed to:
1. Make people aware of the value of heritage
2. Enact legislation to protect heritage
3. Document heritage sites and objects
4. Assess the significance of heritage sites and objects
5. Conserve or preserve heritage sites and objects
6. Interpret heritage
7. Present heritage

to protect heritage sites and objects through legislation and other protective measures, and they have become increasingly active in the presentation of heritage to the public.

Heritage tourism, which has become a multibillion-dollar business, is one aspect of heritage presentation that has created considerable opportunities for archaeologists. For example, the Valley of the Kings in Egypt receives close to two million visitors annually; several Maya sites in Central America are major tourist destinations; and despite a remote and very high altitude, several hundred thousand people visit Machu Picchu each year. Heritage sites throughout North America, Europe, and elsewhere present many opportunities for archaeological research and interpretation. Many sites in North America, including those with UN World Heritage status, have created great opportunities for archaeology. These sites include Head-Smashed-In Buffalo Jump and Mesa Verde, which are discussed more fully in Chapter 3. Governments that control heritage sites that are tourist destinations often support archaeological research to enhance the experience for visitors.

Archaeologists often get involved in the authentic presentation of heritage, another aspect of heritage tourism. Many are active in creating and maintaining authenticity at the hundreds, and perhaps thousands, of **living museums** that now dot the globe. Examples include the reconstruction of eighteenth-century Colonial Williamsburg in the United States, which reportedly has about one million visitors each year, and the very popular Jorvik Viking Centre in Great Britain, where smells have been recreated to increase authenticity.

Archaeologists are also interested in the lack of authenticity in many living museums. Among other things, they often level criticism against sanitized versions of the past, including inadequate representations of poverty, racism, prostitution, alcoholism, and drug use.

Archaeologists are also often critical of **archaeological theme parks**, which, although frequently promoted as educational experiences, lack support from mainstream archaeology. Mystery Park in Switzerland, for example, promotes the notion that many of the great achievements of humankind have resulted from encounters with extraterrestrials, an idea that archaeologists and other scientists generally find preposterous.

Archaeology in the Context of Politics

There are three primary political contexts for archaeology: in the creation of a sense of national identity; the protection and investigation of archaeological sites; and the destruction of heritage sites and objects for political purposes.

First, the link between archaeological sites and national identity is not difficult to observe. Archaeological sites often symbolize their countries. As already mentioned, the Parthenon and surrounding buildings of the Acropolis are firmly tied to Greek identity,

MYSTERY PARK

FIGURE 1.3: MYSTERY PARK, Switzerland. An extreme example of heritage tourism, Mystery Park is an archaeological theme park promoting the notion that some of the greatest achievements of humankind have resulted from interactions with extraterrestrial aliens.

and Machu Picchu has come to represent Peru. Mayan sites often symbolize Mexico; Stonehenge represents Great Britain; and the pyramids are an emblem of ancient Egypt.

In many countries of the world, national identity is strongly tied to heritage sites even though research doesn't always link contemporary peoples of the region with the builders of the sites. Sites of the ancient Maya, for example, are often tied with national identity in Mexico, even though Mayans constitute a minor percentage of the contemporary population; and a recent Honduran presidential inauguration took place at the Mayan site of Copan. Other examples of well-known heritage sites that are used to create a sense of national identity include the sites of Angkor and Great Zimbabwe.

Angkor, located in Cambodia, was the capital of the ancient Khmer empire, which controlled much of what is now Cambodia, Thailand, and Vietnam. Angkor is best known for its complex of more than one hundred temples, built between the ninth and twelfth centuries AD. Some scholars believe the complex to be among the greatest architectural achievements of humankind. Following centuries of neglect and looting, Cambodia began to rebuild Angkor in the 1990s, after a civil war. Angkor has now become one of the world's premier tourist attractions, and one of its temples, Angkor Wat, is the centerpiece on the Cambodian national flag.

The country of Zimbabwe takes it name from the site of Great Zimbabwe. When Europeans first started inhabiting the African country once known as Rhodesia, they

FIGURE 1.4: ANGKOR, Cambodia. Part of a complex of more than 100 temples built from the ninth through the twelfth century AD. After centuries of neglect, Angkor has been designated a World Heritage Site, has become a premier tourist desination, and is a symbol of Cambodia.

dismissed the notion that the stone ruins they found there were the remains of a large settlement constructed by the ancestors of the contemporary indigenous people. During the 1900s, however, archaeologists became convinced otherwise, and one of the largest sites was given the name Great Zimbabwe, which is a word taken from the language of one of the local indigenous groups. The site had such significance in building a sense of identity among the peoples of the region that when Rhodesia gained independence in 1980, the country was renamed Zimbabwe. It is now believed that the site was built between the fifth and fifteenth century AD, and estimates of the prehistoric population range as high as 30,000.

On occasion, using archaeology to create a sense of national identity can have devastating effects, such as when territorial expansion is justified on the basis of archaeological evidence. In the years leading up to World War II, for example, Nazis used archaeological research by German archaeologists in neighboring areas, including Poland, to make claims that those lands rightfully belonged to Germany, since artifacts recovered there appeared to have had a Germanic origin. In some cases, evidence of swastika-like designs was taken to signify German origin, disregarding the fact that the symbol itself probably originated in India. The rationale behind the Iraqi invasion of Kuwait in the late twentieth century provides another example. Linking modern-day Iraq with the ancient Babylonian empire that dominated the region thousands of years ago, Iraq's leader at the time, Saddam Hussein, claimed that Kuwait rightfully belonged to Iraq.

A sense of national identity can also be created and maintained by the way archaeological research is portrayed. Some popular American magazines, for example, have been criticized for the way they use archaeology to foster American values and ideology. A comprehensive examination of articles focusing on archaeology in *National Geographic*, for example, shows that the selective slant of the reporting and the choice of images used to accompany the articles validates the American value of rugged individualism and legitimizes American expansionism (Gero and Root 1994).

Second, the protection and investigation of archaeological sites is often considered political, in part because heritage legislation and research may be seen as a response to pressure from specific interest groups. In many areas of the world, for example, legislation protecting archaeological sites has been put into place or strengthened following an increase in popular support for indigenous claims to rights and territories. Archaeological research, undertaken by both indigenous groups and governments, to investigate legal claims to aboriginal rights and territories can be viewed as being political, since such claims often pit one nation against another (e.g., an indigenous nation versus a national government). This view is particularly common in Canada, where dozens of First Nations (as indigenous groups are called) are negotiating treaties for the first time, and court cases brought by First Nations against governments are common, with archaeology being used to support both sides.

Protection of archaeological sites can also be considered political at the international level. As we will see in more detail in Chapter 3, many international treaties, conventions, and laws under the umbrella of the United Nations cover the protection of heritage sites. It is not mandatory that individual countries agree to abide by the agreements, but pressure to abide from other member countries gives them the appearance of being political.

Finally, archaeologists are concerned about the political destruction of heritage sites and objects. Despite international laws and agreements (see Chapter 3), many significant heritage objects and sites are destroyed from the direct actions of political regimes and during conflicts between groups or nations. The destruction generally falls within the categories of targeted destruction, **collateral damage**, and **subsistence looting**.

Since heritage sites are often used as symbols of identity, they have frequently been targeted for destruction by political regimes new to an area, in a sort of cleansing of previous regimes and ideologies. Examples include multiple attempts at damaging the Acropolis in Greece over the past few millennia, the leveling of the ancient Aztec capital of Tenochtitlan (under present-day Mexico City) by the invading Spaniards in the sixteenth century, and the deliberate destruction of thousands of important artifacts and at least one United Nations-designated World Heritage Site by the Taliban regime in Afghanistan during its reign in the late twentieth and early twenty-first century.

During the 2003 American invasion of Iraq, many important heritage sites were destroyed by what the military calls collateral damage, and a significant portion of the archaeological collection in the Iraq National Museum was stolen in the hours and days immediately following the fall of Baghdad.

Although not generally thought to be one of the primary areas in which the political context of archaeology is considered, the use of archaeologists in espionage is well known. For example, American Sylvanus Morley reportedly used his cover as an archaeologist to search for evidence of German submarines along the coast of Central America during World War I. Harvard archaeologist Samuel Lothrop maintained his cover to spy and coordinate intelligence activity for the United States during World War I and II.

Archaeology in the Context of Global Social Movements

Archaeology and global social movements are often linked, and their association is commonly viewed as mutually beneficial. Archaeologists seeking to increase the social relevance of the discipline often become involved in social movements, bringing with them the data, methods, and theory of archaeology. Conversely, the impact of social movements often challenges mainstream thinking in archaeology and leads to alternative interpretations of the past. Three social movements that have strong links to archaeology are feminism, indigenous empowerment, and the green movement.

The relationship between archaeology and feminism took serious hold in the 1980s and continues to be an integral force in the evolution of both fields. Feminist thought has challenged the basic assumptions about gender roles in the past, such as the perception that men were the dominant tool makers, artists, food providers, and leaders. Feminism has also been integral in significantly increasing the proportion of women in all levels of the profession, from part-time field-worker to university professor. Archaeology has benefited the feminist movement when archaeologists have debunked unsubstantiated claims of male superiority in past societies and focused increasing amounts of research on topics which hitherto received no or little attention, such as child rearing, plant gathering, and other tasks often associated with women.

Indigenous empowerment and archaeology also have a very close relationship. As indigenous groups around the world seek to empower themselves and lessen domination by colonial governments, they often include evidence from archaeological research to support their claims to territory and rights. This has created much employment for archaeologists, to the degree that many are considered to be part of the **Indian industry**.

Although less prominent than either feminism or indigenous empowerment, the relationship between the **green movement** and archaeology is also strong, particularly in Europe. Alternatively known as conservationism or environmentalism, the green movement focuses on environmental sustainability and conservation. Significant contributions made by archaeologists to the green movement include providing data on previous human use of the environment. Archaeologists are able to provide examples of the negative impacts of some subsistence and economic activities, which may ultimately lead to the abandonment of regions and collapse of civilizations. For example, the **archaeological record** shows that irrigation may lead to increasingly saline soils, rendering them useless for farming.

Archaeology in the Context of Popular Culture

Archaeology is very visible in popular culture. As outlined in Table 1.4, this includes many forms of media and entertainment, involving both the results of archaeological research and depictions of archaeologists at work.

Although popular culture presents some authentic depictions of archaeologists and their work, archaeologists commonly observe that these constitute a very small minority and that the portrayal is usually inaccurate, inappropriately sensationalized, and generally presents archaeology as a frivolous activity. Examples include the tendency to emphasize archaeology as a treasure hunt in print and visual media, a common European or North American bias in nonfiction books about archaeology (such as overemphasizing heritage sites that are likely to be of most interest to European and North American readers), a common male bias (focusing on male archaeologists and the male activities they discover), and an almost total neglect of the reasons behind archaeology.

Archaeologists have become increasingly concerned about the depiction of their discipline in popular culture for two principal reasons. For one, if the popular perception is that archaeology is a frivolous activity, then government funding may be reduced. Ultimately, governments pay directly for most of the pure research done by archaeologists and pay most of the costs associated with the teaching of archaeology at colleges and universities. The feeling is that as demands for government funds increase, archaeology may be subject to cuts because of its perceived lack of importance.

TABLE 1.4: Examples of Archaeology in Popular Culture

Category	Examples
Novels of prehistoric fiction	Jean Auel's Earth's Children series (*Clan of the Cave Bear* and others) Kathleen O'Neal and W. Michael Gear's First North Americans series
Television infotainment	*Meet the Ancestors* *Time Team*
Television drama and comedy with archaeologists as major characters	*Young Indiana Jones* *Relic Hunter*
Television drama and comedy with archaeologists as minor characters	*Dr. Who* *Hitchhiker's Guide to the Galaxy* *Star Trek: the Next Generation*
Movies in the genre of prehistoric film	*One Million Years* BC *Cave Man* *Encino Man* *Neanderthal*
Movies featuring archaeologists as lead characters	Indiana Jones series (*Raiders of the Lost Ark* and others) The Tomb Raider series
Games and toys	Board games (e.g., Artifact) Electronic games (e.g., Tomb Raider) Plastic archaeology sets
Advertising	Beer at Machu Picchu Vodka at Easter Island and headphones on its statues Coca Cola as pillars of the Parthenon

The second reason archaeologists are concerned about the depiction of archaeology in popular culture is the fact that the media increasingly determines the kinds of pure scholarly research being undertaken. The media has a long history of funding archaeological projects, the results of which then appear in those media magazines or television documentaries (e.g., *National Geographic*). Print and television media are becoming increasingly involved in archaeological projects. Archaeologists are concerned about this primarily because the type of research conducted may be based on what readers and viewers might find interesting, rather than on what might contribute significantly to our understanding of human behavior, past and present.

FIGURE 1.5: ARCHAEOLOGY IN ADVERTISING: General Paint. Archaeologists have become increasingly concerned about the use of archaeological images in advertising, which often show a lack of sensitivity to indigenous peoples and values.

Archaeologists are also concerned about the use of archaeological sites in advertising, especially the lack of sensitivity to people's identification with the sites and the potential for damage. In the early 1990s, Coca-Cola produced an ad that replaced the columns of the Parthenon with Coca-Cola bottles, causing outrage among many Greeks, some of whom felt that they were being humiliated on an international scale. In 2000, the filming of a beer commercial caused damage to some architectural ruins at Machu Picchu. A crane used in filming damaged a massive carved stone block known as the Intihuatana, which is presumed to have importance in Inka mythology. As Peruvian archaeologist Federico Kaufmann Doig commented, "Machu Picchu is the heart of our archaeological heritage, and the Intihuatana is the heart of Machu Picchu. They've struck at our most sacred inheritance."

Rationalizing Archaeology

Historically, archaeology has been justified on the basis that it is intrinsically interesting; it provides information about the past so we can learn from our mistakes; and all knowledge is good. While these are valid rationalizations and worked well for much of the late nineteenth and twentieth century, for most people in the early twenty-first century, they are not good enough reasons to justify the billions of dollars spent each year on archaeological work, including maintaining the discipline in colleges and universities. The principal contemporary rationalizations of archaeology are outlined in Table 1.5.

To supply context for current global events, archaeology provides a database of more than two million years of human events, including instances of warfare, overpopulation, famine, and responses to environmental disasters. In addition, archaeology provides methods of classification and comparison to make this data meaningful, and it has a variety of conceptual frameworks that can be used to explain events. For example, although there is no consensus among archaeologists, many believe the archaeological record shows that warfare occurs primarily in times of resource shortages.

The framework archaeology had developed for collecting and interpreting data is most obviously applied in the area of documenting heritage. Archaeological techniques have

TABLE 1.5: Contemporary Rationalizations for Archaeology

Rationalization	Example
Archaeology provides context for current global events	Understanding the conditions upon which warfare occurs
Archaeology provides a framework for collecting and interpreting data	Collecting and interpreting information about the past; forensic applications
Archaeology provides a framework for evaluating claims and ideas	Evaluating claims of territory by indigenous groups; evaluating popular ideas about the past such as visits by extraterrestrial aliens
Archaeology provides a framework for assessing the significance of heritage sites and objects	Determining which sites are worth conserving, preserving, or excavating in advance of a development project
Archaeology provides an important economic base	Archaeology is integral to heritage tourism, which is a vital part of the economy in many areas of the world
Archaeology provides an awareness and offers solutions to some important problems associated with living in the early twenty-first century	Marking nuclear waste sites
Archaeology provides support for other disciplines	Provides additional data and approaches useful for studies in history, modern material culture, biology, and geography

found other applications as well, such as forensics. Archaeologists are often employed in such work, including recovering data from fires in buildings, plane crash sites, and crime scenes. Archaeologists were involved, for example, in the recovery of human remains following the destruction of New York's World Trade Center in 2001. Techniques developed in archaeology have further transferred well into studies of modern material culture and have proved beneficial in understanding the effectiveness of recycling and trash disposal programs. Some of these are described in Chapter 3.

Archaeologists are called upon frequently to evaluate data and ideas. On a very practical level, this includes examining claims of indigenous groups to their alleged traditional territory. Archaeologists evaluate these claims based on many variables, including the evidence itself and how it was collected. At a higher, more theoretical level, archaeologists get involved in evaluating ideas put forward by a wide range of groups and individuals, including academics, about the human past. Archaeologists are often able to show that popular ideas have little basis in fact (see Chapter 10).

Assessing the significance of heritage sites is a common task of many archaeologists working in the heritage industry. These assessments are fundamentally important to help determine whether a site will be destroyed without proper excavation, excavated prior to destruction, or preserved. Usually only sites determined to be highly significant are protected. Significance is usually assessed in relation to the site's importance to archaeology, other academic disciplines, particular ethnic groups, and the public.

Archaeology has considerable economic value. Much of it is directly associated with the heritage industry, including archaeological research, education, and presentation. With more than 10,000 people making careers in the North American heritage industry alone, its economic impact is real. In countries such as Mexico, Peru, and Egypt, where visits to archaeological sites are very popular, archaeology has become a vital part of the tourism economy.

Some value is given to the role archaeology often plays in support of other disciplines, in both the social and natural sciences. Archaeologists provide material evidence to our basic understanding of human behavior, which is important to anthropologists, sociologists, historians, economists, human geographers, and psychologists. For example, archaeology is often used to validate claims of people with no history of written records. Another example is that archaeology adds to our understanding of the more recent past by supplementing what can be learned through written records and oral history alone. Through field and laboratory studies, archaeologists study sediments as well as plant and animal remains, which are of interest to physical geographers, geologists, palaeontologists, botanists, and palynologists. In this realm, archaeologists contribute to an understanding of the natural world, including the formation and alteration of landscapes, and studies of biological evolution and diversity.

As a final rationale, archaeologists bring awareness and offer solutions to some important problems associated with living in the twenty-first century. For example, archaeologists have made recommendations to the US government for marking deposits of nuclear waste, based on their knowledge of (i) the kind of materials likely to survive the impacts of nature or looters, (ii) the changes that are likely to occur in the landscape over time, and (iii) the problems that arise when the meanings of symbols change or are lost over time, which is common. Other examples include contributions that archeologists make in debunking popular assumptions about contemporary refuse-discard and recycling programs, and in pointing out the potential problems associated with the ever-increasing amount of space junk in orbit around the earth.

Basic Concepts in Archaeology

Contemporary archaeology rests upon many concepts. The most fundamental of these are **culture**, holism, **deep time**, evolution, reasoning by **analogy**, and using multiple frameworks.

Culture is a concept common to many disciplines in the social sciences. There are many ways to define culture, but one that works well for archaeology is that culture is the learned and shared things that people have, do, and think. There is no minimum number of things that must be shared or number of people sharing to constitute a culture. The things that people have include material objects that are part of the society. In the contemporary world, these include but are certainly not limited to such things as roads, houses, hospitals, churches, colleges, tools, and jewelry. The things that people do include those practices commonly called customs, and involve how they interact with each other, how many hours a day they work, marriage and child-rearing practices, and manners. The things that people think include those commonly linked under ideology, such as beliefs, religion, values, and morals. Sometimes the terms *culture* and *society* are used interchangeably. One way they can be distinguished is to think of the society as the people themselves and culture as those things that are learned and shared by the members of the society.

The reason why culture is a fundamental concept in archaeology is that for the vast majority of archaeologists, their objectives include reconstructing past culture.

The principal spheres of culture are commonly recognized as ecological, social, and ideological. The ecological sphere includes such things as settlement patterns, subsistence strategies, and diet (see Chapter 8), as well as technology (see Chapter 6). The social and ideological spheres include matters of inequality, identity, organization, art, ritual, and religion (see Chapter 9).

In archaeology, **holism** refers to the notion that all components of culture are linked: an understanding of past culture depends on an investigation of multiple components of that culture, and a change in one component inevitably leads to changes in other components. Archaeologists recognize, for example, that understanding the origins of art, ritual, and agriculture depends on an investigation of the earlier technologies, economies, social and political strategies, and belief systems of the people in the region. In many ways, it isn't the individual components of a culture that are under investigation as much as it is the linkages between the components.

In the physical or natural sciences, the phrase *deep time* is generally used to convey the vast billions of years of history of the earth and universe. Also known as **deep antiquity** in archaeology, deep time is used to convey the long history of humans. The outline of deep time, beginning with the origins of the universe but focusing on the time since humans have been leaving evidence of culture, is included in Chapter 7.

The concept of evolution, both biological and cultural, is central to archaeology. Archaeologists understand that the material evidence left behind by humans extends back in time beyond the existence of *Homo sapiens.* Archaeologists also understand that plants and animals used by humans in the past have evolved, and evidence of this can not only be seen in archaeological sites, but it can also be used to make interpretations about such things as whether the plant or animal was wild or domestic. Archaeologists further understand that cultures are continually changing. The rate of change is not constant, and all components of a culture do not change simultaneously, but change in all aspects of the ecological, social, and ideological spheres is continuous.

Reasoning by analogy is one of the ways in which archaeological interpretations are made. Essentially, analogy is a form of reasoning based on the notion that if two things are the same in some respects, they may be the same in other respects as well. Because archaeologists usually deal with the distant past for which no written records or live witnesses exist, they sometimes rely on analogy to interpret their finds. For example, if an archaeologist finds some clay shaped into a bowl that has been determined to be 7,000 years old, they can reason by analogy that it was used to contain something. The analogy is based on the similarity of the clay-shaped bowl with modern bowls made from clay (the things they have in common). Since modern bowls are used to contain things, then the 7,000-year-old bowl was probably used to contain something as well.

Archaeologists recognize some problems with analogy. They are especially aware that the older the things are that they are trying to interpret, the less confidence they can have in their analogies. The two major kinds of analogies archaeologists use are based on ethnographic research and experiments. **Ethnographic analogy** occurs when archaeologists use similarities with contemporary people, or with people whose culture has been documented in an **ethnography**, to make their interpretations. When archaeologists make observations on contemporary people themselves in order to provide a source for comparison, it is known as **ethnoarchaeology**. Many archaeologists do experiments to provide a source of comparison (e.g., creating things that can be described as similar to archaeological finds), which is known as experimental archaeology.

There are many frameworks for discovery and interpretation in archaeology. There is no single right way to do archaeology. No matter what context archaeology is being practiced within, or what the goals of a particular research project may be, there are always alternative strategies to consider. These include such fundamental things as choosing methods for fieldwork and analysis (see Chapters 5 and 6) to conceptual frameworks for understanding why and how cultures change (see Chapter 10).

Because there are many valid methods, there are also many disagreements among archaeologists. Given the restrictions of specific project goals, time, and budget, some strategies may be better than others, but there is rarely a single best way. When it comes to the broad questions archaeologists investigate, such as why people started to farm and why civilizations collapse, differences in explanations are often based on some basic assumptions on the part of individual archaeologists about how cultures work. These are covered in more detail in Chapter 10.

KEY RESOURCES AND SUGGESTED READING

Many excellent sources consider the various contexts and rationalizations of archaeology. *The SAA Archaeological Record* has a special theme issue (volume 4, number 2, 2004) on the status of academic archaeology, and there is a collection of contributions on archaeology as a branch of anthropology in *Archaeology Is Anthropology* by Gillespie and Nichols (2003). Jameson, Ehrenhard, and Finn's (2003) *Ancient Muses: Archaeology and the Arts* focuses on archaeology's relationship to the arts, and Dark's (1995) *Theoretical Archaeology* provides some discussion about the context of archaeology within academia. Views about archaeology as a craft can be explored in Shanks's (1992) *Experiencing the Past: On the Character of Archaeology* and the article "The Craft of Archaeology" by Shanks and McGuire (1996).

There are many books that cover archaeology in the context of the heritage industry, including *Archaeology and Heritage: An Introduction* by Carman (2002), *Archaeological Heritage Management in the Modern World* by Cleere (1989), *Marketing Heritage: Archaeology and the Consumption of the Past* by Rowan and Baram (2004), and *The Constructed Past: Experimental Archaeology, Education, and the Public* by Stone and Planel (1999). Good sources for providing overviews on archaeology in the context of politics include the *The Politics of the Past* by Gathercole and Lowenthal (1994), the article "Nationalism and Archaeology: On the Constructions of Nations and the Reconstructions of the Remote Past" by Kohl (1998), and *Nationalism, Politics, and the Practice of Archaeology* by Kohl and Fawcett (1995). The use of archaeology to support the Nazi agenda is covered in *The Master Plan: Himmler's Scholars and the Holocaust* by Heather Pringle (2006). An excellent book illustrating how an archaeological site can be used foster identity, focusing on the Acropolis, is *The Acropolis: Global Fame, Local Claim* by Yalouri (2001). There are many examples of archaeology in the service of local communities in *Archaeologists and Local Communities: Partners in Exploring the Past* by Derry and Malloy (2003). A good source for the role of archaeology and espionage is *The Archaeologist Was a Spy: Sylvanus G. Morley and the Office of Naval Intelligence* by Harris and Sadler (2003).

There are a dozens of good sources on archaeology in the context of global social movements. Overviews of archaeology and the green revolution include "Archaeology and Green Issues" by Bell (2004) and *All Things Natural: Archaeology and the Green Debate* by Macinnes and Wickham-Jones (1992). Good sources for examining archaeology in the context of feminism include *Gender in Archaeology: Analyzing Power and Prestige* by Nelson (1997), *Ungendering Civilization* by Pyburn (2004), *Reading the Body: Representations and Remains in the Archaeological Record* by Rautman (2000), and *Erect Men/Undulating Women: The Visual Image of Gender, "Race," and Progress in Reconstructive Illustrations of Human Evolution* by Wiber (1997). The relationship between archaeologists and indigenous peoples are covered in *At a Crossroads: Archaeology and First Peoples in Canada* by Nicholas and Andrews (1997), *Archaeological Theory and the Politics of Cultural Heritage* by Smith (2004), and by Watkins in the book *Indigenous Archaeologies: American Indian Values and Scientific Practice* (2001) and the article "Beyond the Margin: American Indians, First Nations, and Archaeology in North America" (2003).

Archaeology in the context of popular culture at a broad level is covered in *From Stonehenge to Las Vegas: Archaeology as Popular Culture* by Holtorf (2005), and the role of archaeology in fiction is the focus of *Digging Holes in Popular Culture: Archaeology and Science Fiction* by Russell (2002). Deconstructions of portrayals of the prehistoric past in fiction include the articles "Bad Hair Days in the Palaeolithic: Modern (Re)Constructions of the Cave Man" by Berman (1999) and "Neanderthals As Fiction in Archaeological Narrative" by Hackett and Dennell (2003).

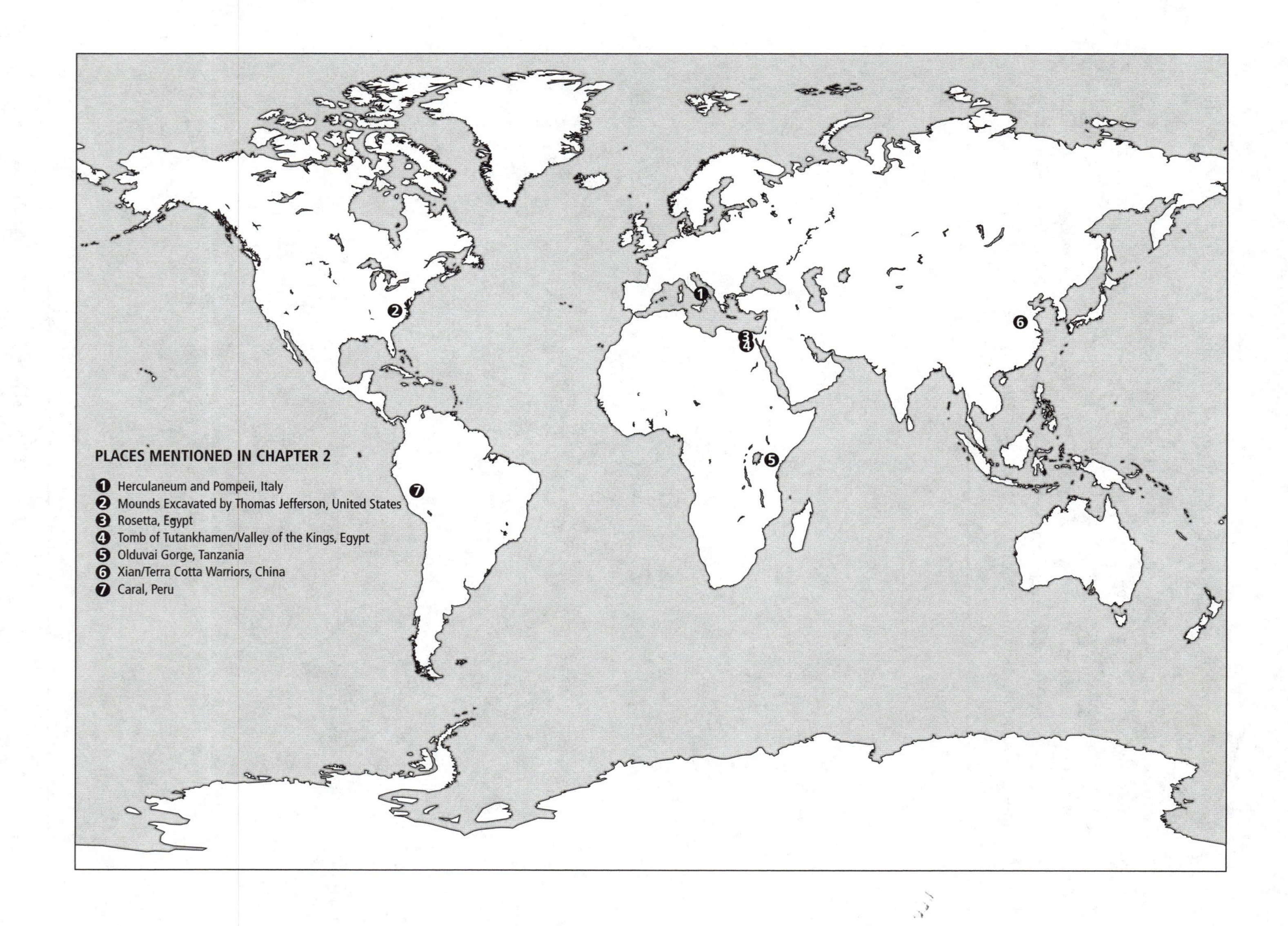
PLACES MENTIONED IN CHAPTER 2
1 Herculaneum and Pompeii, Italy
2 Mounds Excavated by Thomas Jefferson, United States
3 Rosetta, Egypt
4 Tomb of Tutankhamen/Valley of the Kings, Egypt
5 Olduvai Gorge, Tanzania
6 Xian/Terra Cotta Warriors, China
7 Caral, Peru
1
2
3
4
5
6
7

CHAPTER 2

Looking at Archaeology's Past

Introduction

As a widely recognized scholarly endeavor, archaeology has a fairly brief history, extending little more than about 150 years into the past. It has been recognized as a profession for only a few decades. These time frames are somewhat arbitrary, however, and even a cursory examination of the history of archaeology shows that many of the ideas and discoveries upon which the discipline is based come from the distant past, from various fields of study, and from around the globe (even though archaeology has traditionally been considered to be a product of European intellectual history and thought).

This chapter provides an overview of some of the most significant historical events in the emergence and ongoing development of archaeology during three periods: prior to the nineteenth century, during the nineteenth century, and from the twentieth century onward.

From the Ancient Philosophers to the End of the Eighteenth Century

Some historians of archaeology choose to see the first antecedents of the discipline in philosophical speculations about the human past, which can be traced back to the first millennium BC. Surviving manuscripts indicate that in the ancient societies of Greece, Rome, and China, people were speculating on previous "ages" and cultural evolution. Writings from ancient Greece speculate on previous technologies based on stone; a philosopher from ancient Rome suggested something akin to our modern conception of the Stone, Bronze, and Iron Ages; and it is reported that China had its own version of the **three-age system** more than 2,000 years ago.

Rather than focusing on these speculations, other historians choose to see the origins of archaeology in the first examples of concentrated interest in the material remains of past human activities. Like the philosophical speculations, these go back at least a few thousand years. People who lived in the latter days of the ancient Egyptian civilization spent time

TABLE 2.1: Key Events Leading to the Development of Archaeology prior to AD 1800

Time Period	Events
c. AD 1400–1800	Development of science as an explanatory framework
	Recognition of many prehistoric sites and objects in Europe
	Recognition of diverse cultures from around the world
	Formulation of important ideas about biological evolution and principles of geology
	Emergence of antiquarianism
	First systematic excavations
	Discovery of the Rosetta Stone
c. AD 400–1400	Virtually no development of archaeological thought or practice
c. 500 BC–AD 400	Ancient philosophers speculate on cultural evolution

restoring some material remains from earlier times, such as the Sphinx, although it may be stretching the imagination to link this with the development of archaeology. Ancient China and Persia provide stronger ties. It is reported that material remains were used in support of historical records in ancient China. And Nabonidus, a king of the Babylonian Empire, is often cited as the first archaeologist because of his deliberate quest, well over 2,000 years ago, for the material remains of the people who preceded the Babylonians.

According to the records retained in **cuneiform**, Nabonidus, who ruled from 556 to 539 BC, attempted to connect himself with the ancient past by excavating artifacts of his predecessors. Because he was excavating with an explicit design to make links with the past, many people call his actions archaeology, although to most this is a very long stretch.

Public museums date to the fifth century BC in Greece and the first century AD in Rome. The oldest museum still in existence, which has been in operation since the eighth century AD, is in Japan. Despite the close relationship between archaeology and museums, the first public museum did not open in Europe until the late seventeenth century.

The Middle Ages—the period from the collapse of the Roman Empire in the fifth century until the beginning of the Renaissance in Europe at about 1400—was a stagnant period for the growth of archaeology in Europe. Philosophical speculations and interest in the material remains of past cultures gave way to religious doctrine, and the Christian Bible was commonly viewed as the ultimate source of knowledge. Undoubtedly, from the perspective of most people in Europe during that time, speculation about the past was unnecessary. There was little apparent interest in material remains of the past, and little interest or discussion about previous ages.

During the periods widely known as the Renaissance (c. 1400–1600) and the Enlightenment (c. 1600–1800), changes in Europe had important implications for archaeology, beginning with the rise of science as an explanatory framework. As European explorers, traders, and missionaries returned home with tales of foreign places and peoples, Europeans must have found biblical explanations—such as attributing the origin of these cultures to the 10 lost tribes of Israel—increasingly difficult to accept. Parallel developments in the rise of science provided alternative explanations for the natural world. Although the Bible continued to have a prominent explanatory role, it was no longer the ultimate source of knowledge for many.

While the rise of science as a general explanatory framework was perhaps one of the most significant developments in the origins of archaeology, advancements in the more specific areas of geology and biology were equally important. Conventional thinking of the time placed the origin of the earth at somewhere between 6,000 and 3,700 BC. Various people attempted to determine the origin using religious texts. The most well known is the calculation based on the Christian Bible by Archbishop James Ussher, who determined in 1650 that the earth was created in 4004 BC. Subsequent calculations were even more precise, pinpointing the origin as October 23, 4004, at 9 a.m. Advances in geology challenged this notion of such a brief history for the earth and led many people to consider a much longer antiquity. Some of the basic principles of geology were formulated during this period, such as the **law of superposition** (stating that each undeformed sedimentary layer is older than the one above it), which ultimately served as a primary technique for assigning relative ages to archaeological sites.

In addition to suggesting a relatively recent origin for the earth, religious doctrine of the period provided for no such concept as biological evolution. All species were generally considered to have been created in their present form. Discoveries of bones we now recognize as those of extinct animals, and stones we now know were shaped by humans, were commonly explained as freaks of nature. Beginning in the 1700s, some people started believing that biological changes in organisms did occur. By the end of the 1700s, many people accepted evidence of biological change.

Although wide support for the concept of biological evolution did not happen until the late 1800s, the recognition and investigation of the phenomena in the 1700s had profound influence on the development of archaeology. The acceptance of biological evolution opened the door to thinking about cultural evolution. After 1,000 years of relatively little philosophical or intellectual interest in previous ages, Europeans once again became open to new concepts dealing with the cultural past.

Other significant developments during this period in Europe include renewed interest in philosophical speculations and material cultures of the classical civilizations of Greece and Rome. Translations of ancient philosophers who speculated about people progressing through various stages ultimately led to more modern frameworks of the three-age system. By the late 1500s, Europeans were again discussing the possibility of previous ages; and by the late 1700s, many people accepted the notion that European societies had developed in stages now known widely as the Stone, Bronze, and Iron ages. In the sixteenth and seventeenth century, interest in the material culture of ancient Greece and Rome emerged. Collecting art and antiquities from those classical eras became a hobby of the rich throughout Europe, and the collectors became known as **antiquarians**. Eventually the interest spread to antiquities of ancient Egypt as well.

While antiquarians were focused on the ancient civilizations, other people began to document the heritage of their own countries. One of the best known is William Camden, who produced a compendium of archaeological sites in Britain in the late sixteenth century. Edward Lhwyd and John Aubrey also investigated and wrote about archaeological sites in Britain in the seventeenth century.

European societies were introduced to an immense diversity of cultures from around the world during this time. As European explorers, traders, and missionaries returned from their travels to previously unknown parts of Asia, Africa, and the Americas, they brought with them descriptions of vastly different peoples and cultures, generally portrayed as being greatly inferior to European societies. Religious explanations attempted to account for the existence of these so-called morally and technologically inferior peoples: they were among the lost tribes of Israel mentioned in the Bible, and as they wandered from the holy land, they degenerated. Eventually, many would observe some similarities in the material culture of some of the peoples from foreign lands and the finds from earlier times in Europe, suggesting that the non-Europeans were simply not progressing as fast as Europeans (but these views wouldn't be fully worked out until the late 1800s).

The first systematic archaeological excavations are generally considered to have occurred in the eighteenth century. Excavations at three sites are significant for their impact on the development of archaeology. The Roman cities of Herculaneum and Pompeii in Italy were quickly buried by ash from the eruption of Mount Vesuvius in 79 AD. Systematic excavations began at both these sites in the eighteenth century, providing a rich database for understanding everyday life in the Roman Empire.

Another significant excavation took place in the United States. During the eighteenth century, considerable thought was given to the thousands of large earthen mounds that dotted the landscape. Although Europeans had observed indigenous peoples living on some of the mounds and conducting activities on others, and despite that indigenous peoples themselves claimed that they were directly descended from those who built the mounds, many people doubted their origin. Popular explanations included the notion that more advanced civilizations had existed in the mound areas before the indigenous peoples.

Some non-indigenous Americans who were curious about the mounds, including Thomas Jefferson (who would later become the third president of the United States) set out to investigate by excavation. Jefferson's methods, including the recording of mound **stratigraphy**, were remarkable for the time. In many ways, his attention to problem solving (e.g., determining who created the mounds) and his detailed recordings were following scientific method, and he is often credited as the first to undertake scientific excavations. Jefferson determined that the mounds were indeed created by the indigenous peoples in previous times, a conclusion that has withstood the test of time.

Jefferson isn't the only well-known figure from history to have influenced the development of archaeology. When Napoleon Bonaparte, the emperor of France, invaded Egypt in 1798, many people we would describe today as scholars accompanied him. He was interested in Egypt's ancient past, and some of his followers were directed to report on items of potential significance. In 1799, one of Napoleon's officers working in the Egyptian town of Rosetta discovered what was to become one of the world's best-known artifacts. The Rosetta Stone is a large black slab of basalt with an inscription in three languages: an ancient form of Greek, an ancient form of Egyptian script, and hieroglyphics. It is 114 centimeters (44 inches) high, 72 centimeters (29 inches) wide, and 28 centimeters (11 1/2 inches) thick.

The Rosetta Stone was immediately recognized for its potential to help decipher **hieroglyphics**, and although it would take some years, it ultimately did provide the key. Essentially, once it was determined that the ancient Greek and Egyptian scripts said the same thing, the hieroglyphics were assumed to as well, and it was only a matter of time before they were decoded. Despite efforts by the government of Egypt to have the Rosetta Stone returned, it rests today in the British Museum in London.

Archaeology in the Nineteenth Century

The early part of the nineteenth century witnessed further support for the ideas that had begun to form in the preceding centuries. Science was increasingly acknowledged as an appropriate framework for understanding how the world works, and notions of great antiquity for the earth were becoming widely accepted. Although those interested in earth science had developed some basic principles that convinced them that the earth had to be older than several thousand years, as claimed by theologians, the idea of great antiquity, in the order of 100,000 years or more, only became popular after the research and writings of James Hutton in the late 1700s and the publication of Charles Lyell's

BRITISH MUSEUM

FIGURE 2.1: THE ROSETTA STONE. Discovered in 1799 in the town of Rosetta, Egypt, following the invasion of French troops, the stone repeats the same message in three scripts, providing the key for deciphering hieroglyphics.

three-volume series *Principles of Geology* in the early 1830s. These writings were particularly important for establishing the concept of deep time for archaeology. Hutton, often considered the creator of modern geology, developed the principle of **uniformitarianism** (simply, "the present is the key to the past") and wrote *Theory of the Earth*, but by most accounts, his ideas was not easily understood or accepted. It wasn't until the writings of Lyell that theories of geology and geologic time became widely accepted.

TABLE 2.2: Key Events in the History of Archaeology during the Nineteenth Century

Time Period	Events
Late nineteenth century (c. 1865–1899)	Development of unilinear theory of cultural evolution Development of systematic excavation and recording methods
Mid-nineteenth century (c. 1835–1865)	Archaeology emerges as a profession and scholarly discipline People accept concept of biological evolution
Early nineteenth century (c. 1800–1835)	Popularization of three-age system Deep time established

In addition, museums played a very important role in the rise of archaeology in the early nineteenth century. Museums became active in their pursuit of collections. While museums were once generally considered to be passive receivers of finds, the desire to fill them in the nineteenth century became one of the principal reasons for the excavation of sites, both in Europe and the rest of world. The nineteenth century is often seen as the golden age of museums. Some of the collecting was done in a professional manner, but in other cases, it amounted to little more than looting. One of the best-known collectors of the early part of the century was Giovani Belzoni, a purported one-time circus strongman who made a career of looting Egyptian antiquities, some of which made their way to museums. Reports of Belzoni's raids commonly refer to his destruction of tombs and mummies in his quest for specific items, such as **papyri**. Belzoni, who sometimes worked on behalf of the British government, is also well known for his feats of engineering to move huge statues, many of which ended up in Great Britain.

Besides seeking to add to their collections, museums in the early nineteenth century played a role in solidifying thought on cultural evolution and popularizing the notion of the three-age system. Although ideas of cultural evolution can be traced to philosophers more than 2,000 years ago and were rediscovered in the Renaissance, the person usually credited with popularizing the three-age system is Christian Thomsen, who in 1816 was the first museum professional to use it to organize collections. As curator of the Danish National Museum, Thomsen classified objects for public display according to whether they were made from stone, bronze, or iron, and recognized the chronology. The system was quickly adopted by other museums.

Jacob Jens Worsaae was subsequently hired by Thomsen to expand the museum collection. In addition to excavating sites for the collection of objects, Worsaae's work had an intellectual angle: he sought to confirm the chronological sequence of the Stone, Bronze, and Iron Ages. Worsaae also worked for the Danish government, continuing his archaeological research in recording, excavating, and in some cases, preserving archaeological sites. For many, Worsaae is considered the first truly professional archaeologist. He is given this designation because he was paid to be an excavator, had established scholarly research objectives focused on **culture history**, and also was among the first to have a university appointment, beginning his teaching career at the University of Copenhagen in 1855.

Few would dispute that by the mid-1800s, archaeology had not only become a profession involved in the collection of objects of the past, but it had also come to be considered a serious academic discipline. Positions similar to Worsaae's appointment at Copenhagen were being established at other European universities as well.

The mid-1800s were also an influential time for thought about evolution. Many in Europe came to accept the notion of evolution, principally through the publication of Charles Darwin's *On the Origin of Species* in 1859, in which he explained how biological evolution occurs. The widespread acceptance of biological evolution may not have been directly responsible for theories about cultural evolution, since notions of cultural evolution were already in existence, but it likely made it easier to accept that cultures, like organisms, change through time.

If the three-age system is considered the first major archaeological theory, then the second is the **unilinear theory of cultural evolution** developed by Edward Tylor and Lewis Henry Morgan. In 1871, British anthropologist Edward Tylor developed the idea that based on their culture, peoples and societies of both modern and past times could be classified as either savages, barbarians, or civilized.

The American Lewis Henry Morgan further developed this idea with the publication of *Ancient Societies* in 1877. Morgan's system included three stages of savagery and three stages of barbarism before the stage of civilization. Categorization of any group of people was based primarily on its technology and subsistence strategy (Table 2.3). Since this is what is typically best represented in the material remains of people, Morgan's theory became attractive to many archaeologists. An integral part of the theory was that cultural evolution is directional, with all of humankind beginning at the lowest status of savagery. According to the theory, groups moved through the stages, albeit at different rates.

TABLE 2.3: The Unilinear Theory of Cultural Evolution (developed by L.H. Morgan in 1877)

Stage	Description
1. Lower Status of Savagery	From the infancy of humankind to the acquisition of a subsistence strategy that includes fishing and controlling fire No living examples of this stage existed when Morgan developed the theory
2. Middle Status of Savagery	Begins with subsistence that includes fishing and controlling fire, and ends with the use of the bow and arrow
3. Upper Status of Savagery	Begins with the use of the bow and arrow, and ends with the manufacture and use of pottery
4. Lower Status of Barbarism	Begins with pottery and ends with subsistence based on domestic plants and/or animals
5. Middle Status of Barbarism	Begins in the eastern hemisphere with the domestication of animals Begins in the western hemisphere with the cultivation of maize and other plants Ends with the process of smelting iron
6. Upper Status of Barbarism	Begins with iron smelting and ends with the invention of a phonetic alphabet and writing
7. Civilization	Begins with the invention of a phonetic alphabet and writing

While many people chose to accept Morgan's model of cultural evolution, not everyone did. Franz Boas, a pioneer of North American anthropology, was one of the principal people arguing against the model. Boas developed the idea of **historical particularism**, which implies that each group's history is unique and does not follow any general pattern of cultural evolution, contrary the unilinear theory.

The highlight of the last decades of the nineteenth century was development of systematic and detailed methods of archaeological excavation and recording, which remain in place today. Much of this development is attributed to General Augustus Henry Lane-Fox Pitt Rivers, who took the military precision and rigor he practiced as a general in the British army and applied it to archaeological excavation in his retirement. This included paying close attention to, and making detailed recordings of, stratigraphy; recording the precise **provenience** of all finds; keeping detailed notes; working with trained excavators; and publishing the results of his work. Pitt Rivers is generally credited with providing the foundations for contemporary archaeological fieldwork.

While archaeology in Europe and most other parts of the world continued to develop as a distinct discipline, it was largely subsumed within anthropology in the late 1800s in North America. This is likely due to the fact that in North America, unlike in Europe, direct cultural continuity existed between the original inhabitants of sites and the indigenous people of the late 1800s. Archaeology was not the only discipline included in anthropology at this time. Many anthropologists in North America during the late 1800s, including Boas, can be described as generalists, practicing all of archaeology, biological anthropology, cultural anthropology, and linguistics.

From 1900 Onward

Many important developments have taken place in archaeology since the beginning of the twentieth century. These include, but are certainly not limited to, the discovery of new sites; changes in methodological and theoretical orientations; the emergence of archaeology as a profession in addition to an academic discipline; and new interests.

TABLE 2.4: Important Developments in Archaeology since AD 1900

Time Period	Events
Since 1960	Development of processual archaeology Archaeology as a business arises Emergence of post-processual archaeology
Mid-1900s (c. 1940–1960)	Invention of radiocarbon dating Outline of world prehistory becomes established
Early 1900s (c. 1900–1940)	Extensive fieldwork and discovery of sites, including King Tut

Focusing on Description (c.1900–1965)

The first several decades of the twentieth century are often depicted as falling within what some call the culture-historical period (focusing on culture history), which means they emphasized describing the chronological development of cultures. Archaeology was primarily focused on finding and describing archaeological sites and the artifacts discovered within them, and then putting the objects and sites of a region into some sort of chronological sequence. Archaeological reports from this time tend to be thick with description and thin on interpretation. The items of interest were generally objects of stone or clay, obviously made by humans.

Archaeology was practiced for a variety of reasons in the early decades of the century. The tradition of antiquarianism continued, and some wealthy benefactors funded excavations led by professional archaeologists. University professors seeking to add to our knowledge base of past societies led many of the projects, and museums continued to expand their collections. Government funding of archaeology for nationalist purposes was also common.

Although dominated by archaeological description, the early decades were not totally devoid of theory. As the century progressed, the reaction against the unilinear theory of evolution became stronger. **Diffusion** was typically used as an explanation for cultural phenomena, and although it wasn't commonplace, archaeologists did theorize about such things as the origins of agriculture.

By mid-century, many archaeologists came to the conclusion that cultures essentially developed as a way of adapting to the environment, and it became widely accepted that there were multiple effective ways of adapting. The notion of a unilinear model of cultural evolution had been dying during the early decades of the century, and was dead by mid-century.

The early decades of the twentieth century were an exciting time for those involved in archaeology. Many important sites associated with ancient civilizations were discovered, perhaps none more inspiring than that of the tomb of Tutankhamen in Egypt, popularly known as King Tut. Archaeologist Howard Carter had worked in Egypt for many years before coming across the undisturbed tomb of Tutankhamen in 1922. The discovery is significant to archaeology in two major ways. First, it provides the only glimpse we have of an undisturbed royal tomb. All other tombs of royalty that have been discovered were looted long before archaeologists became involved. As such, the tomb of Tutankhamen provides the most comprehensive site of a royal Egyptian burial, and all that we can learn about Egyptian life from that.

Second, the tomb is significant because it marks the beginning of a worldwide fascination with archaeology. Newspapers from around the globe sent reporters to Egypt for the opening of the tomb, bringing the discovery to the attention of readers thousands

GRIFFITH INSTITUTE, OXFORD

FIGURE 2.2: HOWARD CARTER examining the third, innermost coffin of King Tut. The discovery of King Tut was among the most significant events for the development of archaeology in the early twentieth century.

of miles away. Some of the reporters began taking liberties with the facts, and the idea of "the Curse of King Tut," among other things, developed. As the story goes, some newspapers altered the meaning of some of the tomb's inscriptions, leading the public to believe there was a curse. When Lord Carnarvon of Britain, the sponsor of the excavations, died within a year of the opening of the tomb, it was taken as evidence of the curse.

Throughout the middle decades of the century, the fascination with archaeology continued. Archaeology was happening around the world, including in Africa by the well-known husband-and-wife team of palaeoanthropologists Louis and Mary Leakey. They began searching in East Africa's Olduvai Gorge for evidence of early humans. The Leakeys' archaeological projects resulted in dozens of significant discoveries of both skeletal and cultural remains. Louis Leakey was a great popularizer of research into early humans and was widely revered in his home country of Kenya. Many would say he created an archaeological dynasty. After Louis's death in 1972, Mary Leakey continued to make important discoveries into the 1980s. It was Mary who excavated the oldest known hominid footprints (c. 3.4 million years). Their son Richard replaced Louis as the director of Kenya National Museums and directed many significant archaeological projects in Kenya throughout the 1970s and 1980s, before turning his attention to conservation and political issues. The Leakey legacy has continued with Richard's wife, Meave, and daughter Louise (Louis's granddaughter) each making new and significant hominid discoveries in the early twenty-first century.

BARRY KASS/IMAGES OF ANTHROPOLOGY

FIGURE 2.3: FROM ARCHAEOLOGIST TO ARTIFACT: LOUIS LEAKEY. This statue of Louis Leakey sits outside the Kenya National Museum in Nairobi. Leakey was a great popularizer of archaeology, and he and his family have made many significant archaeological discoveries in Africa.

By the middle decades of the century, the basic pattern of cultural chronology around the world had been worked out. With the exception of some recent discoveries in Peru that suggest the presence of a hitherto unknown civilization known as Caral, there haven't been any discoveries of ancient civilizations since the early part of the twentieth century, and our basic understanding of the sequence of events has changed little.

The application of radiocarbon dating at mid-century was one of the most significant developments in archaeology. Radiocarbon dating began to be applied to material remains in 1950, and since that time it has remained one of the most reliable techniques for determining the antiquity of sites and objects. Prior to 1950, few reliable dating techniques existed for prehistoric sites. By providing specific dates, radiocarbon dating significantly increased the accuracy of dating sites and events of the past. The technique is described more fully in Chapter 7.

Archaeology as it was practiced in the early twentieth century was not without its critics from within the profession. It wasn't until the 1960s, however, that significant changes in goals and methods occurred.

A New Archaeology Emerges: The 1960s

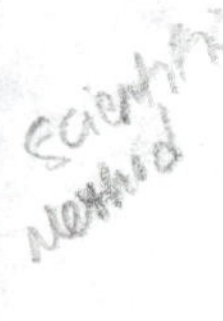

In the early 1960s, archaeology began to change dramatically. Critics argued that instead of simply describing the past, archaeologists should explain the past, focusing on such things as how and why cultures change. Further, the critics argued that archaeologists should use an explicitly scientific approach, which includes testing hypotheses and using quantitative methods. Many archaeologists of the time quickly accepted this new direction, and it became known as the **new archaeology**. Eventually it became more widely known as **processual archaeology**, reflecting the primary focus on understanding **culture process** (that is, how the various components of culture influence each other, how cultures change, and why cultures change).

Whereas the principal goal of traditional archaeology was to simply describe culture history, the new archaeology added two new goals. One was to reconstruct past ways of life, which essentially means to recreate previous cultures in their entirety. This is also known as **culture reconstruction**, which includes more attention to the social and ideological spheres than had typically been considered. Another goal was to explain the nature of culture, with the hope of generating some scientific laws that govern culture change. The essence of the new archaeology was that it could do much more and become more meaningful than traditional archaeology. Documenting culture history was still important, but by doing more, archaeology would become more socially relevant.

The American Lewis Binford and the British David Clarke are the two archaeologists most often associated with leading these changes in archaeology. Lewis Binford continued to make many important contributions to archaeological method and theory over subsequent decades, especially his contributions to **middle-level research**. Tragically, David Clarke died in a traffic accident in the late 1960s.

Culture history certainly wasn't abandoned, but it started to play a secondary role in many archaeological studies, particularly in the United States. The transition to processual archaeology did not occur in a vacuum. Published criticisms of archaeology had begun in the 1940s, but they were virtually ignored until the 1960s.

Archaeology was not the only field that was changing its nature, and some consideration should be given to the influence of changes in other disciplines. It has been suggested, for example, that David Clarke was influenced by changes occurring in the study of geography in Great Britain. Some historians of archaeology have also speculated that new archaeology caught on so quickly in the United States because of the political climate of the time. The argument is basically that the American government and other major funding agencies started to favor projects that were explicitly scientific and socially relevant.

Archaeology Becomes Diversified: The 1970s

The 1970s mark the decade when archaeology became significantly diverse. Throughout the earlier history of archaeology, there was always some degree of specialization, such as focusing on a particular geographic region or time period. The increased diversification that occurred in the 1970s is considered important in two major ways. One is that a split began to develop between archaeology undertaken with scholarly goals (e.g., reconstructing culture history) and archaeology practiced because sites were in danger of being destroyed.

As progressively larger-scale development projects were taking place around the world, people were increasingly concerned that important archaeological sites were being destroyed. During the 1960s and into the 1970s, university- and museum-based archaeologists were called out more frequently to assess potential impacts to sites and sometimes to undertake excavations in advance of their destruction by development. During this time, governments around the world began to strengthen heritage legislation, often making it mandatory that archaeological work be done in advance of development. Eventually, because of increasing development and stronger legislation, a new career track was opened up in archaeology. No longer were employment opportunities restricted to those based in universities or museums. Archaeologists could now work full time in industry: finding sites, assessing their significance, and in some cases, excavating them.

Archaeology also diversified in the 1970s by topical interests. Along with the latest goals and methods of the new archaeology came new topics to be explored. A new type of research known as **middle-range research**, or middle-range theory, began. Middle-range research was designed to bridge the gap between the low-level research of documenting culture history and the high-level research of theorizing about how cultures work. Examples of middle-range research include experimental archaeology and ethnoarchaeology. Analytical specialties also gained in prominence. Most of the major subfields recognized today (detailed in Chapter 3) arose during the 1970s and early 1980s.

A Newer, More Critical Archaeology Emerges: The 1990s

By the early 1980s, it was clear to many that there were problems with processual archaeology. The criticisms included a failure to adequately consider (i) the inherent bias in archaeological research, including gender bias, (ii) non-scientific frameworks for investigating the past, (iii) the multiple stakeholders in archaeological interpretation, (iv) that general laws governing human behavior may not exist, and (v) ideology, ethnicity, and gender in the archaeological record.

Like the development of processual archaeology, this newer, more critical archaeology did not emerge in a vacuum. It is generally considered to have been influenced by what has become known as **postmodernism** in the humanities. Other important and influential developments of the time include assertions of indigenous peoples and the continued rise of feminism. During the 1980s, most of the criticisms of processual archaeology were coming from archaeologists working in Britain, most notably Ian Hodder.

This newer, more critical archaeology was originally called **post-processual archaeology**. It has always been understood that post-processual archaeology is not so much a new way of doing archaeology as it is an umbrella phrase for all those who not only criticize processual archaeology, but do archaeology in scholarly, non-traditional methods. Post-processual archaeology includes, but is certainly not limited to, such things as the widespread belief that all archaeology is political; the use of metaphor in interpretations; the explicit recognition of bias in interpretations; the practice of archaeology in non-scientific ways; and includes the identification and significance of gender, ethnicity, and ideology as principal objectives of research.

It is difficult to know for sure whether the criticisms of Hodder and other British archaeologists were persuasive enough to alter the kinds of research being done throughout the world, or whether that had more to do with other occurrences, such as the rise of feminism and indigenous empowerment, or perhaps a change in the way archaeological research is funded.

It is clear that many who profess to be doing processual archaeology early in the twenty-first century have clearly been influenced by the criticisms. Explicit recognition of bias is now common, and topics such as gender, ethnicity, and ideology are now mainstream. Whether the changes are related to world events, intellectual persuasion, funding, or other means, remains to be seen. It has been pointed out, however, that after a few decades of National Science Foundation funding for archaeological researchers from the United States, subsequent decreases in funding allocations in the 1980s caused researchers to shift their grant proposals to the National Endowment for the Humanities in which research on issues of gender and ethnicity are much more likely to be funded.

Important Discoveries of the Late twentieth Century

In 2005, *Discover Magazine* asked several well-known archaeologists to identify the most important discoveries or trends of the previous 25 years. The responses were diverse and included the growing appreciation of the relevance of archaeology; new technologies relating to finding sites; the increased use of ethnoarchaeology and experimental archaeology; government regulations regarding archaeology; and the use of microscopic particles such as DNA and isotopes in research.

In addition to advances in methods, there were many important archaeological site discoveries and excavations in the late twentieth century. One of the most sensational is the excavation of the terra cotta warriors, near the city of Xian in China. Approximately 8,000 life-size warriors, horses, and chariots arranged in battle formation were uncovered near the tomb of Qin Shi Huang, reported to have been the first emperor of China, dating to between 211 BC and 206 BC. After being discovered

VICKIE PAVLOVICK

FIGURE 2.4: TERRA COTTA WARRIORS, discovered in 1974. About 8,000 life-size terra cotta warriors were deposited in battle formation near the tomb of the first emperor of China.

by Chinese peasants digging a well, the site began to be excavated in the 1970s. The soldiers, horses, and chariots remain in battle formation. Each soldier was baked in a kiln, has a distinct facial expression, and wears a uniform painted in either red or green.

Perhaps the most important discovery of recent years in the Americas is the identification of what may be the hemisphere's oldest city and civilization. Excavations that began in the 1990s at the site of Caral in Peru indicate that it is probably about 4,700 years old. The site itself covers more than 150 acres and includes monumental architecture such as plazas and pyramids, suggesting it reached the stage of cultural complexity commonly known as a civilization.

KEY RESOURCES AND SUGGESTED READING

The most comprehensive history of archaeology, particularly its intellectual development is *A History of Archaeological Thought* by Trigger (1989). Other general histories of archaeology include *A Short History of Archaeology* by Daniel (1981), *A Brief History of Archaeology: Classical Times to the Twenty-First Century* by Fagan (2005), *The Discovery of the Past* by Schnapp (1996), and *Uncovering the Past: A History of Archaeology* by Stiebing (1993). Sources that focus on the history of American archaeology include *The Land of Prehistory: A Critical History of American Archaeology* by Kehoe (1998), the article "The Political Economy of Archaeology in the United States" by Patterson (1999), and *A History of American Archaeology* by Willey and Sabloff (1993). *Archaeology as a Process: Processualism and its Progeny,* by O'Brien, Lyman, and Schiffer (2005) provides an engaging view of the intellectual development of American archaeology since the early 1960s. Kelly and Williamson (1996), in the article "The Positioning of Archaeology Within Anthropology: A Canadian Historical Perspective," focus on the development of archaeology in Canada. *Collecting in a Consumer Society* by Belk (1995) provides some insight into the history of collecting and museums.

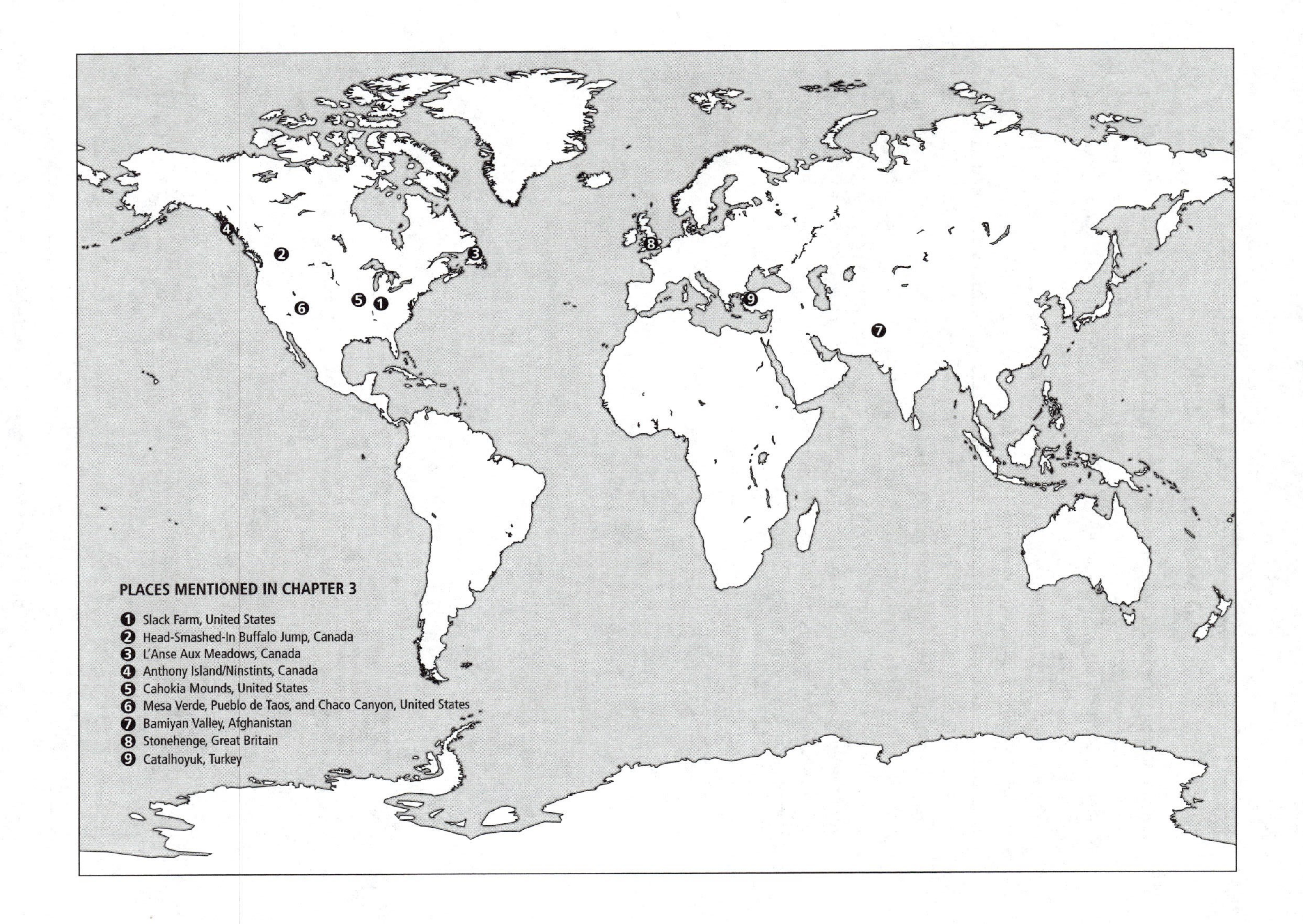
4
2
3
5
1
6
8
9
7
PLACES MENTIONED IN CHAPTER 3
1 Slack Farm, United States
2 Head-Smashed-In Buffalo Jump, Canada
3 L'Anse Aux Meadows, Canada
4 Anthony Island/Ninstints, Canada
5 Cahokia Mounds, United States
6 Mesa Verde, Pueblo de Taos, and Chaco Canyon, United States
7 Bamiyan Valley, Afghanistan
8 Stonehenge, Great Britain
9 Catalhoyuk, Turkey

CHAPTER 3

Managing Archaeology in the Early Twenty-first Century

Introduction

This chapter provides an overview of the diversity of archaeological work and how it is regulated. It begins with descriptions of the four major domains of archaeology, along with the widely recognized subfields and specialties of archaeological research. This is followed by outlines of laws and other instruments that govern archaeology; the codes of ethics to which archaeologists adhere; and the ways in which archaeologists share information.

The Four Major Types of Archaeology

The four main types of archaeology being undertaken today are **academic archaeology**, archaeology in the context of industry (commony known as **CRM**), **indigenous archaeology**, and amateur (or avocational) archaeology. These categories are not necessarily mutually exclusive, and it is possible for a project to have elements of more than one kind of archaeology.

Academic Archaeology

Academic archaeology is undertaken for intellectual or scholarly reasons and is based primarily in colleges, universities, and research museums or institutes. There are two basic components of academic archaeology: education and research.

The education component of academic archaeology focuses on teaching students archaeology at the B.A. (bachelor's degree), M.A. (master's degree), and a Ph.D. (doctor of philosophy) level. Academic archaeology often also includes a component of public education, but this is usually secondary.

The research component usually involves the collection of data from the field, including the identification and recording of sites, as well as the excavation and analysis of recovered remains.

Some projects have elements of both education and research. For example, colleges and universities often operate archaeology field schools. These field schools invariably have explicit research goals and the clear objective of training students in archaeological methods. Similarly, students working on their master's degree or Ph.D. do a great deal of research, and it is often said that they learn archaeology by doing it.

Academic research projects are usually directed by an archaeology professor or a student working on a master's degree or Ph.D. Funding for major research projects often comes from large funding agencies, which are often directly or indirectly tied to government (e.g., the National Science Foundation and the National Endowment for the Humanities in the United States, and the Social Sciences and Humanities Research Council of Canada). To ensure that research proposals to large funding agencies will make a worthwhile contribution to society and have a sound research design, they are usually subjected to peer review. In addition to the project director, there are typically field crews consisting of archaeology students.

Of all the major kinds of archaeology, it is academic archaeology that is most dominant in media. The results of research conducted within the domain of academic archaeology form the basis of published information about the discipline. Results of research are often reported in one of many scholarly or semi-scholarly periodicals that include archaeology (Table 3.1). Most articles about archaeology in newspapers and popular newsmagazines, such as *Time* or *Discover*, are written by journalists, but are reporting on academic research. Archaeology stories produced for television, whether it is a news item or documentary, are also almost always based on academic archaeology.

Academic research often involves multiyear projects, with the amount of time spent doing fieldwork dwarfed by the amount of time involved in analysis and interpretation. The results of academic research projects directed by students are written as master's theses or Ph.D. dissertations, which are held in libraries and are often rewritten as one or more articles in scholarly journals, or as a book. The results of research projects directed by professors are often written as one or more journal articles, a chapter in an edited book, or an entire book.

Archaeology in Industry

Most professional archaeologists make their careers in industry, primarily in the documentation and assessment of heritage sites. In North America, this kind of archaeology is usually described as cultural resource management or simply CRM. Other descriptors are outlined in Table 3.2.

This kind of archaeology is usually done because it is required by legislation, and it involves several stages. Throughout the world, governments have enacted legislation

TABLE 3.1: Periodicals that Include Articles on Archaeology

Scholarly archaeology journals

American Antiquity
American Journal of Archaeology
Antiquity
Archaeologies: Journal of the World Archaeological Congress
Archaeometry
Canadian Journal of Archaeology
Geoarchaeology
Historic Archaeology
International Journal of Historical Archaeology
Journal of Anthropological Archaeology
Journal of Archaeological Method and Theory
Journal of Archaeological Research
Journal of Archaeological Science
Journal of Field Archaeology
Journal of Social Archaeology
Journal of World Prehistory
Latin American Antiquity
North American Archaeologist
World Archaeology

Scholarly anthropology journals in which archaeology articles often appear

American Anthropologist
Current Anthropology

Scholarly multidisciplinary journals in which archaeology articles occasionally appear

Nature
Science

Semi-scholarly periodicals in which archaeology articles appear

Archaeology
Discover
National Geographic
Scientific American

TABLE 3.2: Archaeology as it is Known in the Heritage Industry

Name	Description
Cultural resource management (CRM)	The phrase used most commonly in North America to describe archaeological work being done in industry, particularly due to heritage legislation requiring the identification, documentation, assessment, and in some cases the excavation of sites prior to land-altering developments
Compliance archaeology	Essentially the same as CRM, but used less often Called compliance archaeology because it is done in compliance with heritage laws
Client-based archaeology	Also the same as CRM The clients are the developers or agencies funding the work and hiring archaeologists because they are legislated to do so
Conservation, rescue, and salvage archaeology	Names commonly used to describe archaeology being done in advance of land-altering activities in the 1960s and 1970s
Archaeological heritage management (AHM)	The equivalent of CRM in continental Europe
Archaeological resource management (ARM)	The equivalent of CRM in the United Kingdom
Cultural heritage management (CHM)	The equivalent of CRM in Australia

that requires archaeologists to assess the impact of potential land-altering projects on heritage resources, often leading to the documentation and excavation of archaeological sites. The process generally begins when a proposal for land-altering development of some kind, ranging from the widening of a road to building a dam that may potentially flood thousands of square miles, is given to government for approval. The proposal makes the rounds of many different government departments, including the department responsible for heritage. A bureaucrat reads the proposal and determines whether the developer must hire archaeologists to search and document heritage sites in the area. If heritage sites are discovered, archaeologists then assess their significance and make recommendations about protecting or excavating the sites.

One example of a project done in this context is the archaeological investigations associated with the construction of a gas pipeline in Peru. Thirty-three kilometers (21 miles) of pipeline were added to prevent damage to some sites, but many others were excavated. Close to 1,000 archaeological sites were discovered near the route of the 730-kilometer (454-mile) pipeline. It was reported that over 100,000 pieces of textile, jewelry, weapons, and tools were recovered, as well as dozens of mummies.

Compared to those in academic archaeology, archaeologists working in industry generally spend a much higher proportion of their time doing fieldwork (that is, looking for and excavating sites), and less time in analysis and interpretation. Archaeologists working in industry often attempt to incorporate into their fieldwork a research strategy that will contribute to the broader field of archaeology, but this is usually secondary to fulfilling the needs of their contracts, which usually simply focus on the documentation and assessment of sites.

Whereas field crews and laboratory personnel working on academic archaeology projects are usually affiliated with colleges and universities (as either students or employees), field crews associated with archaeology in industry usually have completed at least a bachelor's degree. Because projects in industry are frequently short term, many field-workers go from job to job with various employers. These workers are sometimes referred to as **shovelbums**.

Reports of the archaeological projects are always prepared for the clients in industry or government, but they rarely become widely available. Instead, they tend to remain in the client's or government's offices and enter what has come to be known as the **gray literature**.

Indigenous Archaeology

Archaeologists have recently begun to work closely with indigenous peoples at all levels of research. This has led to the emergence of indigenous archaeology, which is archaeology that is done either by, with, or for indigenous peoples. It is based primarily out of indigenous organizations, and the objectives of the projects and the research designs are determined in whole or in part by those organizations. Typical objectives of indigenous archaeology projects include (i) providing support for claims of indigenous rights and territory, (ii) archaeo-tourism, (iii) education for their own and other (non-indigenous) communities, and (iv) nation building.

Amateur Archaeology

Amateur archaeology, also known as avocational archaeology, is an umbrella phrase for the work being done by people without educational credentials in the field, and who do not receive direct income for their work on archaeological projects (although they may receive income from books they write or artifacts they sell). The primary kinds of amateurs are those who volunteer or pay a stipend to work on academic archaeology projects, usually under the guidance of an academic archaeologist, and looters, sometimes known as **pothunters**, who essentially dig up sites to find and sell objects of value. Amateur archaeology also includes people with little or no training in archaeological method and theory who nevertheless theorize and sometimes write popular books explaining the origins of famous heritage sites. Many of the people who fall into this category either have little knowledge or choose to ignore the fundamental principles, methods, and research findings of academic archaeology. Their work is often termed **pseudoarchaeology**.

Subfields of Archaeology

There are dozens of widely recognized subfields and specialties in contemporary archaeology. Table 3.3 lists a number of them, but it certainly is not exhaustive. Many of the subfields and specialties, such as classical archaeology, geoarchaeology, historic archaeology, lithic studies, ceramic studies, archaeometry, archaeobotany, forensic archaeology, and zooarchaeology, are commonly offered as third and fourth year courses in university.

Prehistoric archaeology, which is defined as focusing on a time period before written records existed for a given area, has many subspecialties. These include **palaeoanthropology** (the study of early human biology and culture, usually at least several hundred thousand years ago), or study of one of the widely known temporal periods such as **Palaeolithic**, **Mesolithic**, and **Neolithic.**

Historic archaeology, defined as focusing on a time period for which written records do exist, is also known as text-aided archaeology, and similarly has many subspecialties. These include **biblical archaeology** (places and events mentioned in the Bible), **classical archaeology** (sites and objects of the Greek and Roman empires), **Egyptology** (sites and objects of the ancient Egyptian civilization), **Pre-Columbian archaeology** (civilizations of the Americas before the arrival of Christopher Columbus), **colonial archaeology** (study of the time and place of European rule of non-European lands claimed by Europeans), **post-colonial archaeology** (focusing on the time and place since European colonial governments ceased to rule foreign lands), and **industrial archaeology** (machinery and structures of industrial activity, such as mining, power generation, and road building).

TABLE 3.3: Archaeological Subfields and Specialties

Name	Focus
Archaeobiology	Plants and animals in archaeology
Archaeobotany	Plants in archaeology
Archaeometry	Application of physical sciences
Biblical archaeology	Places, people, and events of the Bible
Bioarchaeology	Human remains
Ceramic studies	Baked clay
Classical archaeology	Ancient Greece and Rome
Community archaeology	Local community interests
Ecological archaeology	Adaption to natural environment
Egyptology	Ancient Egypt
Ethnoarchaeology	Contemporary people
Exoarchaeology	Material remains in outer space
Experimental archaeology	Creating data for comparison
Forensic archaeology	Crime investigations
Garbology	Contemporary refuse
Geoarchaeology	Sediments
Historic archaeology	Period since writing began
Indigenous archaeology	Indigenous groups
Industrial archaeology	Heavy industry
Lithic studies	Stone
Maritime archaeology	Sites near or under water
New World archaeology	North, South, and Central America
Old World archaeology	Asia, Africa, and Europe
Prehistoric archaeology	Period before writing
Underwater archaeology	Sites under water
Zooarchaeology	Animals in archaeology

Archaeologists involved in **Old World** archaeology usually specialize in either the continent of Africa, Asia, or Europe, or a specific region within one of the continents. Archaeologists involved in **New World** archaeology often specialize in North, South, or Central America, or a specific region within one of those continents.

Two of the most common types of materials recovered from archaeological sites are fragments of stone and pottery, which have led to the development of the specialties of **lithic** studies and **ceramic** studies. The study of sediments from archaeologi-

ROBERT J. MUCKLE

FIGURE 3.1: FIREPLACE IN A FOREST. Although most people's image of archaeology focuses on ancient civilizations and prehistoric remains, interest in remains of recent times has been on the rise. The fireplace depicted here was from an early twentieth-century cabin on the west coast of Canada.

cal sites is termed **geoarchaeology**, and the study of human skeletons is called **bioarchaeology** or **osteology**.

Archaeobotany (also known as palaeoethnobotany) is the study of plant remains from archaeological sites, and **zooarchaeology** is the study of animal remains from archaeological sites. Together, archaeobotany and zooarchaeology are known as **archaeobiology**.

Forensic archaeology is the application of archaeological methods to criminal investigations, as well as the collection of evidence in cases of mass disasters. **Underwater archaeology** focuses on objects and sites underwater, including but not restricted to shipwrecks. Archaeology that depends on the methods of physics, chemistry, mathematics, and computer science is often referred to as **archaeometry**.

Ecological archaeology focuses on the relationships between people and the environment. **Ethnoarchaeology** refers to when archaeologists apply their observations of the behavior and material culture of contemporary people to interpretations of the patterning they see in archaeological sites.

There are many other subfields and specialties, which although rarely warrant a college or university level course, are common in popular and scholarly writing. These include **dirt archaeology**, which generally is taken to mean working in the field, looking for sites, and possibly excavating them. **Armchair archaeology** is a phrase used to describe both professionals and amateurs who rarely, if ever, do fieldwork, but rather focus their attention on explaining what has been observed by others, without leaving the comfort of their home or office. **Experimental archaeology** involves replicating possible past events to aid interpretation of archaeological sites and objects.

Some archaeologists focus on contemporary refuse, a subfield popularly known as **garbology**. Although often considered trivial, this is one area that garners much popular attention and has great value to American industry and government agencies.

The best-known archaeologist in the field of garbology is William L. Rathje, who founded the Garbage Project, also known as Le Projet du Garbage, at the University of Arizona in the early 1970s. Since that time, members of the Garbage Project have studied fresh household garbage in several cities throughout the United States, as well as in Mexico and Australia. They have also conducted excavations in more than a dozen landfills in Canada and the United States. Their research has been funded by a wide variety of corporations that are interested in patterns of food consumption and waste, including Heinz, Frito-Lay, NutraSweet, and Pillsbury, as well as agencies such as the National Livestock and Meat Board in the United States. Regional governments fund work to measure the effectiveness of recycling programs and the amount of hazardous waste in cities.

The members of the Garbage Project have come up with many interesting and sometimes surprising research results. These include the fact that paper remains a dominant class of material in landfill sites and that fast food packaging, Styrofoam, and disposable diapers make up less than 3 per cent of landfill material. They have also found that the average household wastes about 15 per cent of the food it buys and that recycling programs are not always effective (e.g., instead of using up hazardous materials, people will discard them by recycling). They also have found that the average amount of garbage thrown away by individuals continues to increase substantially and that when people receive larger trash containers (as often occurs when a city moves towards a mechanized system of dumping individual containers into trucks), they throw away more stuff.

Among the most recent subfields to emerge, **exoarchaeology** is the study of the off-earth material remains of space exploration. This includes the study of the tens of thousands of pieces of space junk currently orbiting Earth, as well as the remains of space exploration left on the moon and Mars. Archaeologists are particularly interested in the dozens of sites containing material remains on the moon. One site of particular focus is Tranquility Base, the site of the first landing, where archaeologists funded by NASA have documented over 100 artifacts.

NASA

FIGURE 3.2: MAN ON THE MOON. The documentation of space exploration is an emergent interest in archaeology and includes landing sites on the moon.

National and International Heritage Management

Governments throughout the world recognize the value of **tangible heritage** and have enacted legislation and other instruments to protect it (Table 3.4). In some countries, the penalty for the unauthorized destruction of heritage resources can be execution. In North America, death is not an option given to the courts, but fines and imprisonment are.

TABLE 3.4: National and International Heritage Regulations

United States
Antiquities Act (1906)
Historic Sites Act (1935)
National Historic Preservation Act (NHPA) (1966)
National Environmental Policy Act (NEPA) (1969)
Archaeological and Historic Preservation Act (AHPA) (1974)
Archaeological Resources Protection Act (ARPA) (1979)
Abandoned Shipwreck Act (ASA) (1987)
Native American Graves Protection and Repatriation Act (NAGPRA) (1990)
Canada
Indian Act (1985)
Historic Sites and Monuments Act (1985)
National Parks Act (2000)
Canadian Environmental Assessment Act (1992)
ICOMOS (International Council on Monuments and Sites)
Charter for the Protection and Management of the Archaeological Heritage (1990)
Charter for the Protection and Management of Underwater Cultural Heritage (1996)
International Cultural Tourism Charter (1999)
UNESCO (United Nations Educational, Scientific, and Cultural Organization)
Hague Convention for the Protection of Cultural Property in the Event of Armed Conflict (1954)
Recommendations on International Principles Applicable to Archaeological Excavations (1956)
Recommendations on the Means of Prohibiting and Preventing the Illicit Export, Import, and Transfer of Ownership of Cultural Property (1964)
Convention on the Means of Prohibiting and Preventing the Illicit Import, Export, and Transfer of Ownership of Cultural Property (1970)
Convention Concerning the Protection of the World Cultural and Natural Heritage (1972)
Second Protocol to the Hague Convention of 1954 for the Protection of Cultural Property in the Event of Armed Conflict (1999)
Convention on the Protection of the Underwater Cultural Heritage (2001)
Declaration Concerning the Intentional Destruction of Cultural Heritage (2003)
UNIDROIT (International Institute for the Unification of Private Law)
Convention on Stolen and Illegally Exported Cultural Objects (1995)
UN (United Nations)
Law of the Sea (1982)
Outer Space Treaty (1967)
WAC (World Archaeology Congress)
Vermillion Accord of 1989

There are several government acts controlling archaeological research in the United States, beginning with the Antiquities Act of 1906, which established the protection of archaeological sites on federal lands and a permit system for archaeological work. This was followed by the Historic Sites Act of 1935, in which it became a national policy to preserve historic sites, buildings, and objects. The majority of archaeological research in the United States today is performed under the National Historic Preservation Act (NHPA) of 1966, which stipulates that archaeological investigations should occur in advance of potential disturbances on federal lands or on lands that may be disturbed by any federally funded project.

The National Environmental Policy Act (NEPA) of 1969 requires federal agencies to consider environmental, historical, and cultural values (including archaeological resources) whenever land owned by the federal government is altered or when private land is altered with federal money. The Archaeological and Historic Preservation Act (AHPA) of 1974 made federal agencies responsible for any damage they caused to archaeological sites. The Archaeological Resources Protection Act (ARPA) of 1979 further strengthened heritage legislation by establishing penalties and fees of up to $100,000 and five years' imprisonment for illegally excavating on federal lands. The Abandoned Shipwreck Act (ASA) of 1987 established that the US government owns abandoned shipwrecks in the country's rivers and lakes, and in the ocean up to three miles off the coastlines.

The Native American Graves Protection and Repatriation Act (NAGPRA) of 1990 requires agencies and museums receiving federal funds to work towards returning native skeletal remains and associated burial objects to the affiliated native groups and also provides native burial sites greater protection in that it requires natives to be consulted when archaeological investigations are anticipated or when cultural items are unexpectedly recovered in their traditional territory.

While the United States has several acts that protect archaeological resources on federal lands, it is virtually the only country that gives ownership of archaeological resources to the owner of private land. In other countries, ownership tends to lie with the government. In some jurisdictions, ownership of recovered prehistoric remains lies with indigenous peoples, although the artifacts may be held by the government "in trust."

There is little doubt that the heritage laws in the United States have led to a decrease in the amount of looting on federal lands. But because looting on private land is unregulated, many archaeological resources continue to be unprotected. There are reported cases of people buying "looting rights" to archaeological sites. A well-known example is the Slack Farm in Kentucky, where looters reportedly paid the owner $10,000 for the rights to raid a native cemetery on the property. Landowners of an Anasazi site in Utah charge "guests" more than $2,000 per day if they want to keep artifacts they discover on the site.

In Canada, heritage legislation falls primarily under provincial and territorial power. All jurisdictions impose penalties for the unauthorized removal or destruction of archaeological resources. The Heritage Conservation Act of British Columbia, for example, stipulates that a corporation that violates the act is subject to a penalty of up to $1 million, while individuals who violate the act are subject fines of up to $50,000 and a maximum of two years' imprisonment. The removal of heritage objects on Native reserves is governed by the Indian Act (1985), and archaeological sites and artifacts on other federal lands are protected primarily through the National Parks Act (2000), the Historic Sites and Monuments Act (1985) and the Canadian Environmental Assessment Act (1992).

Although successful prosecutions for looting or otherwise destroying archaeological sites in North America are rare, they do occur. For example, an investigation in the United States that started in 2001 resulted in the convictions of seven people and a corporation for looting. Upon conviction, individuals had to pay restitution ranging from less than $10,000 to more than $100,000 and were given prison sentences of up to 37 months.

At the international level, there are many accords, charters, declarations, recommendations, agreements, conventions, protocols, and laws relating to archaeological sites and objects.

The United Nations Educational, Scientific, and Cultural Organization (UNESCO) has developed several instruments protecting heritage, beginning with the Convention for the Protection of Cultural Property in the Event of Armed Conflict, also known as the Hague Convention, adopted in 1954. This convention was developed in response to the massive destruction of heritage sites during World War II and stipulates that states are bound to safeguard cultural heritage during times of armed conflict. The convention was adopted with a protocol that prohibits the export of cultural property from occupied territory. In response to the continued destruction of heritage sites during armed conflict throughout the latter decades of the twentieth century, particularly that occurring in the former Yugoslavia and the former Soviet Union, a second protocol was adopted in 1999, which essentially improved the safeguarding measures by defining them, created a new category for enhanced protection, and provided specific sanctions for violations.

The UNESCO Recommendations on International Principles Applicable to Archaeological Excavations, adopted in 1956, lays out guidelines for member states to legislate the protection of archaeological sites. These include requiring archaeological work to be subject to authorization, declaring archaeological discoveries to proper authorities, providing penalties for violations, defining the legal status of archaeological finds, preserving archaeological deposits for future archaeology, maintaining repositories, and educating the public.

The UNESCO Convention on the Means of Prohibiting and Preventing the Illicit Import, Export, and Transfer of Ownership of Cultural Property, adopted in 1970, stipulates that countries are bound to return cultural property, including the products of both legal and illegal excavations, to the country of origin. UNESCO asked the International Institute for the Unification of Private Law (UNIDROIT) to create a supplement to the convention. The result is the UNIDROIT Convention on Stolen and Illegally Exported Cultural Objects, adopted in 1995, which makes it clear that anyone who has an illegally obtained artifact in their possession must return it.

TABLE 3.5: Selected UNESCO World Heritage Sites

North America
United States
Mesa Verde
Cahokia Mounds State Historic Site
Independence Hall
Statue of Liberty
Chaco Canyon National Historic Park
Monticello and University of Virginia in Charlottesville
Pueblo de Taos
Canada
L'Anse Aux Meadows National Historic Site
Head-Smashed-In Buffalo Jump
Historic District of Quebec
Old Town Lunenburg
Anthony Island
Central America (including Mexico)
Tikal National Park, Guatemala
Maya Site of Copan, Honduras
Historic Center of Mexico City and Xochimilco
Historic Center of Oaxaca and Archaeological Site of Monte Albán, Mexico
Pre-Hispanic City of Chichen-Itza, Mexico
Pre-Hispanic City and National Park of Palenque, Mexico
Pre-Hispanic City of Teotihuacan, Mexico
Pre-Hispanic Town of Uxmal, Mexico
South America
Tiwanaku: Spiritual and Political Centre of the Tiwanaku Culture, Bolivia
Rapa Nui National Park (Easter Island), Chile

TABLE 3.5: ***continued***

Historic Sanctuary of Machu Picchu, Peru
Lines and Geoglyphs of Nasca and Pampas de Jumana, Peru
Europe
Acropolis of Athens, Greece
Archaeological Site of Delphi, Greece
Archaeological Areas of Pompeii, Herculaneum and Torre Annunziata, Italy
Archaeological Site of Atapuerca, Spain
Altamira Cave, Spain
Archaeological Site of Troy, Turkey
Stonehenge, Avebury and Associated Sites, United Kingdom
Asia
Cultural Landscape and Archaeological Remains of the Bamiyan Valley, Afghanistan
Angkor, Cambodia
Mausoleum of the First Qin Emperor (Terra Cotta Warriors), China
Peking Man Site at Zhoukoudian, China
Archaeological Ruins at Moenjodaro, Pakistan
Africa
Ancient Thebes and Its Necropolis, Egypt
Memphis and Its Necropolis—the Pyramid Fields from Giza to Dahshur, Egypt
Fossil Hominid Sites of Sterkfontein, Swartkrans, Kromdraai, and Environs, South Africa
Great Zimbabwe National Monument, Zimbabwe
Australia
Kakadu National Park

The well-known World Heritage List was initiated through the UNESCO Convention Concerning the Protection of the World Cultural and Natural Heritage, adopted in 1972. This convention established the framework for having sites added to the list and accessing funds and other forms of assistance to aid in the protection, conservation, rehabilitation, and presentation of heritage. To be included on the list, sites must meet several criteria, including having outstanding universal value. Worldwide, there are approximately 1,000 designated **World Heritage Sites**, mostly in the "cultural" category. Some of the well-known archaeological sites with World Heritage status are listed in Table 3.5.

Several locations of past cultural activity in Canada and the United States have been accorded World Heritage status. Head-Smashed-In Buffalo Jump in southern Alberta is an excellent example of the aboriginal practice of driving large animals over a cliff to their death. The site itself consists of a complex of drive lanes that directed buffalo (bison) to a cliff, an accumulation of buffalo bones at the base of the cliff, a butchery location, and camping areas. The site was used for over 5,000 years and is a good example of archaeological tourism in Canada today, with an on-site museum and interpretive programs run by the local Blood and Piikani (Peigan) First Nations, the descendants of the people who operated the jump.

L'Anse aux Meadows is the earliest undisputed evidence of Europeans in North America. Located on the northern tip of Newfoundland, the site consists of the remains of an eleventh-century Viking settlement. Excavated remains include wood-framed, peat-turf buildings like those found in Norse Greenland and Iceland.

Anthony Island (also known as SGaang Gwaii) among the Queen Charlotte Islands (also known as Haida Gwaii) along the north Pacific coast of British Columbia includes the Haida peoples' village of Ninstints (Nans Dins) and the remains of their houses, as well as carved mortuary and memorial poles, offering visual keys to their oral traditions.

Cahokia Mounds is an excellent example of the mound-building peoples of the continent. Located near St. Louis, Cahokia Mounds is the largest prehistoric settlement north of Mexico. It was occupied from the ninth to fifteenth centuries, covered nearly 1,600 hectares (3,952 acres) including more than 100 earthen mounds, and at its peak may have had a population close to 20,000. The largest mound, known as Monks Mound, covered more than 5 hectares (12 acres) and stood 30 meters (98 feet) high.

Mesa Verde in Colorado, as well as Pueblo de Taos and Chaco Canyon in New Mexico, includes remnants of the Pueblo peoples who occupied the southwestern states beginning in the sixth century. Mesa Verde, the best known, consists of both dwellings built into the cliffs as well as villages on top of the mesa. More than 4,000 sites have been recorded in the area, and some dwellings are comprised of more than 100 rooms. Pueblo de Taos, representing the Pueblo Indians of New Mexico and Arizona, is an adobe settlement consisting of dwellings and ceremonial buildings, and Chaco Canyon was a major center of Pueblo culture in the Four Corners area, known primarily for its distinctive architecture and ceremonial buildings.

The International Council on Monuments and Sites (ICOMOS) adopted the Charter for the Protection and Management of the Archaeological Heritage in 1990. The charter establishes basic principles relating to archaeological heritage management. These include frameworks for legislation, fieldwork, conservation, qualifications, and accessibility to information.

FIGURE 3.3: MESA VERDE, Colorado. One of four prehistoric sites the United States with World Heritage Site designation, Mesa Verde comprises the remnants of Pueblo peoples.

Both the United Nations and ICOMOS have instruments that are meant to specifically protect heritage objects underwater. The United Nations Law of the Sea states that countries have an obligation to protect underwater heritage, and the UNESCO Convention on the Protection of the Underwater Cultural Heritage, adopted in 2001, sets high standards for archaeological investigations in international waters and obligates people to report discoveries or illicit activities. The ICOMOS Charter for the Protection and Management of Underwater Cultural Heritage, ratified in 1996, outlines the appropriate methods for archaeological research underwater, and the qualifications and responsibilities of those undertaking the work.

Recognizing the increase in heritage tourism during the late twentieth century, and the potential challenges that come with it, the ICOMOS International Cultural Tourism Charter was adopted in 1999. The charter includes clauses that recognize differing cultural values and significance of sites, the importance of retaining authenticity, and the value of including indigenous peoples in the identification, management, and interpretation of heritage resources.

UNESCO adopted the Declaration Concerning the Intentional Destruction of

Cultural Heritage in 2003. This declaration was in response to what appears to have been an increasing number of intentional acts of deliberate destruction of cultural heritage, including two monumental Buddha statues within the World Heritage designated landscape of the Bamiyan Valley in Afghanistan. In part, the declaration makes it clear that all states should take appropriate measures to prevent intentional acts of destruction, wherever it is located, during peace and in times of war.

The World Archaeology Congress adopted the Vermillion Accord on Human Remains in 1989. While recognizing the legitimate concern that science should have the ability to study human remains, the accord also establishes that the wishes of the dead, the relatives or guardians of the dead, and the local community be respected.

As archaeologists are becoming increasingly interested in the material remains of space exploration, the United Nations Outer Space Treaty (1967) has important implications. Essentially, the treaty states that land in space cannot be owned by any country, but the material remains of space exploration and other forms of space junk are the property of the country that sent the items into space.

Ethics and Archaeology

Most associations of archaeologists have codes of ethics that stipulate how archaeologists should conduct their work. Although the issues addressed for each organization vary (Table 3.6), some generalizations can be made about the protection of the archaeological record, commercialization, and responsibilities to various groups.

Protection of the Archaeological Record

Most professional organizations recognize an obligation to protect the archaeological record. In practical terms, this means that archaeologists should not allow the wanton destruction of archaeological sites or the looting of heritage objects. Some organizations stipulate that archaeologists hold the primary responsibility of protecting and interpreting the human past. Others believe that the responsibility for protecting and interpreting the human past should be shared with or be secondary to **descendant communities**. This brings up the dilemma often expressed in the question, "Who owns the past?" For some, the human past, even if it is the past of one particular group, belongs to everyone. For others, the past of particular groups belongs to the descendants.

The conflicts around the issue of who owns the past can be observed in the example of the prehistoric site of Stonehenge in Britain. Stonehenge, which was constructed between about 4,900 and 4,000 years ago, is comprised primarily of a circular setting of large standing stones, known as megaliths. The first discernible feature in the area

TABLE 3.6: Major Archaeological Associations and Issues Addressed by their Codes of Ethics

Organization	Ethics addressed
Archaeological Institute of America	Responsibilities to the archaeological record, the public, and colleagues
Canadian Archaeological Association	Stewardship; aboriginal relationships; professional responsibilities; public education
Register of Professional Archaeologists	Responsibilities to the public, descendant communities, colleagues, employees, students, employers, and clients; commercialization; standards of research; sharing research
Society for American Archaeology	Stewardship; accountability; commercialization; public education and outreach; intellectual property; public reporting and publication; records and preservation; training and resources
Society for Historical Archaeology	Stewardship; sharing research results; documentation; commercialization; public education
World Archaeology Congress	Responsibilities to Indigenous Peoples

is a circular ditch, about 100 meters (328 feet) in diameter, dug about 4,900 years ago. About 4,500 years ago, an arrangement of dozens of stones, weighing up to 4,000 kilograms (8,800 pounds) each, were transported about 200 kilometers (124 miles) from Wales to the site and placed within the circular ditch. About a century later, 30 or so larger stones, known as the sarsen stones and weighing up 25,000 kilograms (55,000 pounds) each, were shaped and transported from an area about 30 kilometers (19 miles) away to the site and placed in a circle within the circular ditch. Following this, other stones, known as the lintels and weighing about 5,500 kilograms (12,100 pounds) each were shaped and placed on top of the sarsen stones to form a complete ring. Most archaeologists believe Stonehenge was primarily a ritual location, although the alignment of some stones with the rising sun on the summer solstice provides some support for the idea that it was, perhaps in part, an astronomical observatory.

Many groups claim rights to visit Stonehenge. In addition to tourists, tens of thousands of people wish to use Stonehenge as a place of ritual, particularly during the time of the summer solstice. These include several different kinds of groups based on ancient religious practices, most notably druids, but also wiccans and people who

ROBERT J. MUCKLE

FIGURE 3.4: STONEHENGE, England. Constructed more than 4,000 years ago, Stonehenge has come to symbolize the problem of conflicting interests in archaeological sites.

practice ancient Viking and Anglo-Saxon beliefs. Many of these people see a connection between Stonehenge and their own beliefs and rituals, and think it is their right to consider it sacred and practice their own rituals at the site. This presents a dilemma for the archaeologist who is concerned about the harm done to the site during the annual summer solstice festivals, which, in addition to damaging the stones, have also included digging into archaeological deposits to make pits for latrines.

Commercialization

Archaeologists are generally dissuaded from participating in the commercialization of artifacts. Archaeologists are faced with the dilemma of placing value on objects, which then may create a market for looting. Working with looted material is another problem. Some archaeology journals (e.g., *American Antiquity* and *American Journal of Archaeology*) have adopted policies preventing the publication of articles that rely on looted artifacts, although not all archaeologists are in agreement that this is a good thing. Similarly, while most archaeologists acknowledge the severe impact of looting, many sympathize with the relatively poor people who do the looting to feed their families, a practice that has become known as subsistence looting.

Responsibilities to Various Groups

Most codes of ethics recognize that archaeologists have responsibilities to other archaeologists and scholars, descendant communities, funding agencies, and the public. However, there is no consensus on how these responsibilities should be prioritized or implemented. Minimally, it is considered proper practice that archaeologists share the results of their research with each of these groups. Many organizations also include responsibilities to the workers, especially in matters pertaining to health and safety.

Beyond consulting about research objectives and strategies, and sharing the results of research with various groups, ethical issues about intellectual property rights have also emerged in archaeology, particularly among those who work with indigenous populations. As archaeology becomes increasingly commercialized, questions of who owns intellectual property arise. Is it the archaeologist, the funding agency, or the descendant community?

Career Tracks in Archaeology

Tens of thousands of professional archaeologists are working in the world today. The vast majority have a minimum of a bachelor's degree in archaeology or a related field. With rare exception, those in supervisory positions and those in academic positions have a master's degree or a Ph.D.

Most professional archaeologists find employment in industry, either working for large companies that do enough land-alteration development to employ archaeologists; working for large environmental consulting companies that offer archaeological services; or working for companies that specialize in archaeology. A master's degree is usually considered the minimum qualification to obtain a supervisory position in archaeology within the heritage industry. Non-supervisory field and laboratory workers usually have a minimum of a four-year bachelor's degree or a two-year diploma in archaeology technology.

Employment as a college or university professor generally requires a graduate degree. Most universities require a Ph.D., although some universities and colleges only require a master's degree.

Many governments employ archaeologists to make sure heritage regulations are being followed, and in some cases to undertake research. As with working in industry or academia, a graduate degree is usually required for these positions.

Some archaeologists find employment in museums. In large museums, a graduate degree is usually required for supervisory positions.

Sharing Information

Archaeologists share the results of their research in many ways, principally through print media, conferences, and the internet.

Publication in scholarly journals is one way in which the results of academic research projects are shared (see Table 3.1, page 47).

Information is also commonly shared through conference presentations. Many local, national, and international associations of archaeologists have annual conferences, which provide opportunities for sharing research results. One of the most prominent is the annual conference of the Society for American Archaeology (SAA), during which thousands of presentations are given. Another prominent conference is that of the World Archaeology Congress, which has one large conference every four years and many smaller special interest conferences during the intervals.

The impact of the internet on archaeology has been considerable, like it has been with almost all aspects of life in the early twenty-first century. Many journal articles are available online, along with useful archaeology-related websites and discussion listserves. Some government agencies are now making their gray literature more accessible by putting it online. Some archaeologists have created websites for specific projects, for example the website created for the multiyear excavations led by Ian Hodder at Catalhoyuk, a Neolithic site in Turkey. Among other things, the website contains an extensive archive of analytical reports.

KEY RESOURCES AND SUGGESTED READING

Indigenous archaeology is covered well by Watkins in the book *Indigenous Archaeologies: American Indian Values and Scientific Practice* (2001) and the article "Beyond the Margin: American Indians, First Nations, and Archaeology in North America" (2003); and in *At a Crossroads: Archaeology and First Peoples in Canada* by Nicholas and Andrews (1997). Tainter (2004) covers some issues in cultural resource management in the article "Persistent Dilemmas in American Cultural Resource Management." Heritage regulations are covered in *Illicit Antiquities: The Theft of Culture and the Extinction of Archaeology* by Brodie and Tubb (2002) and in *Loot, Legitimacy, and Ownership: The Ethical Crisis in Archaeology* by Renfew (2000). *Ethical Issues in Archaeology,* an edited book by Zimmerman, Vitelli, and Hollowell-Zimmer (2003) provides a good overview of ethics and archaeology. Nicholas and Bannister (2004) focus on intellectual property rights and archaeology in the article "Copyrighting the Past? Emerging Intellectual Property Rights and Issues in Archaeology." The articles "Between Colonial and Indigenous Archaeologies: Legal and Extra-Legal Ownership of the Archaeological Past in North America" by Ferris (2003) and "Who Owns Prehistory? The Bering Land Bridge Dilemma" by McGhee (1989) cover the issue of who owns the past in North America. Those desiring more information on garbology are encouraged to consult works by Rathje (e.g., Rathje 2002; Rathje and Murphy 1992; Rathje, Hughes, Wilson, Tani, Archer, Hunet, and Jones 1992).

The codes of ethics of various associations can usually be found on the association's web site. Similarly, national heritage laws can usually be found on government websites, and international regulations can be found on the websites of the UNESCO, ICOMOS, and UNIDROIT.

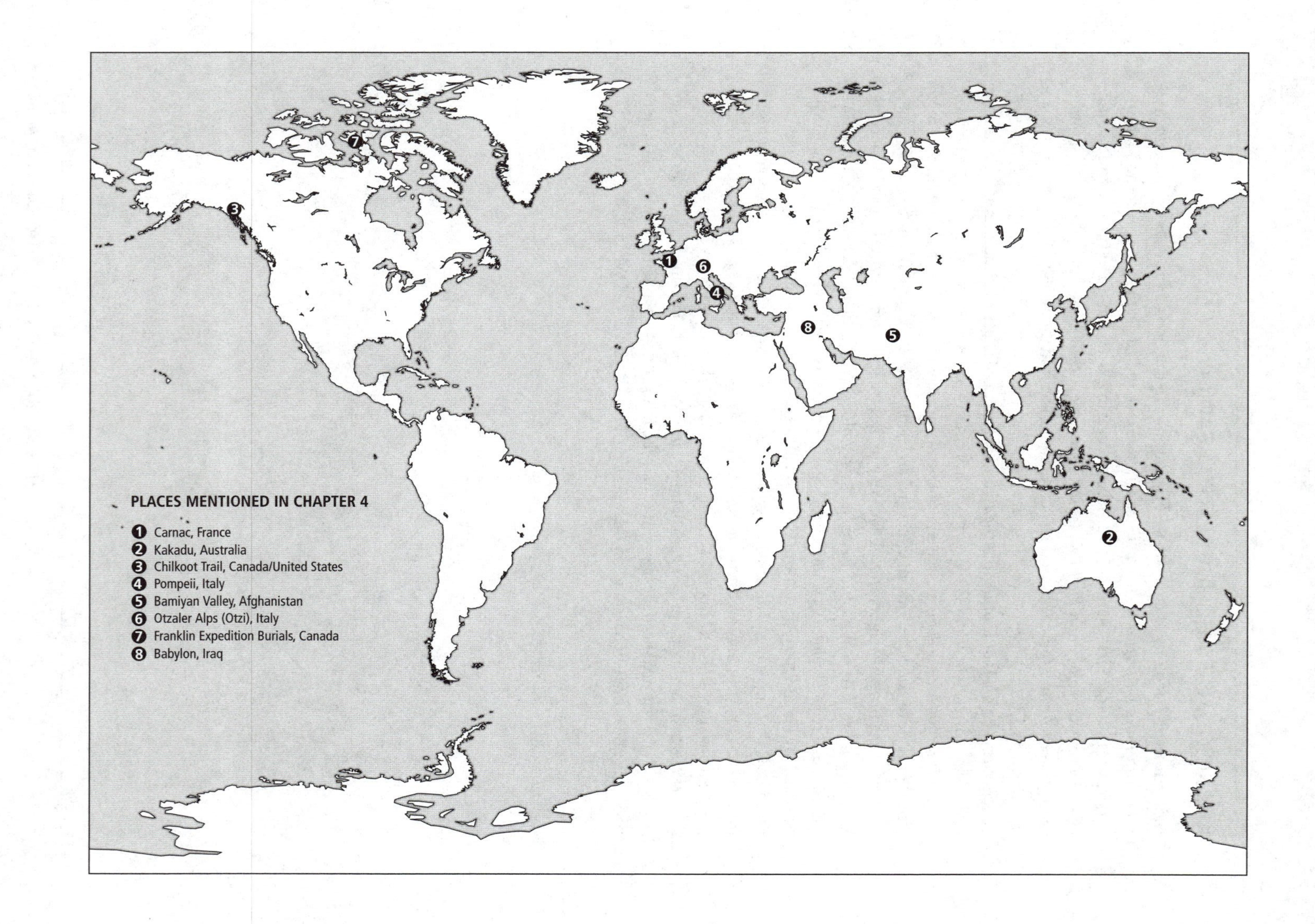
PLACES MENTIONED IN CHAPTER 4
1 Carnac, France
2 Kakadu, Australia
3 Chilkoot Trail, Canada/United States
4 Pompeii, Italy
5 Bamiyan Valley, Afghanistan
6 Otzaler Alps (Otzi), Italy
7 Franklin Expedition Burials, Canada
8 Babylon, Iraq

CHAPTER 4

Comprehending the Archaeological Record

Introduction

This chapter defines the components of the archaeological record. It also outlines the processes that lead to the creation of archaeological sites, the factors that influence what is preserved, and the range of activities that disturb the original patterning in material remains.

Defining the Archaeological Record and Its Components

There is no consensus definition of the archaeological record. At a minimum, it is taken to comprise all the material remains documented by archaeologists. Many expand this definition to include all material remains left by humans, including those remains yet to be documented. Some consider the archaeological record to include the basic facts about the past, based on material remains. For others, all the documentation pertaining to archaeological investigations, including field notes, maps, photographs, and written reports, constitutes the archaeological record.

However the archaeological record is defined, it is understood that the basic components of the material remains are sites, artifacts, **features**, **ecofacts**, and **cultural landscapes**.

Archaeological Sites

Broadly defined, an archaeological site is any location in which physical evidence of human activity exists. In practice, however, archaeological sites are usually defined more narrowly, based on such things as artifact density and time period. Most archaeologists do not routinely record isolated finds of a broken piece of pottery or stone tool as a site, nor do they commonly record deposits less than 100 years old, but they may. Whether material remains are defined as a site is often dependent on the research objectives. Two archaeologists independently looking for sites in an area may see exactly the same material remains, but one may not document any sites, while the other, using different criteria, may document several sites.

There are several common types of archaeological sites. At a very broad level, most archaeologists make a distinction between prehistoric sites and historic sites, each with several discrete categories. The major kinds of sites are listed in Table 4.1.

Classifying a prehistoric site as a habitation indicates that people once lived at the site, but there are no restrictions on the number of people or length of time. Describing a site as a camp suggests a small and temporary occupation, while calling it a village implies at least a **semi-sedentary** pattern of residency. Archaeologists generally refrain from describing a site as a city unless the population is assumed to have been at least 5,000. **Tell** is a term commonly used to describe mounds that have been created by successive settlements in western Asia and northern Africa. Habitation sites usually have large accumulations of refuse, which archaeologists describe as **middens.** When the refuse includes a substantial amount of shell, it is often called a **shell midden**.

TABLE 4.1: Major Types of Archaeological Sites

Prehistoric Sites	Subtypes
Habitation	Open-air; rock shelter; cave; camp; village; city; tell; midden
Earthwork	Embankment; trench; mound
Human remains	Isolated; cemetery
Rock art	Pictograph; petroglyph
Petroform	Megalith; cairn
Resource utilization	Hunting; fishing; gathering; culturally modified trees; quarry; processing; storage
Historic Sites	**Subtypes**
Habitation	Single dwelling; multiple dwelling
Industrial	Mining; logging; other
Commercial	Shop; hotel; bar/saloon; other
Human remains	Isolated; cemetery
Military	n/a
Religious	n/a
Medical	n/a

The term *petroform* refers to alignments of stones. Alignments of very large stones are known as **megaliths**. Other common types of petroforms include cairns, hunting blinds, stone fences, and alignments in rivers and intertidal zones of beaches to direct and capture fish.

GILLIAN CROWTHER

FIGURE 4.1: CARNAC, France. Carnac is an example of alignments of very large stones known as megaliths.

The term *earthwork* is used to describe large, deliberately created embankments or mounds. Earthworks are commonly created for defensive purposes, but some have been shaped into animal forms and others have had habitation structures on top.

Burial was not the only way to treat the dead in the past, but certainly it is the most archaeologically visible method. Distinctions are usually made between isolated graves and cemeteries.

Many different kinds of sites fall within the category of resource utilization. Quarries were used to extract clay for making pottery and stone for making tools. People often did some initial manufacture of stone tools at or near the quarry site, creating a **lithic scatter**. Similarly, people often undertook some preparation and preserving of food where they procured their food resources, leaving evidence such as animals parts from butchering, cooking pits, drying racks, and **cache pits**.

GILLIAN CROWTHER

FIGURE 4.2: PICTOGRAPHS FROM KAKADU, Australia. With an estimated 15,000 sites, and spanning up to 20,000 years in age, Kakadu National Park has one of the greatest concentrations of rock art in the world.

The two main categories of rock-art sites are **pictographs** and **petroglyphs**. Using the term *pictograph* indicates that art has been painted onto a large immovable boulder or bedrock, or onto the wall of a cave, cliff, or rock shelter. The term *petroglyph* means the design was carved or pecked into the stone.

Several other classifications of prehistoric sites include cave sites, rock shelter sites, underwater sites, sacred sites, and open-air sites. Sometimes a site can be designated on the basis of a single artifact, and these sites are often described as isolated finds. Culturally modified trees is a category used to describe the evidence of removing the bark, planks, or small sections of living trees, or cutting the tree down, usually by indigenous peoples before the use of tools from the historic period.

Historic habitation sites are usually described as either a single dwelling, such as a cabin, or multiple dwellings, such as a town site. Industrial sites include those associated with logging, mining, manufacturing, and power generation. Commercial sites include those that show evidence of shops, hotels, and saloons. Other common classifications of historic sites are military, medical, religious, social, transportation, and communication sites.

Artifacts

Any object that shows evidence of having been manufactured, modified, or used by people is an artifact. Many archaeologists assert that the object must also be portable. As they do when defining an archaeological site, archaeologists often use narrower criteria to decide whether to classify objects as artifacts. Some archaeologists working at prehistoric sites, for example, may choose to classify individual **potsherds** and **lithic debitage** as artifacts, while others do not. Similarly, others may choose to label every nail and broken piece of glass as an artifact, but most do not. The usual classification of artifacts is outlined in Chapter 6.

Features

The term *feature* is used in a variety of ways. It is commonly used to describe objects that have all the characteristics of an artifact, except that they are non-portable. Feature is also used to describe material that has been patterned in such a way that the arrangement itself is significant, such as when a group of artifacts or food remains are recovered together in a burial. Patternings of natural sediments are often described as features if the arrangement has been caused by human activity. A pattern of soil discoloration, for example, often reflects that wooden posts were deliberately put into the ground, discoloring the soil as they decayed over centuries or millennia. Cobbles and boulders in a circular pattern often represent the outline of a shelter in which hides were weighted down with stones. Similarly, the term *activity area* describes an area in which evidence of certain types of activities is discerned, such as making stone tools. An activity area is often described as a feature. When the activity involves the manufacture of stone tools, the remains of the waste flakes are usually known as a lithic scatter. Some archaeologists make a distinction between constructed features, which include deliberately built structures such as buildings, fire hearths, and burials, and cumulative features, such as the buildup of trash forming a midden.

Ecofacts

Collectively, **faunal remains**, botanical remains, and sediments from archaeological sites are known as ecofacts. They are collected because, at a minimum, they can provide evidence of the past environmental conditions to which the site's occupants had to adapt. They are also often useful for making interpretations about past lifeways, including settlement patterns, subsistence strategies, diet, and social inequalities, as detailed in subsequent chapters.

Many faunal remains recovered from archaeological sites are bones, but the category includes all parts of animals, including teeth, shell, hide, hair, fur, nails, claws, and soft tissue. Botanical remains similarly include a variety of forms. One of the most commonly recovered botanical remains is wood, usually charred or in the form of wood ash, but also including bark, seeds, nuts, pollen, and **phytoliths**. If faunal and botanical remains have been modified (by food preparation, for example), they could technically be classified as artifacts. In practice, however, unless animal or botanical remains have been made into a tool or piece of jewelry, such classifications are rare.

When discussing sediments, archaeologists usually are referring to non-cultural elements in the archaeological site. This excludes, for example, all artifacts and features. Sediments are often referred to as the **matrix**, and are typically described as clay, silt, sand, loam, gravel, pebbles, and cobbles.

Cultural Landscapes

Although geographers have been using the term *cultural landscape* for over 100 years, archaeologists have only recently begun to commonly use it. Its use has been part of a recent trend to reduce the focus of archaeology on individual artifacts and sites, instead conceptualizing areas as they were likely envisioned by those using them in the past. UNESCO first recognized cultural landscapes as a world heritage category in 1992. The operational guidelines for implementing the World Heritage Convention describe cultural landscapes as "illustrative of the evolution of human society and settlement over time, under the influence of the physical constraints and/or opportunities presented by their natural environment and of successive social, economic, and cultural forces, both external and internal."

One example of a cultural landscape with a UNESCO World Heritage designation is the Bamiyan Valley in Afghanistan. The valley contains many material remains associated with Buddhism from the first to thirteenth century in Central Asia and was an important pilgrimage destination. Material remains include monumental Buddha statues, as well as other forms of art and architecture in the Buddhist tradition. The Bamiyan Valley received international attention in 2001 when the Taliban deliberately destroyed two monumental Buddhas carved into cliffs. The Bamiyan Valley is also inscribed on the UNESCO List of World Heritage in Danger, primarily due to ongoing military action in the area, dynamite explosions, looting, and the presence of land mines.

Although it does not have UNESCO designation, another good example of a cultural landscape is the Chilkoot Trail, which begins on the coast of Alaska and heads inland to Canada's Yukon Territory. The 45-mile (73-kilometer) trail has a long history as an indigenous trade route, but it is more widely known as the gateway to the Yukon goldfields along which tens of thousands of gold-seekers trekked during the late 1800s, scattering many thousands of artifacts along the way. For many archaeologists, it makes

FIGURE 4.3: CHILKOOT TRAIL. Connecting Alaska and the Yukon, the 73-kilometer trail is an example of a cultural landscape.

more sense to envision the trail as a single entity rather than as hundreds of discrete clusters of artifacts, features, and sites.

Creating Archaeological Sites

Principal things to consider about the creation of archaeological sites are the circumstances under which initial material remains enter the archaeological record (e.g., discarded as refuse, intentionally buried, lost, or abandoned), and the different ways that material remains can become buried (e.g., intentional burial, sandstorms, or landslides).

How Sites Are Initially Created

Many processes lead to the creation of archaeological sites (Table 4.2). Collectively, these are known as **site formation processes**. When the focus is on the initial deposition of

TABLE 4.2: Site Formation Processes

Cultural Formation Processes	Natural Formation Processes
Deliberate discard	Natural soil formation
Intentional burial	By water
Loss	Through the air
Abandonment	Over land
	By animals

material remains, the processes are sometimes called **cultural formation processes** or **behavioral formation processes.** Archaeological sites invariably have sediments in them that are brought in by nature, and the processes responsible for this are generally called **natural** or **non-cultural formation processes.**

Most archaeologists use the term **refuse** to refer to the collectivity of discarded items. Some, however, prefer to use the term *trash* to describe dry items such as broken artifacts, *garbage* to describe wet or organic items such as food waste, *refuse* to refer to both trash and garbage and *rubbish* to include all discarded or abandoned items, including house remains.

Archaeologists frequently make a distinction between **primary refuse** and **secondary refuse.** Refuse that was simply abandoned where it was created or used and subsequently found in that precise location by archaeologists is primary refuse. Refuse that was deliberately moved from the area where it was initially created or used and redeposited elsewhere, such as a midden, is called secondary refuse.

In order to understand the conditions in which items were discarded or abandoned, many archaeologists have done ethnoarchaeology, from which a few generalizations can be made. Research indicates that time and size are the two key variables that determine whether refuse will be left ***in situ*** or redeposited in a midden. Generally, if people are occupying an area for a very short time, with little expectation of return, they leave refuse in primary context. For example, people who stop to cook a meal while hunting are not likely to create a midden for their refuse. Conversely, few people like to live amongst their refuse, and if they are going to be staying in an area for at least a day or two, they are likely to create a special area for refuse. Also, people are more likely to leave small items *in situ* and redeposit larger items as secondary refuse. Potential reuse is another important factor that influences whether people will leave items as primary refuse or secondary refuse.

Many items enter the archaeological record through intentional burial. This includes human burials and associated **grave goods**, as well as **caches** of food in storage pits. Human burials were usually meant to lie undisturbed, but caches of food were buried with the intent of removing the food at some future time. Cache pits for food storage are a common type of feature found in prehistoric habitation sites, sometimes dug into house floors and sometimes outside the houses. It is not uncommon to find cache pits in resource utilization sites, where food preserved by drying or smoking would have been left if it was anticipated that members of the group would return that way in the future.

Some artifacts enter the archaeological record because they were lost. However, this is a relatively rare occurrence. Examples include cargo lost during a shipwreck and coins or jewelry that may have fallen onto, and ultimately under, floors or floor coverings (e.g., wooden floorboards or mats). Isolated finds of arrowheads are likely to be the result of loss, for example, by a hunter who missed the target and could not relocate the arrow.

Abandonment is usually considered a site formation process. Most prehistoric sites, including settlements, were abandoned by design, sometimes with the intent of returning and sometimes not. Throughout most of **prehistory**, people moved, at least seasonally, within their territory, and each time they left for an extended period can be considered abandonment. In other situations, such as abandonment due to environmental, economic, or social reasons, return may not have been anticipated. The implication for archaeology is that when a site was abandoned by design, the inhabitants would have had the opportunity to take what they wanted with them. Sites that have been abandoned, therefore, are usually devoid of artifacts that would have had a relatively high perceived value among the inhabitants.

Natural Sediments in Archaeological Sites

In between periods of occupation and after the final abandonment, many different processes bring natural sediments into a site, which often cause its complete burial. The natural decay of organic matter eventually contributes to soil formation, which in itself can bury a site. Sediments are also brought in by water, such as rivers, tides, and rising lake and sea levels; through mass movement, such as slides or flows; and through the air, such as wind blowing sand over a site. Sediments in archaeological sites may also have been transported and deposited by glaciers.

Burials of sites are usually slow, but occasionally they are sudden and can happen almost instantaneously. Many sites throughout the world are buried by mud slides, avalanches, and volcanic eruptions. The most well-known is the site of Pompeii in Italy.

The city of Pompeii, along with Herculaneum and some smaller settlements, was completely buried by ash from the eruption of Mount Vesuvius in AD 79. Because of the quick burial, Pompeii provides a glimpse into everyday life rarely found in the archaeological record. In most cities, people take their valuables when they leave, and environmental

CARMEN WHITE

FIGURE 4.4: POMPEII, Italy. Due to a catastrophic eruption of volcanic ash, Pompeii is one of the best-preserved cities in the world, providing an excellent glimpse into everyday life in a Roman city during the first century AD.

conditions lead to the decomposition of organic remains. The people of Pompeii had no time to evacuate, and the quick covering of ash provided excellent preservation. Excavations at Pompeii have uncovered markets, restaurants, shops, an amphitheatre, villas, and many other smaller residences. The population is estimated to have been about 20,000.

Besides the obvious processes that bring in sediments over the surfaces of sites, archaeologists also consider that processes operating beneath the surface may also result in site burial. In some regions, for example, sites can be buried by earthworms. Earthworms burrow by swallowing the dirt in front of them, often bringing dirt to the surface where it is redeposited.

Understanding Bias in the Preservation of Material Remains

Archaeologists understand that with the rare exception of a quick and complete burial, as in Pompeii, they usually recover a very biased subset of material culture. This is largely due to the fact that the vast majority of the material record was discarded or abandoned deliberately, as previously described. Artifacts of perceived value generally account for a very small percentage of the total items recovered. It is not unreasonable to imagine that for every complete arrowhead or pottery vessel in an archaeological site, there are probably a thousand or more pieces of lithic debitage or potsherds.

Archaeologists also understand that some materials preserve better than others, so that what is recovered is not necessarily an accurate reflection of what originally existed. The major factors that bias the preservation of material remains are the material itself and the environmental conditions.

Material Bias

Items recovered from archaeological sites are often broadly classified as organic or inorganic, and it is widely recognized that inorganic materials will almost always preserve better. However, even within the category of inorganic materials, there are clear differences in preservation qualities.

The three most common types of inorganic materials recovered from archaeological sites are artifacts and features made of stone, clay, and metal. Stone is often characterized as being "hard" or "soft," and the harder varieties such as obsidian, basalt, and chert are the most durable and therefore less susceptible to weathering than softer varieties. Fired clay is as hard as stone in some cases, but tends to be more easily broken and crushed. Metals have varying degrees of durability. Objects made of iron and tin tend to rust and corrode relatively quickly, while objects of gold, silver, bronze, and copper preserve well.

Many types of organic remains are also commonly recovered. Various skeletal elements of animals are recovered, but the parts that preserve the best tend to be bones, teeth, and antlers. Similarly, many types of plant remains are recovered, but the ones that preserve the best tend to be wood (often burned), pollen, and seeds.

In order to interpret the relative abundance of different types of organic remains in archaeological sites, many archaeologists have become involved in taphonomic studies. Broadly defined, **taphonomy** is the study of what happens to organic remains after death. It involves examining the differential rates of decomposition between different organic materials. At a very general level, it is apparent that bone density is a key variable affecting preservation, and since the bone density of large animals tends to be greater than in small animals, the bones of larger animals are more likely to be preserved. Similarly, since mammal bones tend to have greater density than bird or fish bones, mammal bones are more likely to be preserved.

Environmental Conditions

Many environmental conditions affect the preservation of organic remains, including the rapidity of burial, microbial activity, burning, the chemistry of the matrix, and extreme environments.

Organic remains that are buried quickly often preserve better than those that are left on the surface of the ground. This is particularly true for animal remains, since dead animals left on the ground surface are generally eaten by a variety of other animals, large and small. Rapid burial, whether it occurs deliberately (as in buried garbage) or naturally (as in snowfalls, windstorms, or mudslides) removes the first agents of destruction—scavengers. Rapid burial also generally takes the remains from an aerobic environment to an anaerobic environment, where organisms that eat organic remains are less active. Exposure to air and chemicals at the surface promotes decomposition and weathering. If rapid burial takes place, this exposure is limited, and materials are preserved better.

Although less active in anaerobic environments, many organisms feed on dead matter. These life forms are called saprophytic organisms, and although they include large scavengers, such as rodents, the term is more commonly used to describe much smaller forms, such as bacteria, fungi, and insects. These microbial saprophytic organisms need water and air to stay alive, so anaerobic environments inhibit their survival.

Besides an anaerobic environment, several other conditions inhibit the activities of saprophytic organisms. One of these is burning, which removes the nutrients from the remains, making them unattractive to those that feed on dead matter. This is why wood charcoal, for example, is found so frequently in prehistoric archaeological sites.

Very cold environments also inhibit saprophytic activity, which is the usual explanation for the existence of very well preserved bodily remains throughout the world, dating from hundreds to thousands of years ago. The body of a man commonly known as Otzi (named after the Otztaler Alps in Italy, where he died) is an excellent example. He was discovered in a melting glacier in 1991, having died about 5,500 years ago. Current research suggests that after death he probably was covered by a slight layer of snow, dried in the high altitude of the Alps and was eventually frozen within a glacier. Many of the organic objects he had with him were preserved as well, including clothing and shoes made from animal hides, a grass cloak, and a longbow and arrow shafts. Otzi has become one of the most studied individuals from prehistory, and his excellent preservation has allowed researchers to examine rare soft tissue. Researchers were able to conclude from his intestines that he dined on goat, cereal, and deer shortly before his death. Parasites indicate he was probably suffering from diarrhea, and his fingernails suggest a recent history of illness. X-rays reveal what appears to be an arrowhead in his back, evidently shot from behind and likely the cause of his death.

Another example of human remains preserved in a cold environment comes from northern Canada, where some crew members of an ill-fated nineteenth-century journey through Arctic waters were buried in permafrost. In what is known as the Franklin expedition, two ships set sail from England in 1845 carrying 129 men to Canada in search of a sailing route through the north of the continent. Despite the apparently well-equipped ships and experienced crew, including Captain John Franklin with his previous arctic experience, all met their demise in the doomed expedition. It has long been a mystery what led to the relatively quick death of many expedition members shortly after reaching northern Canada, and the seemingly bizarre decision of some to hike out of the Arctic on foot, burdened with luxury items. Owen Beattie sought the answer to these mysteries by investigating both the material remains (including middens) and skeletal remains of expedition members. He concluded that they likely died of lead poisoning due to the poorly manufactured cans in which much of the food provisions were stored for the expedition (evident from the cans found at the sites). Neurological damage is one symptom of lead poisoning, which may explain why some made the bizarre decision to hike out of the Arctic when it would have made much more sense to wait for rescue ships.

Mummy is a term often used by archaeologists to describe human remains that have been preserved by drying. A distinction is often made between deliberate and natural mummification. Deliberate mummification has a several-thousand-year history, and usually involves some sort of intentional drying of the body before burial, as was practiced in ancient Egypt, as well as in South America, Southeast Asia, and elsewhere.

OWEN BEATTIE

FIGURE 4.5: MAN IN ICE. An example of excellent organic preservation in extreme environmental conditions, this is a member of an ill-fated nineteenth-century Arctic expedition in which all 129 men perished.

Natural mummification has a similarly long history, with remains being preserved through naturally dry environments in North and South America and parts of Asia.

Yet another important condition affecting preservation is matrix chemistry. The precise effects that chemistry has on the variety of organic remains typically found in archaeological sites do not appear to be well understood. In general, however, it is apparent that bone usually preserves best in alkaline soils, and some types of botanical remains survive better in acidic soils.

Organic remains submerged in water or buried in waterlogged sediments tend to preserve well, although not normally for more than a few thousand years. Peat bogs, which are sometimes considered a special class of waterlogged sites, provide excellent conditions for some types of preservation, especially soft tissue. The famous **bog men** of northern Europe are particularly good examples of this. The highly acidic nature of peat bogs generally makes them unsuitable for the long-term preservation of bone, but leads to good preservation of plant remains.

Site Disturbance

In addition to the biasing effects of material and environmental conditions, archaeologists recognize that many other factors potentially alter the original patterning of material culture left by a site's occupants. Collectively, these processes are known as **post-depositional disturbance processes**, sometimes simply called site disturbance processes. They are further subdivided into the categories of natural disturbance and cultural disturbance.

Natural Disturbance

Alternatively known as **non-cultural disturbance processes** or **N-transforms**, natural disturbance processes include a wide range of activities that may alter the patterning of the material record.

Bioturbation is a term used to describe disturbance by plants and animals, sometimes more specifically called **floralturbation** and **faunalturbation**, respectively.

TABLE 4.3: Site Disturbance Processes

Cultural Disturbance Processes	Natural Disturbance Processes
Reusing	Bioturbation
Recycling	Cryoturbation
Trampling	Aeroturbation
Construction	Aquaturbation
Looting	Graviturbation
Collateral damage during war	

Disturbance by plants involves such things as the roots of trees and other vegetation growing through archaeological deposits and displacing items of the material record. Tree-throws are a particularly active force in altering the deposits because when the tree falls over, it typically takes a substantial portion of the deposits around the roots and redeposits it on the ground surface. Bioturbation, by aerating the deposits, also allows more oxygen, water, and chemicals into the ground, which can lead to increased rates of physical and chemical weathering of the material remains.

Many types of animals also commonly alter the patterning. This includes the digging and scavenging activities of dogs, rats, and other small animals on or near the surface of a site, as well as the activity of rodents and other burrowing animals, which often creates internal pathways or voids in the matrix where artifacts can fall or be displaced by the animals themselves. Earthworms alone can make significant changes in patterns. One experimental study showed that earthworms buried lithic and ceramic fragments as much as 18 inches (45 centimeters) deep after only 5 years. In addition to the burial of artifacts, geoarchaeologist Julie Stein observed that earthworms can obliterate stratification and obscure boundaries of sedimentary layers, alter the botanical assemblage within sites, and alter the chemistry of the soils.

The effect of rodents on site disturbance is illustrated in an experimental study reported by Barbara Bocek in 1992. After excavating a 1 x 2 meter (3 ¼ x 6 ½ foot) unit, the unit was backfilled with clean (culturally sterile) sediment. After 7 years, the unit was re-excavated and found to contain 390 pieces of shell, bone, and **debitage**, as well as 3.4 kilograms (7.48 pounds) of burned and unmodified rock, presumably transported laterally to the unit from the surrounding areas. A simple calculation showed that in the 1,000 years since the site was last occupied, the cultural contents of a single excavation unit could have been totally replaced more than 11 times.

Besides moving artifacts, animals may also mark or break bones in a pattern that could potentially be mistaken for human activity. Archaeologists are aware that the breaks and marks on bones caused by scavenging could be mistaken for deliberate butchery by humans. Similarly, when animals trample over a site, they can easily cause bone breakage.

Archaeologists working in what are now or were once cold environments are usually aware of the potential for cryoturbation to influence the patterning of the material record. Studies have shown that objects can move substantial distances due to frost activity alone. M.R. Hilton (2003), for example, undertook some experiments showing that in a control plot designed to minimize the impacts of wind and other natural processes, freeze-thaw cycles caused artifacts to move an average of almost 8 centimeters (3 ¼ inches) over a 3-year period. Without the constraints to minimize other processes, artifacts in another plot moved an average of almost 32 centimeters (12 ½ inches) over the same period.

Archaeologists working in windy areas are aware that relatively light items may be displaced or buried by wind, a process known as aeroturbation. Similarly, archaeologists working in areas which are now or once were associated with moving water, whether along a tidal beach, creek, or through simple groundwater percolation, are aware of the potential for water to move material remains, a process known as aquaturbation. And archaeologists working in hilly environments are generally aware that material remains may be displaced as they move downhill, either by slipping down the surface of a slope or when substantial amounts of sediments move, a process sometimes known as graviturbation or mass wasting.

Other natural processes that may influence pattering of material remains are weathering and erosion. Chemical weathering includes the processes that alter the composition of remains when they react with water, oxygen, and other elements. These reactions may weaken the structure of large artifacts and features made of stone, clay, or mud-brick. Physical weathering involves the mechanical breakdown of material into smaller pieces, and erosion means the transport of residual sediments. Extensive wind and water movement potentially removes the matrix surrounding artifacts and features, which makes them more susceptible to displacement by a wide variety of other processes. Wind and water may also erode surfaces of artifacts and features, potentially causing them to break. Physical weathering also describes artifacts that break due to natural fires.

Cultural Disturbance

Alternatively known as **behavioural disturbance processes** or **C-transforms**, cultural disturbance processes include a wide range of post-depositional human activities.

A large proportion of sites have been used again after periods of abandonment, a process widely known as reuse. By their very presence, those who occupy a site after a period of abandonment, whether it is measured in years, decades, centuries, or millennia, often disturb it in significant ways. They often modify the site surface and dig in older deposits while involved in such activities as clearing the site of trees; moving shell from a midden to provide increased stability or drainage in another area; using a midden as a burial ground; constructing semi-subterranean houses, cooking pits, and cache pits; or inserting poles for shelters, fences, and enclosures.

Recycling of material remains is commonly recognized as a potential site disturbance process. This includes when people disturb their own middens or those created by previous inhabitants while searching for bone, shell, charcoal, or ceramics to create artifacts such as jewelry, or other items to make dyes, pigments, or pottery temper.

Human trampling is a process widely recognized for its potential to both break and displace material remains. Experimental studies have shown that ceramics and shells are particularly susceptible to breakage by trampling, and that depending on a wide variety of variables, items are also subject to considerable vertical displacement. One study showed that in sandy deposits subjected to human trampling, large artifacts had a tendency to move upwards while smaller artifacts tended to move downwards.

Many contemporary human activities disturb sites in significant ways. It is likely that hundreds and perhaps thousands of archaeological sites are destroyed every day by industrial activities such as mining, logging, and various sorts of construction; albeit not all of the sites are necessarily significant. Many of these sites are unknowingly destroyed or destroyed with the permission of regulatory authorities because they are of low significance and they stand in the way of development projects.

Many sites are mined for the value of the materials in contemporary construction. In various parts of the world, shell middens are mined because the shell is useful for road building. A recent study of Mayan sites in Belize showed that the remains of temples were often used for road fill, and at least one entire Mayan site has been almost completely destroyed by the search and removal of material to build roads.

Deliberate looting of sites for artifacts of a variety of materials and values, often referred to by the generic term **pothunting**, is a major source of site disturbance and results in the total destruction of many thousands of sites, the removal of at least tens of thousands of significant artifacts, and the displacement of artifacts in many thousands more. This practice extends back at least several thousand years to the robbing of ancient tombs for items buried with Egyptian pharaohs, and similar burial sites throughout the world. It continues today around the world, ranging from people collecting arrowheads as a hobby in North America to using metal detectors to search for gold coins in Roman era sites and deliberate looting to fuel the trade in illicit antiquities.

The impact of warfare on the archaeological record is also significant. Despite the Hague Convention and other instruments to protect archaeological sites during times of conflict, the destruction of many significant sites continues in contemporary times. Bombing of sites, whether intentional or not, is one way they are disturbed. But contemporary warfare affects on the archaeological record in many other ways, such as making it logistically difficult to prevent looting, and other disruptive effects of conflict, in remote locations and by constructing military bases on or near sites. For example, the ancient city of Babylon has been disturbed by the construction of a military base following the 2003 US conflict with Iraq. The site, which dates back about 2,600 years, was disturbed in a variety of ways: military vehicles damaged much of the brick pavement; trenches were dug into the deposits; deposits were used as fill for sandbags; and large amounts of gravel and other sediments were brought to the site to use as fill in the construction of such things as helipads, parking lots, and accommodations.

KEY RESOURCES AND SUGGESTED READING

The nature of the archaeological record is discussed in the article "Is There An Archaeological Record? by Patrick (1985). There are many studies that deal with the creation and subsequent disturbance of archaeological sites. Hayden and Cannon (1983) report on ethnoarchaeological observations among the Maya in the article "Where the Garbage Goes: Refuse Disposal in the Maya Highlands." "A Survey of Disturbance Processes in Archaeological Site Formation" by Wood and Johnson (1978) and *Formation Processes of the Archaeological Record* by Schiffer (1987) provide good overviews of site formation and disturbance processes. In "Shaw's Creek Shelter: Human Displacement of Artefacts and Its Significance" Stockton (1973) describes a simple experiment on artifact mixing caused by trampling. Hilton (2003) reports on the results of an experiment with freeze-thaw processes on artifact movement in "Quantifying Postdepositional Redistribution of the Archaeological Record Produced by Freeze-Thaw and Other Mechanisms: An Experimental Approach." The impact of earthworms is discussed in "Earthworm Activity: A Source of Potential Disturbance to Archaeological Sediments" by Stein (1983) and in "Earthworm Activity and Archaeological Stratigraphy: A Review of Products and Processes" by Canti (2003). Bocek (1992) discusses artifact mixing by rodents. *The Handbook of Archaeological Sciences*, edited by Brothwell and Pollard (2001) includes several contributions on the preservation of material remains. Readings about Otzi include *The Man In the Ice* by Spindler (1994) and "The Iceman Reconsidered" by Dickson, Oeggl, and Handley (2003). The excavation and analysis of frozen bodies associated with the Franklin Expedition is covered in *Frozen in Time: The Fate of the Franklin Expedition* by Beattie and Geiger (1988).

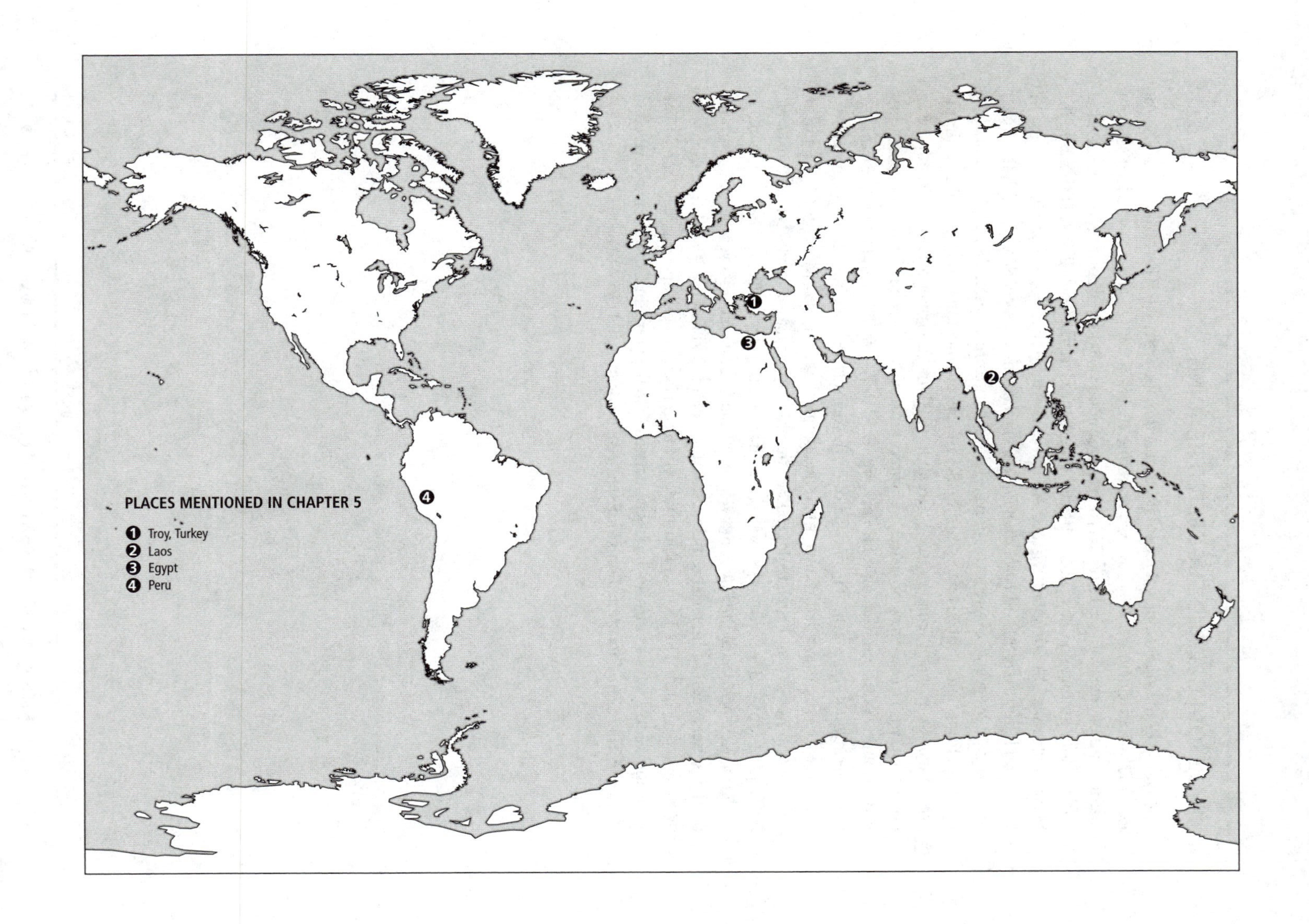
PLACES MENTIONED IN CHAPTER 5
1 Troy, Turkey
2 Laos
3 Egypt
4 Peru
1
2
3
4

CHAPTER 5

Working in the Field

Introduction

This chapter focuses on archaeological fieldwork. It includes sections on archaeological research design, site discovery, excavation, ethnoarchaeology, and the hazards of field archaeology.

Designing Archaeological Field Projects

Archaeological projects are always guided by research design, unless amateurs are undertaking them. Research designs are critical for a variety of reasons. Most importantly, they establish (i) the significance of the project, (ii) the kinds of information being sought, (iii) the preferred methods for obtaining that information, and (iv) the plan for making the research meaningful.

There are always choices to be made in research design. Not only does the design guide the archaeological project director and crew once they begin fieldwork, it also provides a mechanism by which others can evaluate the project.

Archaeological projects that involve the discovery and excavation of sites follow nine basic stages (Table 5.1). Planning the details of each of these stages in advance is what constitutes the research design. Although the basic stages of archaeological research outlined here include excavation, it is important to understand that excavation is not always considered or carried out. Indeed, many purely academic research field projects are based on finding and mapping surface features alone. For cultural resource management (CRM) archaeology, the purpose of most fieldwork is to evaluate the threat development poses to archaeological sites and to work towards avoiding impact on significant sites. In CRM archaeology, excavation is usually undertaken only as a last resort, such as when it is evident that the site will be destroyed.

TABLE 5.1: Basic Stages of Archaeological Research

Stages of Research
1. Identifying the need for research
2. Doing background research
3. Generating hypotheses or research questions
4. Determining the types of data to collect
5. Determining the field and laboratory methods to use
6. Detailing the logistics of making the project work
7. Collecting data
8. Making the data meaningful
9. Making the research meaningful

Identifying the Need for Field Research

In academic archaeology, identifying the need for research generally comes after recognizing the need for more data. Additional data can fill significant gaps of knowledge in a plethora of things that interest archaeologists, whether considered low level (e.g., culture history), mid level (e.g., reconstructing past lifeways), or high level (e.g., explaining culture change). Although individual archaeologists generally identify the need for research, other archaeologists confirm that need before work proceeds, through peer review of research proposals.

For archaeologists working within the context of CRM, the need for fieldwork is usually determined by proposed land-altering activities such as road building, pipeline construction, logging and mining activity, or residential and business development. Major land-altering development proposals are generally sent to governments, where they are subject to review. Typically, a bureaucrat determines whether the person, company, or agency responsible for the proposal is required to fund an archaeological project to assess the impact of the project on archaeological sites and possibly excavate the site as well. Essentially, the need for fieldwork in the context of industry is based on the fact that archaeological sites may or will be destroyed by an impending land-altering development.

Background Research

After the need for fieldwork has been identified, the next stage is background research. This typically involves a literature review, which includes searching for and reading relevant written reports, articles, and books on the geographic area and time period of interest. At a minimum, a literature review takes in all archaeological reports on the area. It often also includes area history, as well as ethnographies of its indigenous peoples.

Background research also involves reviewing all the archaeological site records for the study area and consulting a wide variety of people. The site records include completed archaeological site inventory forms as well as reports of site investigations usually held on file with the local, regional, or national government agency responsible for heritage. People consulted are usually those who are potentially very knowledgeable about the location of unrecorded archaeological sites, such as members of local descendant communities and others who spend a good deal of time in the area's outdoors. Historians and anthropologists are often consulted if there is reason to believe that a relatively recent site may be discovered. If an archaeologist is focusing on an area where ancient sites may be discovered, he or she is likely to consult with geologists and palaeontologists familiar with the region.

When the project is being undertaken in the context of CRM, background research further includes a detailed review of the development proposal. Most importantly, archaeologists examine the proposal to identify the precise nature and scope of potential impacts to archaeological sites, should they be discovered.

Formulating Hypotheses and Stating Research Questions

Academic archaeologists usually create one or more hypotheses to guide the research. Essentially, the hypothesis is an explanation of some phenomena that makes some sense to the archaeologist based on background research (e.g., which group of people created a site or why a site was abandoned), but lacks sufficient data to fully support it.

Rather than formulating hypotheses, archaeologists in CRM tend to state research questions in their research design. Typical questions include how many sites are likely to be found in the study area and how will the development project impact the sites.

Determining the Types of Data to Collect

It is certainly not practical and not very realistic to think that archaeologists can collect data on matters of interest to all archaeologists while in the field. For example, archaeologists cannot collect and classify every piece of lithic debitage, potsherd, or ecofact recovered during excavations. Thus, while they often take representative samples of the various components of the archaeological record, they focus on the data that can be used most effectively to test their hypotheses or answer their research questions. Basically, archaeologists list in their research designs the kinds of data that they desire to test their hypotheses. Some archaeologists refer to this as **ideal data**.

Different archaeologists will not always collect the same kinds of data. An archaeologist focusing on diet, for example, may recover, classify, and analyze every animal or botanical remain seen during excavations, but take only samples of potsherds and lithic debitage. Conversely, an archaeologist interested primarily in pottery technology, is likely to recover, classify, and analyze every potsherd, but take only representative samples of ecofacts.

In addition to determining what material to collect, archaeologists must also consider which variables of the material will be most appropriate to address their hypotheses or research questions. An archaeologist interested primarily in stone tool technology, for example, will seek different sorts of data than one interested primarily in stone tool function. The archaeologist interested in technology is likely to consider such variables as the size and shape of the flakes removed to make the tool, while the archaeologist interested in function is likely to consider whether there is residue on the tool, and if so, what kind (e.g., plant, bone, hide, etc.).

Determining the Methods to Collect and Analyze Data

Once the ideal data is determined, the next stage of the research design is to decide the most appropriate methods of obtaining that data, both in the field and in the laboratory. Some archaeologists refer to these as the **ideal methods**. Principal factors that ultimately determine the choice of methods include time and money.

Logistics

Logistics are the details for putting the plan in place. For those working in academia, this usually includes an application for money to undertake the research. Normally, funding agencies subject the proposal to peer review to ensure that the project is important from an intellectual stance, and that ideal data and methods are appropriate.For those working in industry, logistics involve submitting a proposal of their work to the government or the developer, and the government agency responsible for archaeology will act as the reviewer to ensure that the methods are appropriate.

Logistics also involve obtaining necessary permissions and permits to conduct fieldwork. This almost always entails obtaining a permit from government and often also means getting approval from landowners and other stakeholders, including indigenous groups.

Logistics also include hiring the field crew, arranging transportation and accommodation, and buying field supplies.

Collecting Data

The search for sites, their excavation, and laboratory work all produce data. Data collected during the search for archaeological sites typically includes basic information on the sites discovered, including their location, number, type, and condition. Data from excavation consists of numbers and types of artifacts, features, and ecofacts. Data from laboratory analysis may include a wide variety of information, as outlined in Chapter 6.

Making the Data Meaningful

Raw data is usually made meaningful after it has been manipulated in some way. This usually involves systems of classification, described in Chapter 7. It also often entails statistics. Essentially, data is made meaningful through its application to the stated hypotheses or research questions.

Making the Research Meaningful

Making the research meaningful brings the project full circle. It is incumbent upon archaeologists to report their research in a timely manner. For those in academic archaeology, this generally means a report to the government and others who have issued the permits or permissions for research, the funding agency, and other archaeologists. Reports to other archaeologists usually take the form of presentations at conferences, journal articles, chapters in edited books, or monographs. Although it does not happen routinely, academic archaeologists are increasingly making their research meaningful to the public, through film productions and articles written for the popular press.

For those in CRM, making the research meaningful generally means reporting the results of the project to the government and others who have issued permits or permissions for research.

Discovering Archaeological Sites

Archaeological sites can be discovered in many ways. They are generally classified in six major categories: fortuitous discovery, predictive modeling, consultation, aerial-based remote sensing, ground-based remote sensing, and surface survey (Table 5.2)

TABLE 5.2: Methods of Discovering Archaeological Sites

Category	Examples
Fortuitous discovery	Plowing fields; during development
Predictive modeling	Using computer programs; maps; knowledge of natural and cultural history
Consultation	With local residents, members of descendant communities, and other academics; written records
Aerial-based remote sensing	Air photos; satellite images; thermography; radar
Ground-based remote sensing	Manual testing with shovels or trowels, augers and corers; geophysical methods such as metal detectors and magnetometers; chemical methods
Survey	Identifying features and artifacts as well as vegetation patterns and anomalies in stratigraphic profiles

Fortuitous Discovery

Fortuitous discovery happens when sites are found without any deliberate attempt to do so. Common examples include farmers discovering sites as they plow fields, construction workers uncovering sites as they build roads, bridges, and buildings, and people casually detecting artifacts in eroded embankments or lying along the water's edge.

Predictive Modeling and Consultation

Predictive modeling involves forecasting where sites are likely to be found by factoring in such things as terrain, weather, and access to resources and transportation routes. **Geographic Information Systems (GIS)** software is often incorporated in predictive modeling.

Consultation involves seeking information from historical documents and advice from other people. Many sites have been discovered based on historical records. Perhaps the most famous occurrence of this was Heinrich Schliemann's search for, and ultimate discovery of, the city of Troy, based on the description written by the ancient Greek author Homer. In North America, many sites have been found based on the readings of ethnographies written in the late 1800s and early 1900s, which often detailed the site locations of previous generations.

Consultation also involves talking to people. Members of descendant communities often provide information on site locations, as do non-indigenous residents familiar with a region's unmodified landscapes. Archaeologists interested in specific time periods often consult geologists and physical geographers to find out where sediments laid down during that period are now exposed. For example, if an archaeologist is interested in finding cultural remains initially deposited between 500,000 and 700,000 years ago, it would make sense to consult with geologists to find out where deposits of that time period are now exposed. Similarly, if an archaeologist is interested in finding evidence of prehistoric coastal or river sites, it may be worthwhile to consult with a geographer to determine the location of past coastlines and river courses. Archaeologists interested in discovering organic remains consult palaeontologists and other palaeoenvironmentalists to find areas with good organic preservation.

Aerial-Based Remote Sensing

There are several aerial-based remote sensing techniques. The most common is the simple use of regular aerial photographs. Occasionally these photographs can be used to identify archaeological features, but more often they are used to locate patterns in the landscape that may have been caused by human use and occupancy. Human impact on the environment often involves changes in natural sediments through such activities as constructing features and discarding food refuse. Human impact can also alter the soil chemistry and soil density so that it is not suitable for supporting certain kinds of plants. Thus, archaeological sites can often be distinguished in aerial photographs by patterns of vegetation. For example, linear patterns of vegetation that differ from surrounding areas may indicate an ancient path or road; an isolated patch of shrubs within a forest of trees may indicate a village or field; and a canopy of vegetation that thrives on soils with a high pH may lie over a shell midden.

Other aerial-based remote sensing techniques are generally more sophisticated and involve methods of detecting subsurface features. These include infrared photography, airborne multispectral scanners, shuttle imaging radar, airborne thermography, and synthetic aperture radar.

Ground-Based Remote Sensing

Ground-based remote sensing techniques are categorized as manual, geophysical, or geochemical. Manual techniques include simply digging holes with a trowel or shovel to check for subsurface cultural remains. This is the simplest technique and is often employed in combination with surface survey. Twisting augers and corers, which are essentially hollow tubes, into the ground is another manual method commonly used both in the search for sites and in attempts to delineate site boundaries. The hollow tubes retrieve the buried sediments, which are then examined for cultural materials.

Geophysical techniques use a wide range of instruments to measure properties of the subsurface sediments, such magnetism, density, and soil chemistry. Common examples include metal detectors and magnetometers, which sense metals and other materials with magnetic properties. Other instruments are used to send electric currents, sound waves, and radar into the ground, which can identify dense materials such as walls and roads. Typically, with all of these techniques, archaeologists first determine the measurements that can be expected in non-cultural sediments and then rely on anomalies to identify subsurface features and artifacts.

Geochemical techniques examine the soil chemistry to identify cultural deposits. As with geophysical techniques, archaeologists first determine the chemistry of non-cultural sediments in the area and then use anomalies in the measurements to identify cultural deposits. Most commonly, it is phosphorous that is measured in geochemical sensing. The basic premise is that human settlements tend to have significantly higher measurements of phosphorous in the sediments than occurs naturally. Reasons for this include the substantial amounts of organic matter deposited as waste, refuse, and ash; extensive deposits of manure applied to fields; and the high phosphate content in human skeletons.

Surface Survey

Also known as ground reconnaissance and field walking, surface survey is undeniably the most usual way in which archaeologists discover sites. It involves physically walking over the ground surface looking for evidence of past human activity.

Despite the vast changes in landscapes as a result of industrial and other activities, it is still common for archaeologists to identify features and artifacts on the ground surface, particularly in areas where there as been little or no deposition of natural sediments.

In places where cultural deposits are likely to have been buried by natural processes, archaeologists sometimes incorporate one or more of the ground-based remote sensing techniques into their survey. Because human occupation alters soil properties, those doing site surveys usually pay very close attention to changes in vegetation patterns.

Surface survey also involves examining natural or culturally created soil profiles for subsurface deposits. These commonly include, for example, eroding river banks and cuts made into the sediments for road building.

An archaeologist doing a survey typically covers several miles per day, often in difficult terrain. Survey work is frequently done in groups, with people evenly spaced and walking roughly in the same direction, often by compass bearing. When sites are found, surveyors complete an archaeological site inventory form, which typically requires

FIGURE 5.1: LOOKING FOR SITES IN A FOREST. Archaeological surveys often involve working in groups, with people spaced evenly apart.

details about location and access, as well as descriptions of the site surface and a map. Typical field supplies carried by archaeologists during survey include topographic maps, a compass, and a global positioning system (GPS). Measurement tools such as a 30 meter tape are carried to measure site boundaries and locations of features within a site. Flagging tape is often carried to mark locations where artifacts or features are found. Cameras are also usually taken on survey.

FIGURE 5.2: FINDING AN ARTIFACT AMONG THE TREES during archaeological survey.

Using Samples to Search for Sites

When searching for archaeological sites, it is often not practical to cover the entire study area by ground-based remote sensing or surface survey. In most cases, the study area is sampled using either a **judgmental sample** or a **probabilistic sample.**

With judgmental sampling, also known as **non-probabilistic sampling**, the area chosen for investigation is based on the archaeologist's judgment of where to search. For example, if a study area was 100 square kilometers (39 square miles) and the research design called for a surface survey of 10 per cent of the area, an archaeologist using a judgmental sample would simply choose the best 10 square kilometers (3.9 square miles) to examine based on his or her judgment. The judgment could be based on any number of factors, including past experience working in the area. It may be the case, for example, that 90 per cent of the study area is made up of rugged terrain and 10 per cent is river valley. The project director may reason that since it is unlikely that there were any sites outside of the river valley, the entire 10 per cent sample will be carried out in the valley.

There are both advantages and disadvantages to judgmental sampling. The advantages include the fact that because of the archaeologist's previous background and reasoning skills, more sites are likely to be discovered. Archaeologists can choose to leave out areas with difficult access or low archaeological visibility, so this strategy is also generally easier and less expensive to undertake than probabilistic sampling.

Judgmental sampling has two principal disadvantages. For one, the results cannot be used to make predictions with confidence. If, for example, archaeologists found 5 prehistoric settlements using a 10 per cent sample, they could not then extrapolate the data to infer that there are about 50 settlements in the entire study area. The only inference that can be made with confidence is that there are at least 5 settlements in the study area. Another disadvantage is that since the archaeologists are looking in areas where they expect to find permanent or semipermanent habitation sites, then they are not likely to find other sorts of sites, such as quarries or temporary camps.

When the area chosen for investigation is not biased by anyone's judgment, it is called probabilistic sampling, or statistical sampling. There are three basic types of probabilistic sampling: simple random, stratified random, and systematic.

Simple random sampling occurs when each part of the study area has an equal chance of being selected for investigation. For example, a 20 per cent sample of a study area could be determined by dividing the entire area into 100 units of equal size, assigning each unit a number on a piece of paper, putting the pieces in a container, and drawing out 20. Those areas with the corresponding numbers will be investigated.

Stratified random sampling involves subdividing the entire study area, usually based on geographic features such as river valleys and mountains, and sampling a predetermined proportion of each area. For example, if half the study area is river valley and half is mountains, then each area is sampled separately. Stratified sampling is generally used to give greater attention to areas where there is a higher probability of discovering sites (e.g., the valleys), and less attention to those with a lower probability (e.g., the mountains). Thus, 30 per cent of the valley may be chosen for sampling, while only 10 per cent of the mountain areas may be sampled.

When areas are subdivided and sampled at regular intervals it is called systematic sampling. For a 10 per cent sample of a 100 square kilometer area, the entire area may be divided into 100 distinct units and every tenth unit is investigated.

Probabilistic sampling has two main advantages. One is that predictions can be made with confidence. Because the areas chosen for investigation are based on chance, extrapolating the data to make predictions about the total number of sites is valid. Archaeologists who find 6 resource utilization sites and 2 settlements using a 10 per cent sample can reasonably infer that approximately 60 resource utilization sites and 20 settlement sites existed in the entire study area.

Another advantage to probabilistic sampling is that archaeologists are more likely to obtain a realistic sense of the variety of sites in the area, because it forces them to look where they might not have based on their own preconceptions.

The principal disadvantage to probabilistic sampling is that it is usually more time consuming and costly than judgmental sampling. Even if a unit chosen for investigation is on a mountaintop or in a marshy area, the archaeologist is still obligated to search there, which often means more time and money.

Excavation

Michael Shanks (1992: 68–69) offers this evocative description of excavation in his book *Experiencing the Past: On the Character of Archaeology.*

> Excavation is striptease. The layers are peeled off slowly; eyes of intent scrutiny. The pleasure is in seeing more, but it lies also in the edges: the edge of stocking-top and thigh. There is the allure of transgression—the margin of decorum and lewdness, modesty and display. The hidden past brought into stage-light of the present. Audience keeps its distance; the stage is for the performer only. The split heightens the enticement. Just as the gap between past and present draws us to wonder in fascination. Discovery is a little release of gratification. A pleasure comes from interruption, costume tossed to the side little by little.... Perhaps above all is the excitement of not seeing, of anticipation.... The performance ends not with seeing and knowing all, but with desire.

One of the many things that distinguishes professional excavators from looters, pothunters, and other treasure seekers is that those trained in archaeological method and theory appreciate how necessary it is to carefully choose where to dig and how to recover and record the material remains uncovered during excavation.

Deciding Where and How Much to Dig

By its very nature, archaeological excavation is destructive, and careful attention should be given to both the location and extent of the digging.

Deciding where to dig within a site depends on the research goals. An archaeologist interested primarily in the diet of the site's inhabitants, for example, is likely to excavate in a midden comprised of food refuse; an archaeologist interested in pottery technology may focus on areas around kilns; and an archaeologist interested in reconstructing social inequality may choose to excavate burial sites.

Unless a site is likely to be totally destroyed in the near future, it is usually considered unethical to excavate the entire area. In addition to being costly, it violates the principle of preserving portions of sites for other archaeologists who may wish to excavate in the future.

Deciding how much to dig is also dependent on time and money. In CRM work, it isn't unusual for less than five per cent of a site to be excavated before being destroyed by development. A number of archaeologists have pointed out the problem inherent in such as small sample size. One study of a midden site from southern California demonstrated that despite a systematic sampling pattern and a total number of artifacts exceeding 65,000, **diagnostic artifacts** from the earliest and the most recent occupations were not revealed until almost half the site had been excavated.

As they did when conducting site surveys, directors of excavation projects make an initial choice between using judgmental or probabilistic sampling to decide where to dig. As with site surveys, judgmental sampling is likely to uncover more of what the archaeologist is expecting to find, while probabilistic sampling is generally better for providing statistics to make inferences.

There is no universal way to excavate, but some methods are more suitable than others, depending on research goals and time, among other things. These methods range from small test pits to large-scale excavations.

ROBERT J. MUCKLE

FIGURE 5.3: SMALL-SCALE EXCAVATIONS IN EGYPT. There are many reasons why archaeologists may excavate only a small area, including time restrictions. Small areas are often excavated to test for the presence of subsurface cultural materials.

Many features are excavated as a unit. Figure 5.4, for example, illustrates the excavation inside a mud-brick building that was originally used as a pottery kiln but eventually served as a receptacle for pots that broke during the manufacturing process at a newer kiln.

ROBERT J. MUCKLE

FIGURE 5.4: EXCAVATING A BUILDING. Excavators are inside a circular building that evidently began as a pottery kiln and ended up as a place to dump broken pottery.

Excavations sometimes involve creating trenches, and square holes are usually dug. Trenches are often excavated through portions of a site in order to provide a sense of the overall site stratigraphy. Excavation units are commonly rectangular, measuring one or two meters along each side. Large, continuous areas of excavation are known as block excavations or horizontal excavations.

An excavator's tool kit contains many pieces of equipment. The standard tool is a trowel, typically used to scrape sediments into a dustpan, which in turn is emptied into a bucket. The sediments in the bucket are then usually sieved through a mesh screen. Quarter-inch (6 millimeter) mesh is generally considered the maximum size to use in archaeology. Most sieving involves merely shaking the screen and letting the smaller-sized particles fall through, while artifacts, ecofacts, and other particles larger than the mesh screen are retained. When sediments are difficult to sieve by shaking and water is nearby, water pressure may be used to break apart the smaller particles and push them through the screen.

A number of researchers have pointed out the bias in screen size. Muckle (1994) observed radically different recovery rates of various species of bivalve mollusk shells using 4-millimeter and 2-millimeter screens, and James (1997) suggests that 90 per cent of fish remains are likely to fall through quarter-inch (6 millimeter) mesh.

SUZANNE VILLENEUVE

FIGURE 5.5: LARGE-SCALE EXCAVATIONS IN PERU. Excavations of large, continuous areas allow archaeologists to observe patterning of the material remains that they might not otherwise see in small-scale excavations. Large excavation units as depicted here are sometimes known as block excavations.

In addition to trowels and screens, the tool kit contains many other items. For particularly delicate items, dental picks and small brushes are often used to clear away particles from an object. In extreme cases of highly compacted sediments, archaeologists have been known to use jackhammers. Archaeologists will often use shovels when there is relatively little time to excavate, or some will use backhoes to dig a trench through a site to get a quick idea of the stratigraphy, knowing that objects recovered from the trench will be in secondary context (that is, not in their original location).

Ideally, artifacts and ecofacts are recorded as they are exposed, and it is only the very small ones that are recovered from the sieves. Generally, once artifacts are uncovered, an inventory form is completed, which minimally includes the artifact's provenience, description, and assigned number. Artifacts are then usually bagged separately. Provenience is established in relation to a site datum. At one extreme, this is accomplished by simply measuring with a tape. At the other extreme, provenience is established with a **total station**, which can record both horizontal and vertical provenience electronically.

Excavators periodically stop and make detailed notes about what they have found, recording such things as the number and types of artifacts and ecofacts, and describing the texture and color of the matrix. These are commonly referred to as level notes. Excavators also typically draw top-view sketches and take photographs of the unit during these intervals.

The timing of these periodic stops for detailed recording is determined by whether the excavation is done by arbitrary levels or by natural levels. Excavating by arbitrary levels means that the detailed notes will be taken at regular intervals, such as every 10 centimeters, arbitrarily chosen by the project director. Excavating by natural levels means the notes will be taken when the matrix changes, such as when a layer of silt overlies a layer of sand.

Excavating by arbitrary levels has both advantages and disadvantages. The advantages are that it is fast and easy. Essentially, all that is required to follow this system is the ability to read a tape measure. The principal disadvantage to this system is that if the matrix changes partway through the predetermined interval, artifacts and ecofacts from significantly different time periods may be grouped together.

The principal advantage of excavating by natural levels is that material remains from the same matrix, and thus time period, are grouped together. The disadvantage is that it requires very skilled excavators and more time. Differences in the matrix are often very minor and difficult to recognize, such as the difference between sandy silt and silty sand. The ability to recognize such differences in the field generally only comes with considerable experience.

As excavators dig through each level, they often come across ecofacts or other material remains such as potsherds or **microdebitage** that for the purpose of the project may not be classified as artifacts, but are nevertheless important. These objects, or at least a representative sample of them, are usually placed in **level bags.**

Field Laboratories

Field laboratories are common on excavation projects. Mostly, they provide a place where initial sorting and cataloguing occurs. Typically, for example, items from level bags are sorted in the field lab, separating such things as organic remains from lithics and ceramics. It is also where initial conservation measures can be made on fragile objects. In some cases, especially where it is logistically difficult or illegal to remove material remains from the country, more in-depth analysis occurs in field laboratories, including illustration, photography, detailed description, and microscopic analysis.

Ethnoarchaeology and Experimental Archaeology: Research Design and Field Methods

Ethnoarchaeology projects, which observe contemporary people to promote an understanding of the past, are invariably academic in nature. Some large-scale archaeology projects incorporate ethnoarchaeology as one of several research activities that may also include the discovery and excavation of sites and laboratory analysis. Many projects, however, are entirely ethnoarchaeological in nature.

Ethnoarchaeology can assist our understanding of how archaeological deposits are created and explain the patterning of material remains that archaeologists observe. One of the primary objectives of ethnoarchaeology is to understand the various human behaviors and motivations of contemporary people associated with material remains, in order to develop models that attempt to explain such processes in the past. In the article "Where the Garbage Goes: Refuse Disposal in the Maya Highlands," Brian Hayden and Aubrey Cannon report on the disposal of refuse among contemporary Maya, noting that their system is influenced by economy of effort and the potential value or hindrance of the refuse. Once refuse from a household is sorted, it may be dumped in different locations. Hayden and Cannon outline the ways in which their observations assist archaeologists focusing on past communities in that area, by helping them to determine (i) differential sorting and deposition methods, (ii) refuse locations, (iii) biases in the refuse found, (iv) useful quantification techniques, (v) types of behavior the artifacts left in houses or other structures most likely represent, (vi) the significance of refuse found in pits, and (vii) the principles of human behavior which most likely explain major variations in refuse disposal.

Most ethnoarchaeological fieldwork is classified as **participant observation**, a technique borrowed from cultural anthropology in which the researcher becomes immersed in a culture, as both a participant and an observer. In participant observation, the researcher usually relies on one or a few key members of the group being studied, who often serve as interpreters of both the language and the behavior being observed.

The primary differences between participant observation as practiced by archaeologists and cultural anthropologists are those of time and focus. With the exception of some notable multiyear ethnoarchaeology projects, archaeologists usually spend much less time interacting with a group of interest than cultural anthropologists. Archaeologists also tend to be much more focused on material culture than cultural anthropologists, particularly when it comes to observations of site formation processes in general and refuse discard in particular. In some cases, ethnoarchaeologists serve as apprentices to potters and metalworkers to better understand how the material remains become part of the archaeological record.

Conducting interviews and asking questions is another method used by ethnoarchaeologists. For some projects, this may constitute the only fieldwork, while other projects consider it supplemental to participant observation.

As with ethnoarchaeology, experimental archaeology (which attempts to replicate past conditions and events) is primarily academic in nature and may take place in the context of a complete project or be a single component of a large-scale project that might also include the discovery and excavation of sites and laboratory analysis. While some experiments may be done in laboratories, the majority are not. Many experiments are undertaken at archaeological sites, while excavations are ongoing. The most common types of archaeological field experiments involve manufacturing and using stone tools, constructing buildings, and taphonomy. Other field experiments study the effectiveness of early tools in food production, metal working, the creation of pictographs, and the movement of large stones.

Hazards of Fieldwork

Archaeological fieldwork can be hazardous. Injury, illness, or death may come from several sources. Few areas in the world offer fieldwork without some level of danger. For those doing fieldwork in developing countries, precautions against malaria and other diseases common to the area are routine.

Depending on the geographic location, other common hazards include encounters with bears, poisonous snakes, spiders, and ticks and other insects. Particularly for those

TABLE 5.3: Hazards of Archaeology

Hazards	Examples
Exposure to disease	Exposure to disease-carrying insects, contaminated buried remains, rusty nails, and infected needles
Exposure to toxic wastes of various kinds	Ranging from nuclear waste to the legacies of many sorts of industrial sites
Wildlife encounters	Spiders, snakes, ticks, insects of many kinds, bears, and cougars
Working in difficult terrain and deep units	Falling down cliffs, collapsing walls of excavation units
Field living in general	Extreme weather, unsanitary water, contaminated food, poisonous plants

doing historic archaeology, toxic chemicals are a real hazard, and it is not unusual for archaeologists to wear full protection clothing, including hazardous-material suits, when working in areas suspected of containing toxic substances. Archaeologists working in areas with a history of warfare must also be very careful. For example, between 1964 and 1973 about four billion pounds of bombs were dropped in and around the Southeast Asian country of Laos. As many as one third of them never exploded, and they remain on the land surface today, countless in close proximity to areas of archaeological interest.

Archaeologists working with burials from the nineteenth and early twentieth centuries must also be particularly cautious. From the mid-1800s to 1910, arsenic was a prime ingredient in embalming practice, with some embalmers using as much as 12 pounds per body. Because arsenic does not degrade, it has become an extreme health hazard for those who may come in contact with burial grounds of the period. John Konefes and Michael McGee suggest if 2,000 people were buried in a single cemetery over a 30-year period and if only half of those were embalmed with even a very conservative amount of arsenic for the time (about six ounces), then it is reasonable to assume that there is about 380 pounds of arsenic in the cemetery today.

In the introduction to *Dangerous Places: Health, Safety, and Archaeology*, David Poirier and Kenneth Feder (2001) give the following description of just some of the hazards involved in contemporary archaeological fieldwork:

> Bacterial and viral infections rest quietly hidden in the soil, are concealed in the animals that roam through our sites, reside in the insects that desire our blood, or even lie in wait in the organic remains we discover. Parasites that once resided unharmoniously within the intestinal tracts of past populations may now be lying in wait, ready to blossom once again.... The mortal remains of individuals who died of historical scourges that once afflicted humanity may still host the pathogens that killed them.... Historically disposed of outside the factory and mill door, toxic chemical wastes and manufacturing by-products may continue to permeate.... Infectious diseases, radioactive and chemical contaminants, and volatile explosives are replacing the traditional and somewhat pedestrian archaeological health concerns of poison ivy, sunburn, and mosquito bites.

Despite the fact that shoring the walls of deep excavation units is becoming standard practice in North America and is often required by legislation or government policy, inadequate shoring is another potential problem for fieldworkers. Many archaeologists in even shallow units have experienced collapsing walls and some have been buried up to their waist or higher in moderately deep units. In 2005, a European archaeologist was buried alive when the walls of the unit he was excavating collapsed and his coworkers could not dig him out quickly.

FIGURE 5.6: WORKING IN NARROW, DEEP PIT. One of the hazards of archaeology is the collapsing walls of deep pits.

KEY RESOURCES AND SUGGESTED READING

The Handbook of Archaeological Sciences, edited by Brothwell and Pollard (2001) includes several contributions on archaeological prospection. Good overviews of field archaeology include *The Archaeologist's Field Handbook* by Burke and Smith (2004) and *Field Methods in Archaeology, 7e* by Hester, Shafer, and Feder (1997). Orton (2000) focuses on sampling in *Sampling in Archaeology* and Roskams (2001) focuses on excavation in *Excavation.* David and Kramer (2001) provide a comprehensive overview of ethnoarchaeology in *Ethnoarchaeology in Action.* Poirier and Feder (2001) are the editors of *Dangerous Places: Health, Safety, and Archaeology.* The *Handbook of Archaeological Methods v.1*, edited by Maschner and Chippendale (2005) includes chapters on survey, excavation, ethnoarchaeology, geographic information systems, and experimental archaeology.

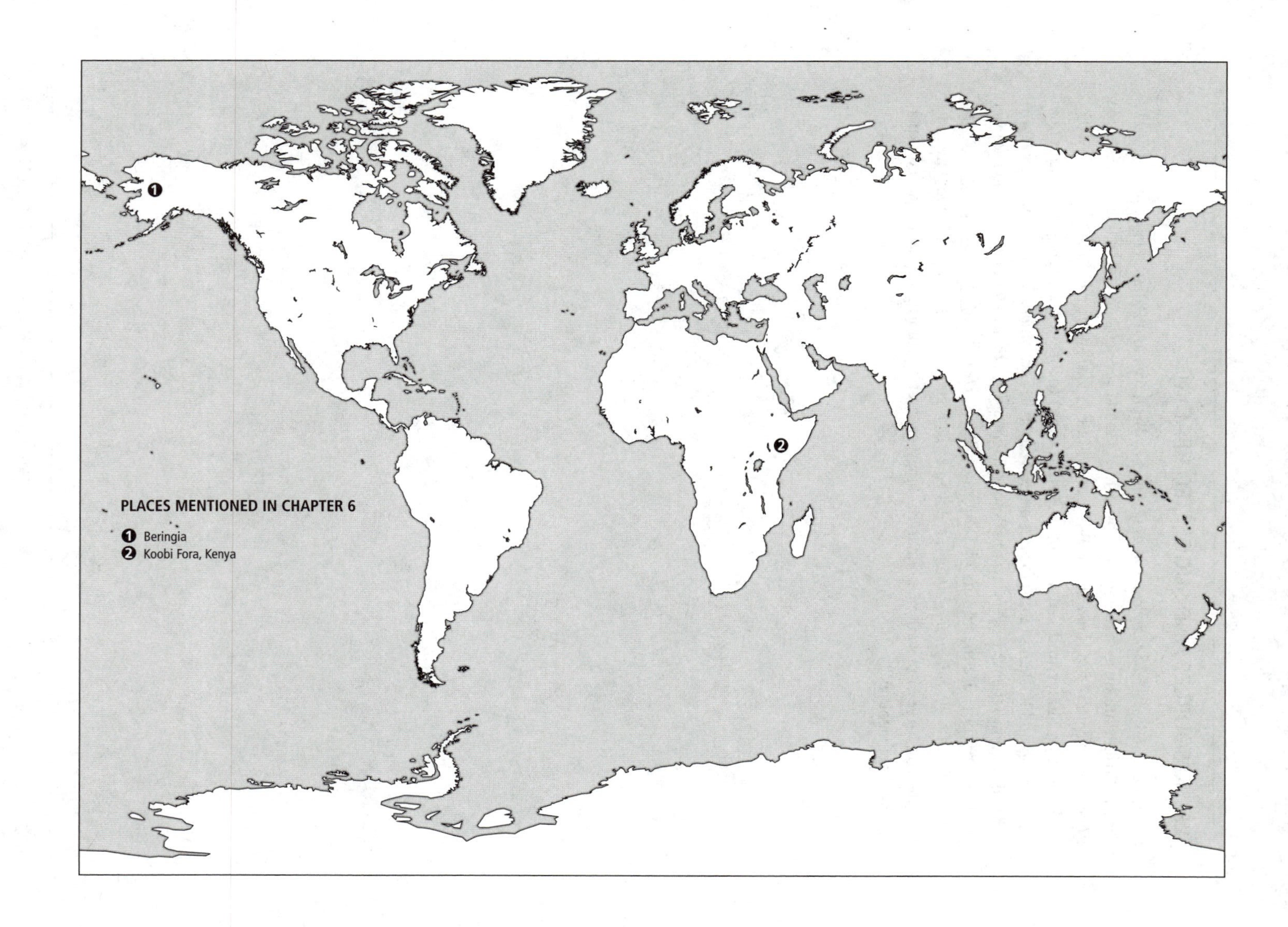
PLACES MENTIONED IN CHAPTER 6
1 Beringia
2 Koobi Fora, Kenya

CHAPTER 6

Working in the Laboratory

Introduction

The most common popular perception of archaeology is the image of the archaeologist at work in the field. It is primarily in the laboratory, however, that the material remains recovered during excavation are made meaningful.

As described in this and subsequent chapters, laboratory analysis provides the basis for the archaeologist's reconstructions of culture history, technology, palaeoenvironments, subsistence strategies, diet, social and political systems, and ideology.

This chapter provides an outline of the common types of laboratory work archaeologists do, beginning with the initial processing of recovered material and then focusing in particular on the analysis of artifacts, ecofacts, and human remains. Methods of determining antiquity are covered in Chapter 7.

Laboratory Processes

Archaeological laboratories may be categorized as either field laboratories or regular laboratories. Field laboratories are most common on large-scale academic research projects, especially where it is logistically difficult or illegal to remove archaeological remains from the area. For example, field laboratories are used for excavations in remote or difficult to access locations, such as on islands or in high altitude regions where archaeologists may want to leave all or a portion of the collected material behind so as not to be burdened by transporting it. In areas where authorities permit excavation but do not wish artifacts to leave the area, field laboratories are used. Field laboratories typically are set up for the duration of the excavation.

Regular laboratories are permanent rooms with specific analytical materials and equipment, and are commonly found in colleges, universities, and CRM firms. It is not unusual to use a variety of laboratories for analyzing different types of recovered material, such as sediments, faunal remains, botanical remains, human remains, ceramics, and lithics. Besides equipment for various types of measuring, archaeological

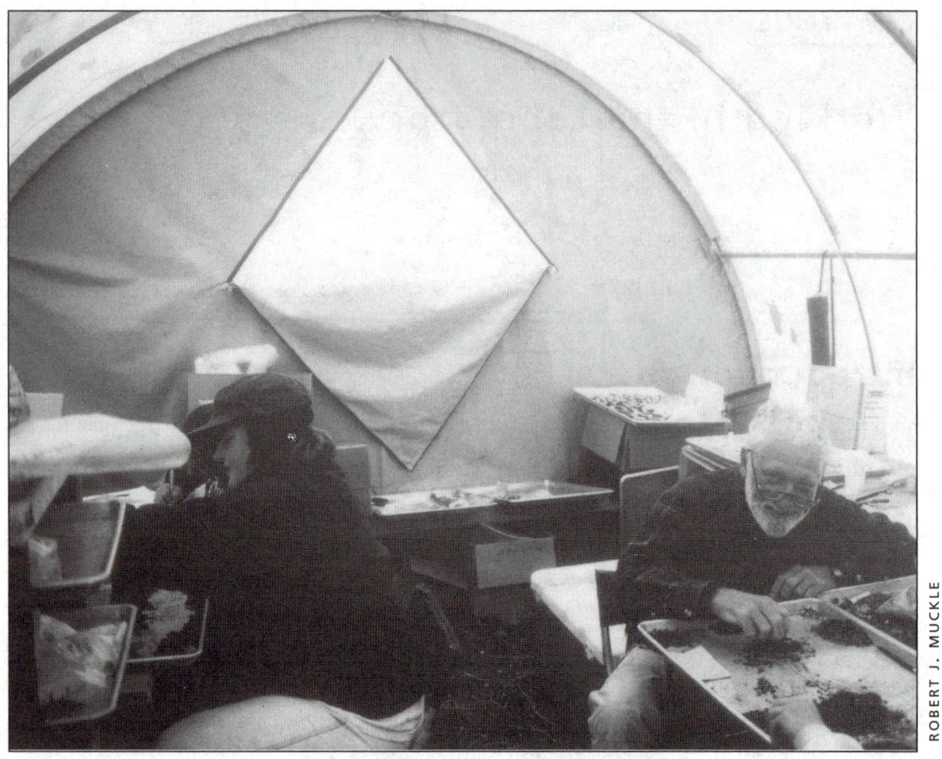

ROBERT J. MUCKLE

FIGURE 6.1: ARCHAEOLOGY FIELD LABORATORY. Field laboratories are common, especially for long-term projects and where transporting large amounts of material remains is difficult. This lab was set up on a remote island in Alaska where the only viable transportation was by float plane.

laboratories generally have comparative collections to aid the identification of various types of material remains.

Laboratory processing generally begins with sorting. This includes sorting items from level bags, typically into the categories of faunal remains, botanical remains, potsherds, and lithic debitage. If the excavations were undertaken at an historic site (from the time for which written records exist), the additional categories of glass and metal pieces are common.

Depending on the research objectives and the skill of the laboratory workers, it is not uncommon to use subcategories in the initial sort, for example, classifying bones as either mammal, bird, or fish, or subdividing the artifacts into lithics, ceramics, glass, metals, or organics. Recognizing that residues on artifacts may provide important clues for current or future studies, artifacts are usually cleaned only to the degree necessary for analysis.

Individual artifacts are entered into a permanent catalog. This process usually begins by looking at the artifact inventory forms completed in the field and adding more detail about the artifacts than could reasonably have been provided when they were first collected. This commonly includes making more precise descriptions of form. The initial processing of artifacts in the laboratory also often includes making line drawings and taking photographs. Perishable or fragile artifacts are often treated with one of a variety of preservatives, and pieces of once-intact objects are often refitted and glued. Artifacts are typically labeled with permanent ink in an inconspicuous place, and if they are not going to be analyzed in the near future, they are packed for storage. The entire process of cataloging, labeling, conserving, and storing artifacts is known as **curation**.

ROBERT J. MUCKLE

FIGURE 6.2: ARTIFACT PHOTOGRAPHY. Photographing artifacts is standard procedure in archaeology. This photo was taken at a field laboratory in Egypt.

Artifact Analysis

Artifacts are analyzed in many ways. This section provides an overview of the major types of analysis, beginning with classification and including the basic ways in which archaeologists analyze lithic, ceramic, organic, and historic artifacts.

Classification

Artifact analysis often begins with a system of classification known as **typology**, which may be descriptive, functional, or a hybrid of both.

Descriptive typology classifies artifacts according to observable, measurable traits, such as its material, shape, size, and any evidence of its manufacture. Using a descriptive typology, a stone artifact may be classified, for example, as a small, triangular, lithic **biface**. These attributes constitute an artifact **type**. Using a functional typology, on the other hand, this artifact might be classified as an arrowhead. A hybrid classification could categorize the artifact as a small, triangular arrowhead.

There is no consensus on how to best classify artifacts. Some archaeologists believe that typology should be standardized, with everyone using the same criteria to describe artifacts. Others believe that typology should be designed to fit the specific research objectives of the project. Many archaeologists do both, using standard attributes such as material, size, shape, and color to broadly communicate the results of their work, while at the same time using criteria to specifically address the hypothesis or research question of interest.

In general, prehistoric archaeologists are more inclined to use descriptive typology, and historic archaeologists are more likely to use functional typology. This is partly because historic archaeologists work with material from more recent times, so they have more confidence in their inferences of function.

Creating and identifying artifact types allows archaeologists to make sense of the almost infinite number of characteristics prevalent in the recovered remains. Attributes to be recorded are established in the research design on the basis of how important they are to the researcher's objectives. An archaeologist interested in determining how stone tools were made, for example, will likely want to focus on a completely different set of attributes than an archaeologist wanting to focus on how stone tools were used. Attributes such as the position of flake scars on the tools and the size of debitage will be important to the archaeologist interested in lithic technology, while attributes such as linear striations and polish on the tool will be more important to the archaeologist interested in determining the tool's function.

It should be appreciated that there is no one correct way to determine artifact types.

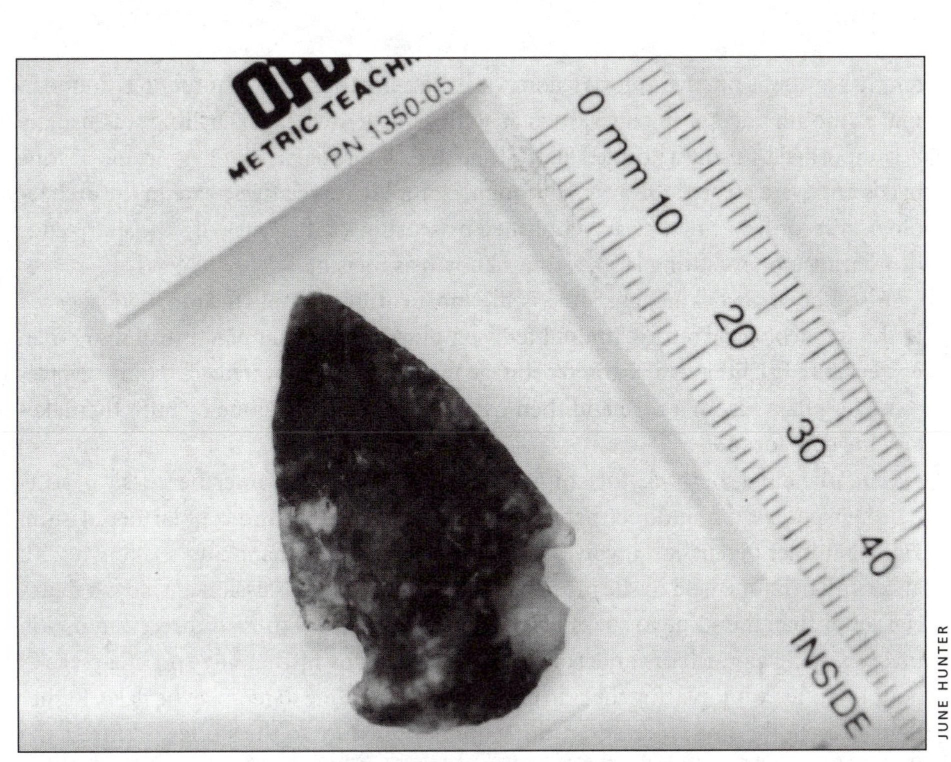

JUNE HUNTER

FIGURE 6.3: PROJECTILE POINT. Thorough descriptions of artifacts, including measurements, are routine in archaeological laboratory work.

It is generally accepted that a minimum of two attributes is required to make a type, but there is no maximum. Provided the same assemblage of 1,000 artifacts, one archaeologist might create 3 types, and another might find 100 types, and another might generate 500 types—and they all would be valid.

Lithic Analysis

In addition to being classified by typology, lithic artifacts are generally analyzed to determine the way they were made and what they were used for, as well as to identify the specific kind of stone.

Archaeologists recognize several ways of making stone tools, including pecking, grinding, drilling, cutting, and chipping. Pecking involves pulverizing one stone with another to rough out a shape, the technique most commonly used to make petroglyphs, as well as stone bowls and statues. Grinding uses an abrasive stone to shape another and was often employed alone or in combination with another technique to make smooth and sharp edges, such as with slate arrowheads. Drilling was usually accomplished by using a pointed, hard stone to drill through a softer stone; most stone beads and were created this way. Although examples are relatively rare in the archaeological record, cutting was accomplished by scoring a soft stone with the sharp edge of a harder stone. Cutting is sometimes known as incising.

Also known as flaking, chipping is the most common lithic technology observed in the archaeological record, undoubtedly employed in the manufacture of more than 99 per cent of all lithic artifacts and debitage that has been recovered. Chipping involves removing flakes from a core and then using either the core alone or both the flakes and the core for tools.

The principal methods for chipping stone are hard-hammer percussion, soft-hammer percussion, indirect percussion, pressure flaking, and bipolar percussion. Hard-hammer percussion involves holding the core in one hand and striking it with another hard stone held in the other hand. Soft-hammer percussion employs a material softer than the stone to strike blows, typically bone or antler. Indirect percussion involves using a punch of some sort to remove flakes by hitting one end of a piece of bone or antler, while placing the other end against the stone to remove the flake. Rather than striking the stone, pressure flaking applies pressure to the stone and forces the flakes off, usually with a piece of bone or antler.

Analysis of stone tool technology usually focuses on determining the method of manufacture, with key variables including the size and shape of waste flakes, including debitage (Table 6.1).

The process of making stone tools by chipping or flaking is known as **flintknapping**, and there are some standard terms used to describe materials produced by this

TABLE 6.1: Attributes of Various Methods of Chipping Stone

Method	Typical Attributes
Bipolar percussion	Damage at both ends of flake or core
Hard-hammer percussion	Flakes of various sizes and shapes; most large and thick flakes created this way
Soft-hammer percussion	Flakes of various sizes and shapes, although thick flakes are rare
Indirect percussion	Very small flakes and microdebitage
Pressure flaking	Very small flakes and microdebitage

technique. **Core tools** are tools produced by removing flakes from around the original cobble (block of stone). **Flake tools** are tools that have been made from one of the flakes chipped off the original cobble. **Unifaces** are tools that have had flakes removed from only one side, and bifaces are tools in which flakes have been removed from both sides. **Blades** describe flake tools that are at least twice as long as they are wide, and have at least roughly parallel sides. Debitage or **detritus** refers to the waste flakes (i.e., flakes that have been created during flintknapping and recognized as trash). Very small, usually microscopic pieces are often referred to as microdebitage.

When it is not obvious from the shape, determining the use of a stone tool depends upon magnified views of the tool's edges or chemical analysis of residue on it. It is not unusual to be able to distinguish the type of blood on stone tools. Researchers Thomas Loy and E. James Dixon (1998), for example, detected the blood of a variety of large mammal species, including mammoth, on artifacts at least several thousand years old from eastern Beringia—a large mass of land in northwestern North America and northeastern Asia that was freed from ice during the last ice age. Most archaeologists believe the initial migration of people into the Americas was via Beringia.

Based on many experiments over the past few decades, a few generalizations can be made about some physical attributes found near the edges of stone tools. Linear striations running parallel to the sharp edge of a stone artifact, for example, generally indicate that it was used for cutting. A polished or glossy surface along the sharp edge is usually taken to mean that it was used for scraping. When the traits are observed under magnification, they are often termed **microwear**.

Some researchers believe they can use microwear to distinguish tool use for very old artifacts. Lawrence Keely and Nick Toth (1981) reported that they were able to confidently identify microwear distinctive of meat cutting on some artifacts, and microwear distinctive of cutting soft plant material on others, as well as microwear distinctive of scraping or sawing wood. Artifacts with microwear have been determined to have been used about 1.5 million years ago in the Koobi Fora region of East Africa, which has been studied extensively and where some of the earliest known members of the genus *Homo* and their tools have been uncovered.

Identifying the kind of stone is often dependent on a comparative collection. In general, the coarser the grain of stone, the more difficult it is to control the way it breaks. For very coarse-grained material, such as granite or sandstone, pecking is usually the only effective way of shaping the stone, but it can rarely make a sharp-cutting edge.

One of the most common stones used to make sharp-cutting edges is basalt, which can also be further classified as coarse, medium, or fine-grained. Many projectile points and other fine tools made with sharp-cutting edges are made from a variety of very fine-grained stones. Among the most common are those known as quartzite, chert, flint, chalcedony, and **obsidian**. Occurrences of these stones are more restrictive, and archaeologists can often trace the original source of the stone through **trace-element analysis**.

Archaeologists often use the same term to describe different things when classifying stone. Although there is no consensus, most American archaeologists and geologists use *chert* as a general term for a wide variety of fine-grained stones, including flint, chalcedony, and jasper. British archaeologists and geologists, on the other hand, usually consider flint to be a distinct from chert.

Ceramic Analysis

Ceramic is a large category of material that is broadly defined as clay baked, through the process known as firing. Ceramics include figurines, bricks, tiles, and pipes. The majority of ceramic analysis is undertaken on the class of ceramics known as pottery, defined as ceramic containers. Essentially, if the ceramic artifact was meant to hold something, then it is classified as pottery, even if it is flat like a plate.

In addition to typology, ceramic analysis commonly involves identifying the ceramic body (the composition of the clay) or **fabric**, the method of manufacture, use, and style. The main categories of fabric are **terra cotta**, **earthenware**, **stoneware**, **china**, and **porcelain**. These categories are based on the type of clay and level of porosity, which is dependent on the temperature at which the ceramic was fired. Measured in Celsius, the firing temperature for terra cotta is less than 1,000 degrees (1,832 Fahrenheit); for earthenware it's between 900 and 1,200 degrees (1,652 to 2,192 Fahrenheit); for stoneware, between 1,200 and 1,350 degrees (2,192 to 2,462 Fahrenheit); for china, 1,100 to 1,200 degrees (2,012 to 2,192 Fahrenheit); and for porcelain, 1,300 to 1,450 degrees (2,371 to 2,642 Fahrenheit). Terra cotta is often considered to be a kind of earthenware.

The primary method of determining ceramic body type involves an examination of color: terra cotta and earthenware usually retain a reddish color; stoneware a light brown or gray; and the categories fired at higher temperatures become white and in some cases translucent. Higher firing temperatures also cause the ceramics to become vitreous.

The vast majority of prehistoric pottery is terra cotta or earthenware, likely because it is difficult to create heat in the extreme temperatures required for stoneware, china, and porcelain.

Five primary methods are used in the manufacture of pottery. Pinching and drawing involves manipulating a lump of clay by hand, primarily by using fingers and thumb to pinch the clay while drawing it upwards to form a bowl shape. When separate pieces of clay are rolled or patted flat and then joined, it is called slab modeling. Molding involves pressing clay firmly into or over a mold. Coiling is the technique of winding worm-like segments of clay upwards in a circular fashion. Throwing refers to pottery manufactured

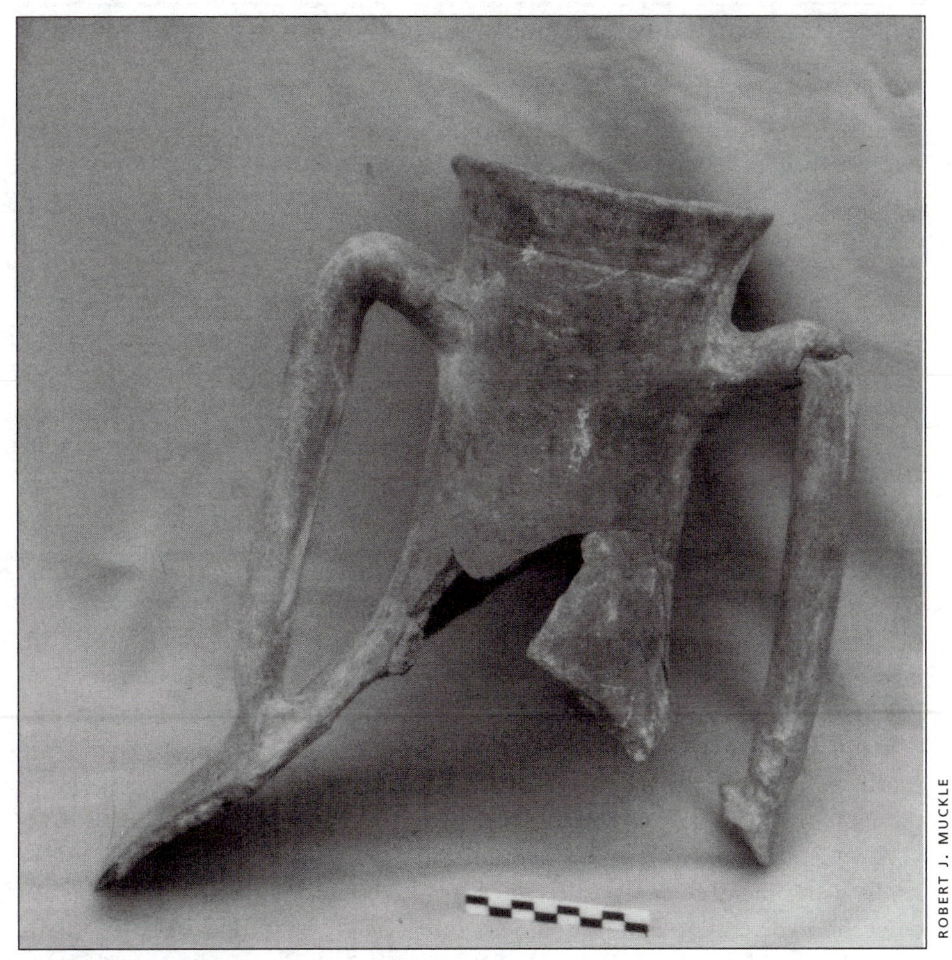
ROBERT J. MUCKLE

FIGURE 6.4: BROKEN POT. Broken pots are among the most frequently encountered types of material remains in archaeology.

with the use of a pottery wheel. Complete pots and potsherds exhibit several attributes that can be used to distinguish the method of manufacture (Table 6.2).

Archaeologists generally recognize that pottery function falls into four major categories: storage, transport, food preparation, and serving. There are several attributes that distinguish function. Storage containers, for example, usually have restricted openings or closures at the top and, if used to hold liquid, a slip or glaze to reduce permeability. Pots used for transport usually have handles and little or no decoration. Pots

TABLE 6.2: Attributes of Various Methods of Pottery Manufacture

Method of Manufacture	Attributes of Pots or Potsherds
Pinching and drawing	Small pots; uneven walls; indentations on walls left by finger and thumb
Coiling	Cracks or breaks along parallel lines; variations in wall thickness; round/smooth edges of potsherds
Slab modeling/building	Rectangular containers; seams; differences in thicknesses of slabs
Molding	Differences in texture between inside and outside of pot or potsherd; parting agents (to prevent clay from sticking to the mold); seams
Throwing	Rilling (a series of small ridges and grooves on the outside of the pot); flat bases; walls may be uneven from top to bottom but not around the circumference

used for food preparation generally have wide openings and little or no decoration. Pottery used for serving is relatively flat (e.g., plates) or has unrestricted openings (e.g., bowls), and often has some sort of decorative design. Charring or burning on the base usually indicates the pot was used for cooking, and extensive wear on the interior of the pot is often indicative of food processing.

As with lithics, the study of pottery function occasionally includes residue analysis. By using chemical analysis to identify proteins and lipids, archaeologists are often able to determine the types of foods and liquids the pots once held. For example, residue analysis of pots is used to determine the antiquity of beer and wine in a region.

Analysis of Organic Artifacts

The most common types of organic artifacts are those made from bone, wood, shell, and plants. The analysis of organic artifacts usually focuses on taxonomic identification of the material, the technology used in making the artifact, and style.

Identifying the type of material is usually done using a comparative collection. In many cases, it is only possible to distinguish fairly broad categories, such as mammal bone or antler, but identification to the level of genus and species is also common.

As with lithics and pottery, the manufacture of organic artifacts often leaves

ROBERT J. MUCKLE

FIGURE 6.5: WOVEN BASKET. Although not as common as lithic or ceramic remains, organic materials such as this basket are occasionally recovered from archaeological sites.

evidence pointing to the method on the artifact itself. For example, stone and metal tools will leave different sorts of scarring on carved wood artifacts.

Because of the highly perishable nature of **textiles** and woven baskets, they are not commonly discovered and analyzed. When they are, the focus tends to be on the nature of the weave (e.g., coiling, plaiting, or twining). As with pottery, stylistic analysis tends to focus on overall shape and decoration.

Analysis of Metal and Glass

While metal and glass recovered from archaeological sites may be analyzed for its mineralogical components, this is not common. Typically, metal and glass artifacts are subjected to typological studies only.

Metal artifacts are usually sorted into broad categories such as nails, cans, apparel accessories, coins, and household items, and then further classified according to size and manufacturing technology. Nails, for example, are often classified as hand-forged, early machine-cut, and modern machine-cut, in addition to being categorized by size.

The analysis of glass from historic archaeological sites is common. The major categories are flat glass, typically used for windows, and bottle glass. Bottle and bottle-fragment analysis is particularly common. Attributes such as lip form, type of closure, mold marks, and existence and location of seams and can often be traced to specific years and places of manufacture.

Quantification of Artifacts

Since most material remains recovered from sites are broken pieces, one laboratory task for archaeologists is to determine how many original artifacts the assemblage of pieces represents. Although there are various ways of quantifying the number, they usually involve refitting as many pieces as possible and then looking at several variables to determine the minimum number of artifacts represented. For example, three potsherds of the same clay fabric and style of decoration conceivably may have come from the same pot and therefore are calculated to represent one pot, whereas three potsherds with different clay fabrics would be calculated to represent three pots. The names and acronyms of some of the methods include the following: estimated vessel equivalent (EVE), estimated tool equivalent (ETE), minimum number of intact tools (MNIT), minimum number of tools (MNT), and minimum number of items (MNI). As described in the next section, the acronym MNI is also frequently used in the analysis of animal remains, where it has a different meaning (minimum number of individuals).

Ecofact Analysis

The analysis of ecofacts in archaeological laboratories is routine. This section covers the most common types of analysis for animal remains, botanical remains, and sediments recovered from archaeological sites.

Animal Remains

Animal remains in archaeological sites include a variety of things such as bone, teeth, claws, shells, hair, and soft tissue. However, it is clearly bone that dominates most assemblages of animal remains and thus receives most attention. The analysis of animal remains routinely involves taxonomic identification and quantification. Taxonomic identification is usually done with the use of a comparative collection. Minimally, a simple list of the species or genera represented is determined in the laboratory. Often, however, there are further, more meaningful quantification calculations to be made.

Although a few standard methods do exist, there is a great deal of diversity in how archaeologists quantify animal remains. In a study of the various methods used to quantify animal remains and the names of those methods R. Lee Lyman (1994) found more than 100 terms.

The two most common ways of quantifying animal remains are **NISP**, which is the acronym for the number of identified specimens; and **MNI**, the acronym for the **minimum number of individuals**. Determining the NISP is simply a matter of counting the number of bone pieces, whether complete or fractured. A single, non-fractured rib, for example, would be counted as one piece. If that same rib had been broken into 15 pieces, the count would be 15.

MNI is a method of quantification that indicates how many individuals are represented by all of the remains identified as belonging to one species. The MNI is usually determined by counting the number of bones for which there is only one per individual, such as a pelvis or otherwise distinctive bone (e.g., the front right forelimb of an animal is different than the front left and back forelimbs). For archaeologists, MNI is usually considered the more meaningful statistic. It prevents overrepresentation of animals with more bones or bones that are subject to breakage.

Botanical Remains

Many types of botanical remains are recovered from archaeological sites, including pollen, phytoliths, seeds, nuts, bark, and wood. Laboratory analysis usually focuses on taxonomic identification using a comparative collection. Quantification is usually limited to a listing of species or other taxonomic categories present, although some researchers calculate the proportion that individual taxonomic categories such as genus and species represent for each of the types of remains. Proportions are calculated by weight, volume, or number of specimens.

Sediment Analysis

A variety of compositional, **pedological**, and chemical analyses are done on sediments from archaeological sites. The most common, however, determine texture, color, and **pH**.

Texture is a description of the particle sizes that make up the sample, typically described as a clay, silt, or sand (Table 6.3). A combination of sediment sizes is often described as a loam. Determining the texture involves sifting samples of sediments through a series of nested sieves with various mesh sizes, and then classifying the sediments based on the proportion of different-sized particles. As outlined in Chapter 8, soil texture is important for reconstructing palaeoenvironments, especially for determining whether the

TABLE 6.3: Particle Size Classification

Category	Individual Particle size
Clay	less than 0.002 mm (0.000078 in); difficult to see without magnification
Silt	0.002–0.05 mm (0.000078–0.00195 in); difficult to see without magnification
Sand	0.05 –2.0 mm (0.00195–0.078 in); can see particles without magnification
Gravel or granule	2.0–7.0 mm (0.078–0.273 in)
Pebble	7.0–64 mm (0.273–2.96 in)
Cobble	64–256 mm (2.96–9.98 in)
Boulder	Over 256 mm (9.98 in)

processes of deposition were high energy, like wind storms or fast-flowing rivers, or low energy, like gentle breezes and meandering rivers.

Descriptions of color are usually based on comparisons with standard color charts widely used by archaeologists and other earth scientists throughout the world.

The **Munsell system**, which measures three different dimensions of color known as hue, value, and chroma, is the most common. Color is represented by a series of numbers and letters, such as 10YR 5/4. Such a standard system of color identification is useful for communicating information on color in textual form (with Munsell charts, one can see precisely what 10YR 5/4 looks like).

Soil color reflects the major soil-forming processes and can indicate concentrations of certain elements or compounds. White generally indicates calcium carbonate, and red indicates oxidation. Distinctions in color are also useful for identifying natural and cultural stratigraphic layers within a site, with even minor changes often indicating a distinct process in the formation of archaeological deposits.

Measurements of pH involve determining the acidity of sediments. Since the preservation of organic remains is affected by pH, such measurements are routine. Because pH levels within a site can be altered by human activities, such as the introduction of gardens and middens, pH tests are also sometimes done to help identify areas of human habitation.

A scale from 0 to 14 is used to categorize pH: a level less than 7 is acid; 7 is neutral; and a level higher the 7 is alkaline or basic. All techniques to determine pH involve mixing the sediment with distilled water, which is pH neutral. The simplest and most inaccurate method involves dipping litmus paper into a solution of the sediment mixture, watching the paper change color, and then matching the color against a standard chart. A better method involves mixing a liquid pH indicator with the sediment mixture and comparing the resulting solution color against a standard chart. The most precise tool for measuring pH is an electronic pH meter, which is a glass electrode that is immersed in the sediment mixture and produces a digital value.

Analysis of Human Remains

Although soft tissue is sometimes preserved, the vast majority of human remains recovered from archaeological sites are bone and teeth. When such remains are excavated, they are commonly in need of preservation and are often in fragmentary condition. Once the remains are stabilized, attempts will be made to identify the particular bones and teeth represented, as well as to infer how old the person was when he or she died and whether the person was male or female. Thus, archaeologists generally are very familiar with human osteology, including not only the characteristics of each bone and tooth of the human skeleton, but also how those characteristics can be used to distinguish the age and sex of the individuals.

Determining Age at Death

It is difficult to determine precisely how old an individual was when he or she died based solely on skeletal remains. Instead, individuals are usually classified into general age categories. While there is no standard, the basic categories are fetal (before birth), infant (0–3 years), child (3–12), adolescent (12–17), young adult (18–30), middle adult (30–50), and old adult (over 50).

Determining age at death includes examining both bones and dentition. Bone analysis focuses on closure of individual bones and bone parts of both the cranial and post-cranial skeleton. Dental analysis examines both tooth eruption and tooth wear.

The analysis of cranial bones looks at those of the top part of the skull, known as the cranial vault. The main bones of the cranial vault are separate at birth but gradually fuse together during a person's lifetime. The places where the bones come together are known as cranial sutures. By looking at the degree of closure and ultimate fusion at the sutures, archaeologists are able to estimate age. Typically, the bones of adolescents and young adults are interlocked like a jigsaw puzzle, but they can still be pulled slightly apart. For people in the middle adult range, the bones are usually fused, and in old adults the sutures themselves are often difficult to distinguish.

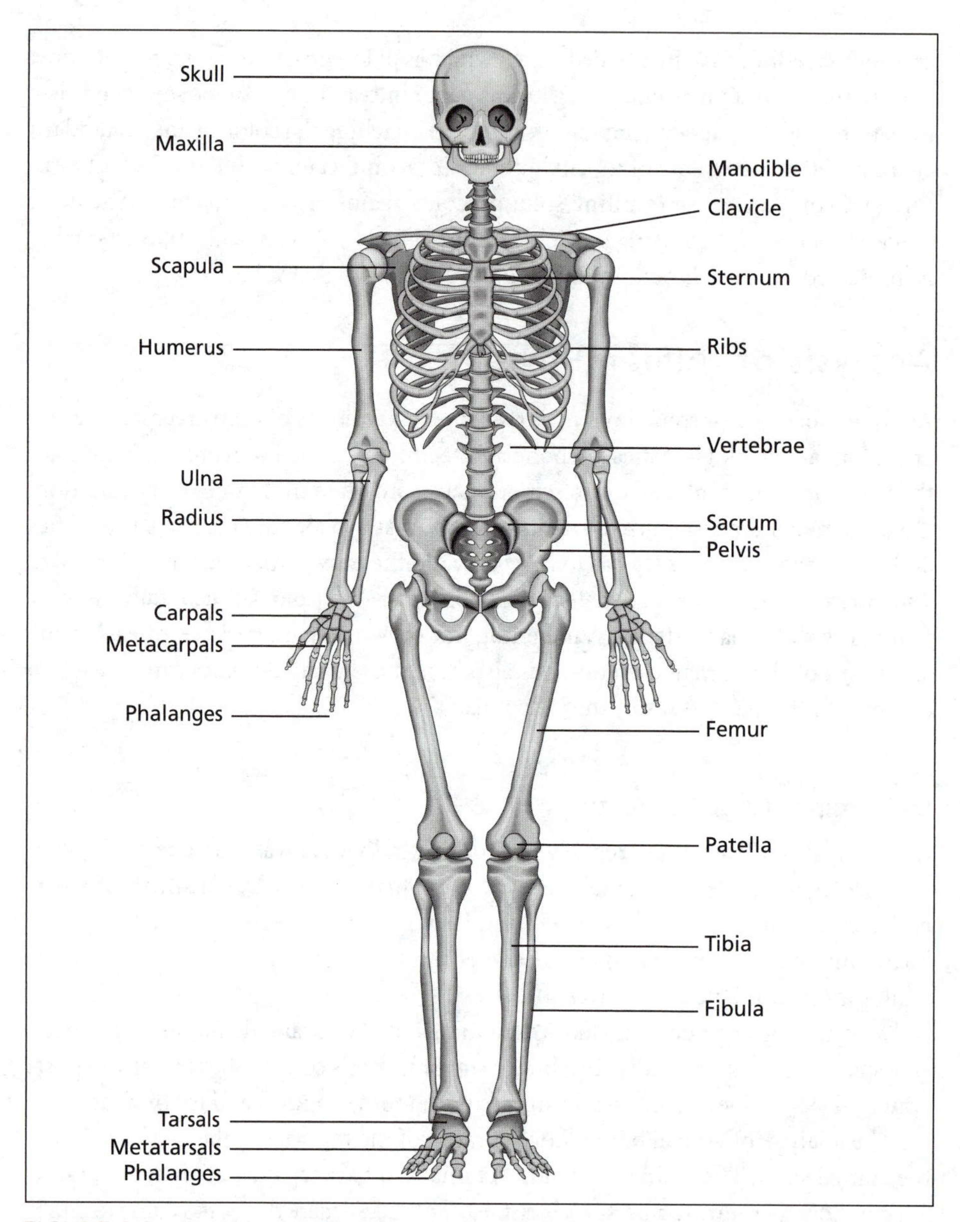

FIGURE 6.6: HUMAN SKELETON. Archaeologists must know how to identify the bones and teeth of the skeleton in order to distinguish them from other animals in fragmentary form. Most have learned how to use the characteristics of a skeleton to determine how old the individual was when they died and whether they were male or female. Human skeletons are often used in the analysis of diet, disease, status, and ideology.

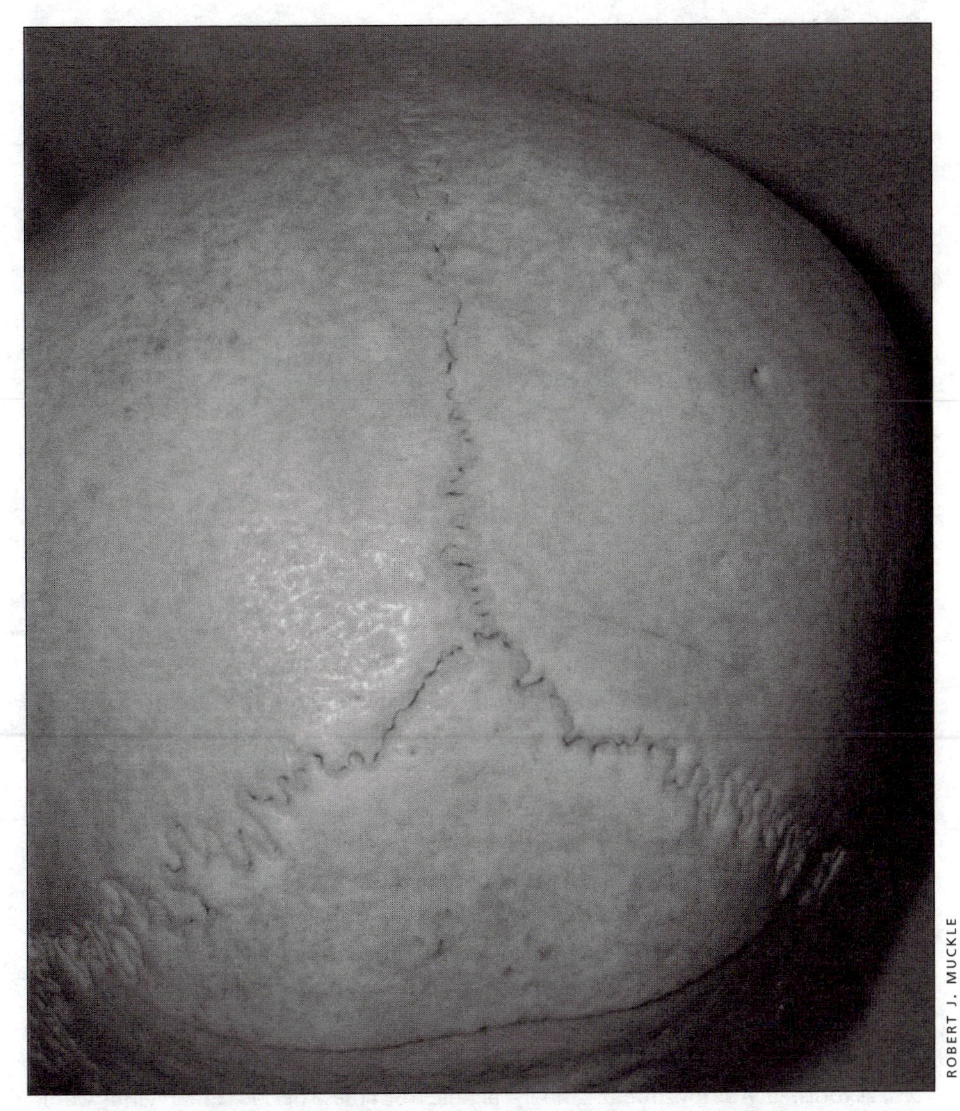
ROBERT J. MUCKLE

FIGURE 6.7: CRANIAL SUTURES. One way of estimating how old an individual was when he or she died is to look at the degree of closure of the cranial sutures.

The analysis of the post-cranial skeleton involves examining the degree of fusion of various bones, often known as epiphyseal union. Many post-cranial bones, especially those of the arms, hands, legs, and feet, grow in sections, such as the shaft growing independently from the epiphyses of the long bones. The cartilage separating the pieces turns to bone and fusion is complete by an approximate age. Most unions are completed in adolescence, but some, such as the clavicle (commonly known as the collarbone) and parts of the pelvis, don't fuse until young adulthood.

The most reliable common method using teeth to determine age of death is identifying deciduous and permanent teeth (alternatively known as baby teeth and adult teeth). The common age ranges at which deciduous teeth erupt and fall out is well established. All the incisors, for example, generally erupt between 6 and 16 months and fall out between 6 and 8 years. Canines and the first molars usually erupt between 16 and 24 months and fall out between 9 and 12 years; and the second molars usually erupt between 23 and 33 months and fall out between 10 and 12 years.

The age of eruption of adult teeth is also well known. Incisors and the first molars generally erupt between the ages of 6 and 9; canines between 8 and 11; premolars between 9 and 12; the second molars between 11 and 13; and the third premolars, commonly known as the wisdom teeth, between 18 and 22. Although some people in the contemporary world never have a third molar eruption and many others find it necessary to have their third molars removed because there is not enough room in their mouth, the third molars remain a part of the human dental formula, and they are commonly found in skeletal remains from archaeological sites.

Since the timing of eruption for all teeth, and shedding in the case of deciduous teeth, is so well known, archaeologists can make inferences about the age of individuals simply based on which teeth are present.

Archaeologists sometimes also use the degree of wear to determine age, but this typically allows only very general inferences and often requires some knowledge of the person's culture. Examining molars is particularly useful, as there is a characteristic pattern of wear on the cusps. Examining the wear on the cusps can give clues to an approximate age. A person whose 6-year molars are worn flat, whose 12-year molars show some wear but with visible cusps, and whose third molars (wisdom teeth) still exhibits prominent cusps probably died as an early adult.

Since it has been the custom of many people in past societies to effectively use their teeth as tools, such as for softening fibers, people from these periods and regions would tend to show considerably more wear than those who did not.

Determining Sex

There is no single characteristic that indicates with certainty whether an individual was male or female. The pelvis is considered the best indicator, followed by characteristics of the skull and overall robusticity (ruggedness) of the entire skeleton. Most archaeologists would probably agree that with a skull alone, and knowledge of the

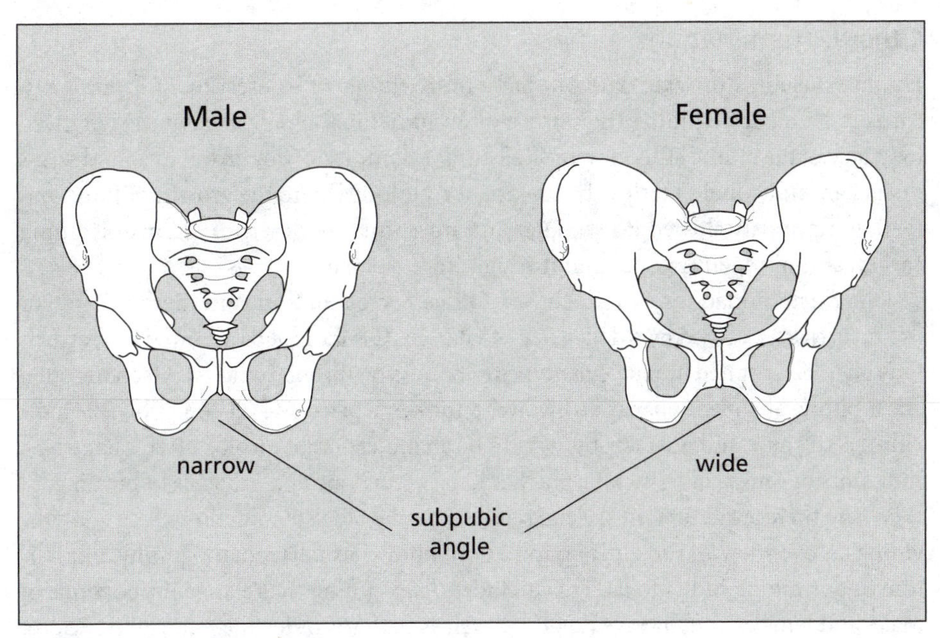

FIGURE 6.8: MALE AND FEMALE HUMAN PELVIS. Compared to a male, the pelvis of a female is usually wider overall and has a wider subpubic angle.

region from which it came, the sex should be determined accurately about 90 per cent of the time. With the pelvis alone, the sex should be determined accurately about 95 per cent of the time, and with both the skull and pelvis, the sex should be determined accurately 99 per cent of the time.

Of course, what makes the pelvis so good for identifying sex is that the female pelvis typically has many features to facilitate carrying and delivering babies. Two of the most prominent characteristics are that it is wider and more basin-shaped. The subpubic angle is also a key indicator. This is the area of the birth passage and is necessarily wider in females. The angle in females in typically U-shaped, while the angle in males is usually V-shaped.

Compared to many other animals, the degree of sexual dimorphism among humans is generally slight, but it does exist, and it varies on a regional and ethnic basis, at least in prehistory. Differences in skeletal characteristics between males and females among prehistoric indigenous populations of North America are quite distinct, for example, with the males typically being considerably more robust or rugged than females. Differences in robusticity in Asian populations are very slight by comparison, and differences in those of European ancestry are midway.

Other Determinations

Human skeletons provide data on many more things of interest to archaeologists. These include determining the stature of an individual by measuring the length of long bones; the ethnic affiliation by looking at a complex of characteristics; and stress during an individual's lifetime by looking for periods where the growth of bone and teeth temporarily slowed down. Diet and nutrition are determined by examining carbon and nitrogen isotopes and through trace element analysis (see Chapter 8).

Other determinations include those of disease, **trepanation**, and cannibalism. For example, rickets, caused by a deficiency of vitamin A, is indicated by bowed legs; arthritis is often determined by particular types of bone growth; and bacterial infections often create pitting of bone. Trepanation involves removing a piece of skull bone while the individual is still alive and is widely thought to be an indication of ideology (see Chapter 9). Indicators of cannibalism include butchery marks on bone and evidence of burning.

Where there are abundant skeletal remains, archaeologists sometimes focus on providing an overview of the entire population, known as palaeodemography, in addition to examining individuals. This includes determining the relative proportions of males and females, and the age ranges, as well as patterns of fertility, mortality, health, and disease.

KEY RESOURCES AND SUGGESTED READING

A good lab manual for archaeology is *The Archaeologist's Laboratory: The Analysis of Archaeological Data* by Banning (2000). The *Handbook of Archaeological Methods, v.2*, edited by Maschner and Chippendale (2005) includes chapters on pottery, lithics, palaeoethnobotany, and zooarchaeology. There are several contributions on residue analysis and bioarchaeology in the *Handbook of Archaeological Sciences*, edited by Brothwell and Pollard (2001). *Archaeobiology* is the title of a book by Sobolik (2003). *Human Osteology, 2e* by White and Folkens (2000) provides a good comprehensive overview of human osteology. Larsen (1997) discusses the wide range of behaviors that can be deduced from human remains in *Bioarchaeology: Interpreting Human Behaviour from the Human Skeleton.* Lithic analysis is covered well by Odell (2004) in *Lithic Analysis* and pottery by Rice (1987) in *Pottery Analysis: A Sourcebook.* The study of sediments from archaeological sites is covered well in *Geoarchaeology: The Earth Science Approach to Archaeological Interpretation* by Rapp and Hill (1998) and in *Archaeological Sediments: A Survey of Analytical Methods* by Shackley (1975).

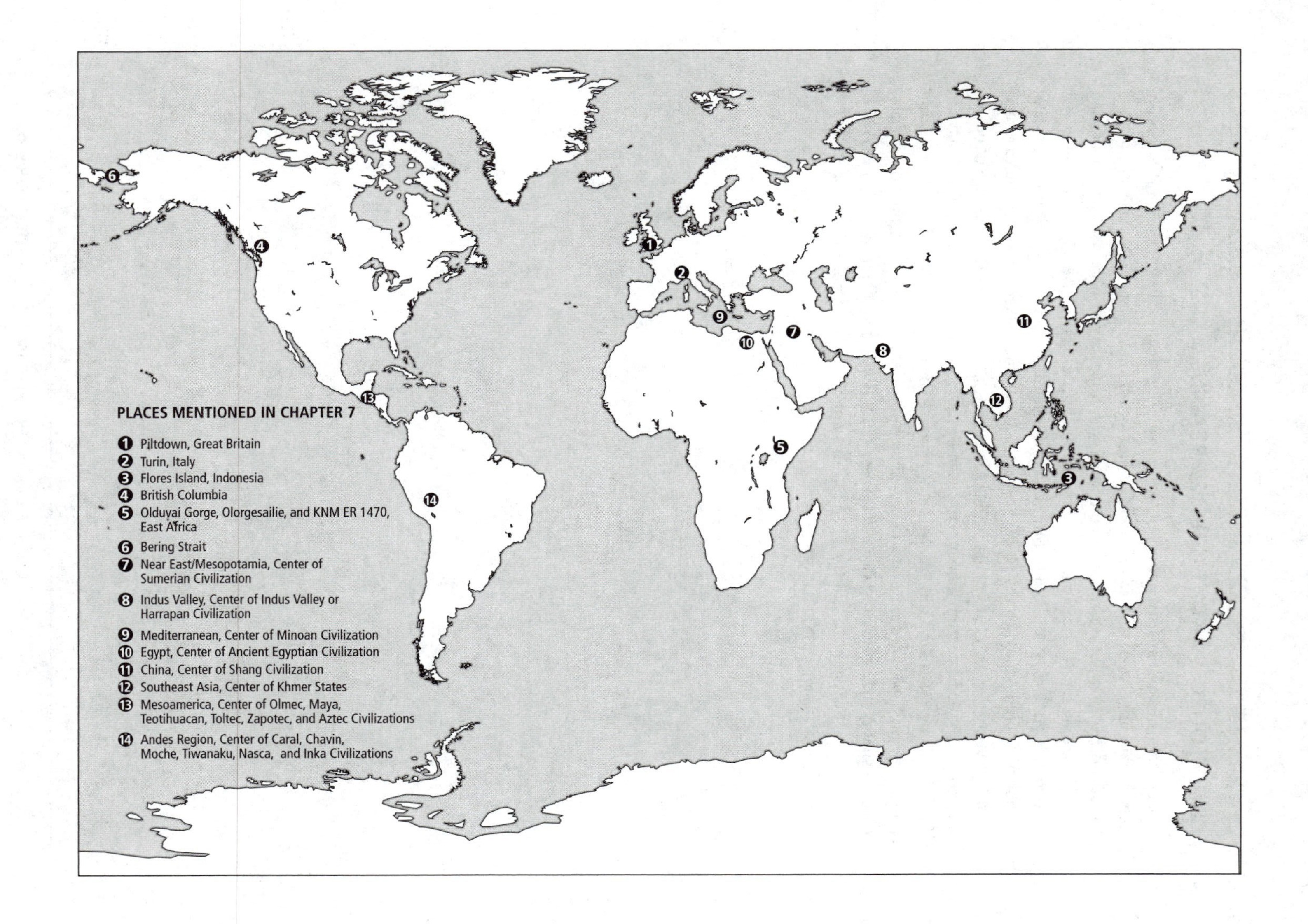
PLACES MENTIONED IN CHAPTER 7
1 Piltdown, Great Britain
2 Turin, Italy
3 Flores Island, Indonesia
4 British Columbia
5 Olduvai Gorge, Olorgesailie, and KNM ER 1470, East Africa
6 Bering Strait
7 Near East/Mesopotamia, Center of Sumerian Civilization
8 Indus Valley, Center of Indus Valley or Harrapan Civilization
9 Mediterranean, Center of Minoan Civilization
10 Egypt, Center of Ancient Egyptian Civilization
11 China, Center of Shang Civilization
12 Southeast Asia, Center of Khmer States
13 Mesoamerica, Center of Olmec, Maya, Teotihuacan, Toltec, Zapotec, and Aztec Civilizations
14 Andes Region, Center of Caral, Chavin, Moche, Tiwanaku, Nasca, and Inka Civilizations
1
2
3
4
5
6
7
8
9
10
11
12
13
14

CHAPTER 7

Reconstructing Culture History

Introduction

Archaeologists deal with time in many ways. This chapter begins with an overview of the practical methods of determining how old things are. It follows with a brief description of how archaeologists conceptually organize time and ends with an outline of world prehistory and early civilizations.

Determining Antiquity

Relative dating and **absolute dating** are the two broad categories of dating methods used in archaeology. Relative dating methods have the advantage of being generally cost-free or inexpensive (other than the archaeologist's time), and are applicable to a wide variety of materials. The main disadvantage is that they do not provide precise dates. Conversely, the main advantage of absolute dating methods is that they provide specific dates, but they are often expensive and can only analyze specific kinds of material.

Relative Dating

There are four principal subcategories of relative dating techniques: **chronological sequencing, dating by association, calibrated relative**, and ***terminus quem*** (Table 7.1).

Chronological Sequencing

Chronological sequencing provides assessments of antiquity in relation to other artifacts and sites, and is thus comparative. Chronological sequencing, for example, enables archaeologists to determine that site A is older than site B, or one arrowhead is older than another, but without specific dates attached.

One of the common methods of chronological sequencing is to apply of the law of superposition, sometimes known as **stratigraphic dating**. This method is based on the

TABLE 7.1: Relative Dating Techniques

Category	Techniques
Chronological sequencing	Law of superposition/stratigraphic dating Stylistic seriation Frequency seriation Fluorine, uranium, nitrogen dating
Dating by association	Association with animals of known age Association with artifacts of known age Association with geological features of known age
Calibrated relative	Obsidian hydration
Terminus quem	*Terminus post quem* *Terminus ante quem*

fact that layers of sediments are normally laid on top of each other through time. Accordingly, as archaeologists excavate, they are encountering successively older deposits. In other words, the deeper the deposit, the older it is. Of course, archaeologists recognize that deposits can be mixed after initial deposition and sediments are not always deposited in uniform or horizontal layers, so they are cautious when drawing inferences from this technique alone.

Seriation, or placing objects in chronological order, is another chronological sequencing method with a long history in archaeology. There are two commonly used types: **stylistic seriation** and **frequency seriation**. Stylistic seriation is based on the knowledge that artifact styles change through time, and by knowing what the end or starting styles are, archaeologists can put artifacts in a chronological order. If an archaeologist started with a pickup truck manufactured in 2006 and was given 50 other pickup trucks manufactured over the previous century by the same manufacturer, that archaeologist should be able to put them in chronological order by comparing their styles and looking for the evolution of characteristics. Similarly, if an archaeologist found 50 clay pots of roughly the same size and shape in a site, he or she should be able to put them in a chronological sequence based on stylistic attributes.

Frequency seriation is based on the premise that artifacts of similar function typically go through an initial period of acceptance, then begin to flourish as they become widely used and manufactured (displacing competing styles in the process), and eventually decline as they themselves are replaced by another style or form. A twentieth-century example is the use of music-recording technology. In the early twentieth century, vinyl was dominant. In the 1960s and 1970s, various forms of tape recordings (e.g., reel-to-reel, cassette, eight-track) rose and flourished, and computer disks emerged as the material of choice for recording music in later years. An archaeologist of the future who discovers a deposit with 10 per cent of the music recorded on vinyl, 40 per cent on tape, and 50 per cent on computer disk would be able to determine that it is more recent than a deposit with 90 per cent of the recordings on vinyl and 10 per cent on tape. By comparing the relative proportions of various styles of lithic projectile points or clay pots, archaeologists can place different sites in a region in a relative chronology in the same manner.

In addition to **stratigraphic dating** and **seriation**, there is third chronological sequencing technique, which is not commonly used any more but is of historical interest: **fluorine, uranium, nitrogen dating**. It is based on the premise that after the death of an animal, the amount of nitrogen in the bones continually decreases over time through the natural processes of decay. Conversely, the amounts of fluorine and uranium increase over time as they enter the bones from the surrounding matrix, especially through groundwater percolation. This technique is used to assess the relative ages of various bones in a site, reasoning that the bones that have been in the deposit longer will have more fluorine and uranium and less nitrogen than bones deposited more recently.

The fluorine, uranium, nitrogen technique was most famously applied to the **Piltdown Man**, discovered in the early twentieth century in Piltdown, England. The Piltdown Man had characteristics of a human skull but with a very ape-like lower jaw. The skull was widely touted by experts of the day as a "missing link" between modern humans and our apelike ancestors. After decades of controversy over the authenticity of the find, both the lower jaw and the rest of the skull were subjected to fluorine, uranium, nitrogen dating in the mid-twentieth century, reasoning that if the parts belonged to the same individual they would have the same proportions of the three chemical elements. They didn't, and it eventually became clear that the Piltdown Man was a hoax and that the lower jaw was that of a recently deceased orangutan, while the rest of the skull was from a prehistoric human.

Dating by Association

Many artifacts and sites are dated by their association with objects of known age, such as bones of animals, particular types of artifacts, and geological features. This technique is also known as cross-dating.

It is not unusual to find artifacts and bones of an animal that is now extinct in the same stratigraphic layers. Sometimes, palaeontologists will have already used absolute dating techniques to establish the time range for the extinct animal, and this then becomes the basis for dating the cultural deposits as well. If, for example, artifacts are found in the same stratigraphic layer as the bones of an extinct form of elephant presumed to have only existed between 600,000 and 200,000 years ago, then the artifacts are presumed to fall within that range as well.

Similarly, archaeologists have used absolute dating techniques to firmly establish the age range for some types of artifacts. The presence of those artifacts in a site, or in a layer within that site, is used to date by association all other material remains.

In many cases, earth scientists assign dates to landforms, including specific dates or ranges of dates to features created during particular ice ages, floods, or other geological events. By their association with these geologic features, cultural remains found by archaeologists are assigned the same dates. For example, a shell midden along a palaeo-coastline dated by geologists to 8,000 years ago may be assumed to be the same age.

Calibrated Relative Dating

Calibrated relative dating essentially involves techniques that combine those of relative and absolute dating. The most widely applied of these is **obsidian hydration**, which is based on the knowledge that a freshly fractured face of obsidian will adsorb water from the surrounding environment into the core of the stone, creating an observable hydration layer. Because the amount and rate of water adsorption is dependent on the local environment, there is no widely recognized standard against which the thickness of the hydration layer can be measured, and thus obsidian hydration is considered a relative technique. However, at many sites, some of the obsidian pieces with thick hydration layers and some of the pieces with thin layers have been dated by absolute techniques. Researchers are then able to make assumptions about the rate at which hydration layers thicken and can use this to assign dates to other pieces of obsidian.

Terminus Quem Dating

Two types of *terminus quem* dating are commonly used in historic archaeology. ***Terminus post quem***, often abbreviated as TPQ, literally means the date after which material remains must have been deposited. Assuming there was no post-depositional disturbance, a Roman coin dating to AD 100 could not possibly enter a deposit prior to that time, so if a coin of that date is found, this technique indicates that the deposit dates to AD 100 or later.

Terminus ante quem, often abbreviated as TAQ, is applied in two different ways. In one sense, when a specific date is assigned to an artifact found in a particular layer in an archaeological site, archaeologists can use that date in combination with the law of superposition to infer that all materials beneath that layer must be older. In the case of the Roman coin, for example, all deposits below the level in which the coin is found must be older than AD 100. TAQ is also applied to the absence of widely used artifacts to infer that a deposit must have been created before that product became available. For example, an archaeologist working at a site in which all the nails were made by hand may reasonably infer that the buildings were constructed before machine-made nails became common.

Absolute Dating Techniques

Also known as chronometric dating, there are several absolute dating techniques widely used in archaeology. Three of the most important are **dendrochronology**, **radiocarbon dating**, and **argon dating**.

TABLE 7.2: Absolute Dating Techniques

Absolute Dating Techniques
Dendrochronology
Radiocarbon dating
Potassium/argon dating
Argon/argon dating
Thermoluminescence
Archaeomagnetism
Electron spin resonance
Uranium dating
Fission track dating

Dendrochronology

Also known as tree-ring dating, dendrochronology is widely acknowledged to be the most accurate technique for dating prehistoric deposits. However, because wood with identifiable tree rings does not normally preserve well, this technique is also one of the most rarely used. The technique is based on the fact that annual growth rings in trees vary in thickness each year, depending on local environmental conditions. In some regions, such as parts of the American Southwest and northern Europe, tree ring sequences have been established for the past several thousand years. Starting with trees of modern age where the years corresponding with each growth ring are known, the sequences are created by working backwards by matching corresponding growth rings with successively earlier fragments recovered from archaeological or natural sites. Researchers working in areas where a master chronology of tree rings exists simply have to take a wood sample from a site and match it to determine when the tree from which the wood fragment derived lived.

Dendrochronology is used very effectively in the American Southwest, where preservation of organic remains is excellent due to the dry climate and people used wooden beams in house construction. Archaeologists take samples of beams from prehistoric houses to determine when the tree lived. Of course, archaeologists also must consider that ancient peoples may have recycled beams from older houses.

Radiocarbon Dating

Also known as **Carbon 14** or **C 14 dating**, radiocarbon dating is undoubtedly the most commonly applied absolute dating technique in prehistoric archaeology. It is based on the principle that carbon 14 (a radioactive isotope of carbon) decays at a known rate. All living things contain the same relative proportions of carbon 14, and at the instant of death, carbon 14 begins to decay. The rate of decay of radioactive materials such as carbon 14 is often measured in terms of half-lives, which is how long it takes half of the material to decay. For carbon 14, the half-life is 5,730 years, which means that half of the carbon 14 is gone in that time, half of the remaining half goes in the next 5,730 years, half of that half goes in the next 5,730 years, and so on.

Because anything that was alive can be dated by radiocarbon dating, it is widely used. Since wood charcoal is common in archaeological sites, it is frequently used to date deposits. However, anything organic can be used, including human remains, shells, animal bones, and botanical remains, including materials made of plant fiber.

Radiocarbon dating is applicable for the time period from about 300 to 50,000 years ago. Due to the usual margin of error in calculating radiocarbon dates, which is normally in the order of 200 to 500 years, materials which are presumed to have died within the last few centuries are not usually subjected to this technique. Radiocarbon dates are always expressed with a plus-or-minus figure, such as 15,700 ± 150. At the other end of the scale, current techniques simply are not capable of measuring the very low quantities of carbon 14 remaining in an organism 50,000 years after its death.

For the first few decades of radiocarbon dating in archaeology, beginning in 1950, it was widely assumed that the relative amounts of carbon 14 in organisms had always been exactly the same. We now know that there have been some minor fluctuations in those amounts over time, and archaeologists have sought to correct errors through calibration with tree-ring dates where possible.

Dates produced by radiocarbon dating are always given as "years before present" (meaning 1950), usually expressed as **bp** or **BP**. Using a specific year as a baseline from which all dates are taken is useful to archaeologists because they do not have to know when the lab work was done in order to calculate the age of the object.

Tens of thousands of dates have been obtained by radiocarbon dating throughout the world. The most famous application of this technique, however, involved dating the Shroud of Turin, a cloth made of plant fibers embedded with the imprint of a man purported to be Jesus Christ, alleged to be the shroud in which he was buried. The authenticity of the shroud has always been in doubt since it was first mentioned in historical records of the Middle Ages. In 1988, several independent radiocarbon dating laboratories throughout the world became involved in tests to determine its age. Samples of various materials from a variety of known ages were submitted to the laboratories without those of the real shroud being identified, so as to not bias the results with expectations. The three laboratories that tested the actual shroud all dated the age of the materials from which it was made to the fourteenth century. Controversy about the authenticity of the shroud still exists, with those that dispute the fourteenth-century date usually focusing on problems of radiocarbon dating or science in general.

Argon Dating

Argon dating involves measuring the amount of argon in volcanic sediments. The most widely known technique is **potassium/argon dating**, commonly known through the abbreviations for the two elements, K/Ar. The basic principle is that radioactive potassium turns into argon gas at a known rate. When volcanic sediments are initially formed, they do not have stable argon gas. Over time, the potassium turns into argon gas. The half-life of radioactive potassium is 1.3 billion years. Accordingly, by measuring how much potassium and argon are in volcanic sediments, the date at which sediments formed can be calculated.

Another argon dating technique is known as argon/argon, or Ar/Ar dating, which is based on the known rate of decay of radioactive argon into stable argon gas.

The primary limitations of argon dating are that it can only be used for dating volcanic sediments, and because the rate of decay is so slow, it is not considered viable for dating materials less than 200,000 years old. Like radiocarbon dating, a margin of error is always given with the dates.

Most applications of argon dating are to determine the ages of early hominid sites, especially in East Africa, where the stratigraphy of deposits often includes multiple layers of volcanic sediments. Therefore, a discovery of human biological or cultural remains can often be dated by subjecting samples from a volcanic sediment above and a sample from a volcanic sediment below to argon dating.

Other Techniques

Many other absolute dating techniques are commonly used in archaeology but are not generally considered to be as accurate or are not as widely applicable. These include **thermoluminescence**, which measures the amount of energy trapped in material since it was heated to very high temperatures. The date of the original firing can be calculated by measuring the amount of energy released in the form of light when reheated. This technique is sometimes used for dating lithics but is used most frequently for dating the manufacture of pottery.

Archaeomagnetism is a technique that correlates the alignment of magnetic soil particles with known locations of the North Magnetic Pole (which is slowly drifting across the Canadian Arctic) during the past few thousand years. In principle, small magnetic particles in sediments align themselves to the Magnetic North when heated to very high temperatures. By correlating the direction of those particles in specific archaeological features with the historic records of the location of Magnetic North, a fairly accurate dating should be possible. For obvious reasons, archaeomagnetism can only be used on features like pottery kilns or soils on which very hot fires have been built.

Other techniques with even more restricted applications include electron spin resonance, which is based on the premise that some types of electrons accumulate in material only after they are buried and is used primarily for dating teeth. Uranium dating is based on the radioactive decay of uranium and is used for dating limestone caves. Fission track dating is based on the measurable fission of uranium particles, and used for dating stone.

Conceptualizing Time

Archaeologists have many ways of conceptualizing time. This section illustrates how the vastness of the time can be symbolized by calendars and linear measurement, provides the ranges of dates for geological epochs, and outlines the major descriptive and analytical units in prehistory.

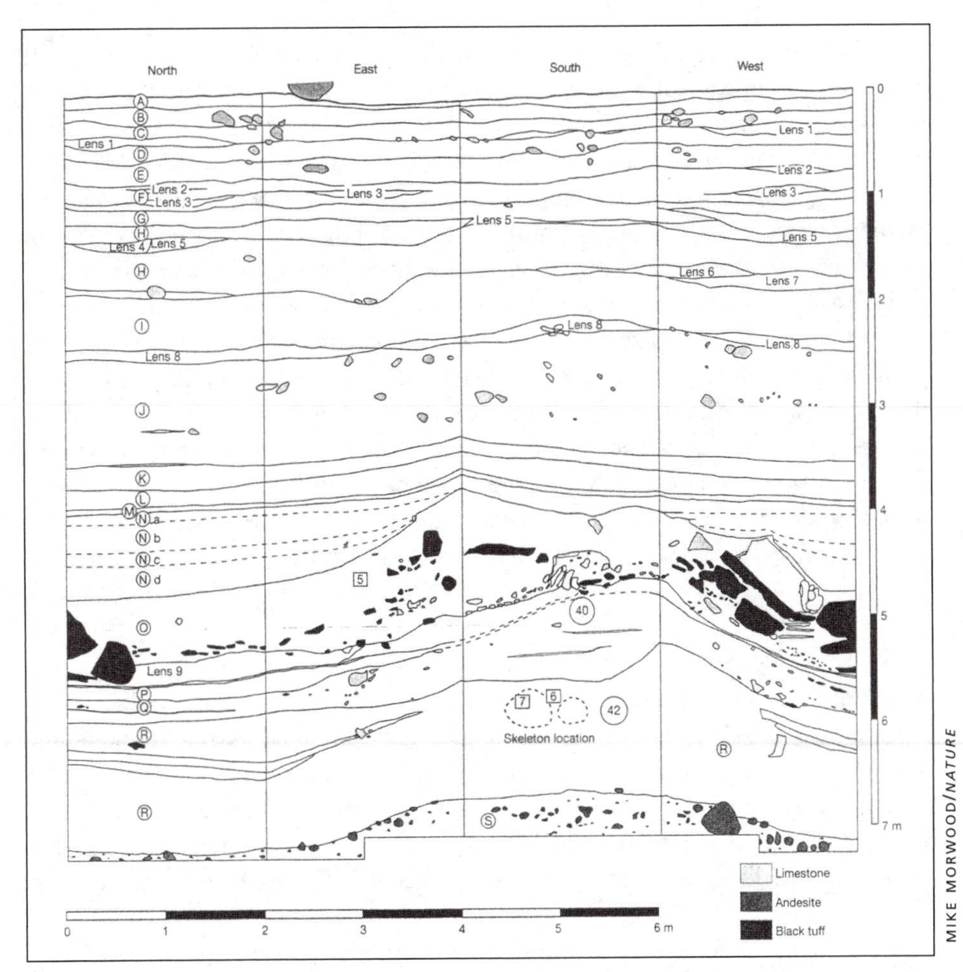

MIKE MORWOOD/NATURE

FIGURE 7.1: PROFILE OF FLORES ISLAND SITE. Skeletons and artifacts attributed to a potentially new species of humans dating to as recently as 13,000 years ago were found at this site, making it one of the most controversial discoveries of the early twenty-first century. The profile illustrates stratigraphy, which can be used for relative dating, and shows the location of samples taken for radiocarbon dating.

Conceptualizing Deep Time

Relative to the entire time span of the universe as we know it, the period during which humans have existed barely registers a blip. It is often difficult for people to contextualize humankind within the 15-billion-year history of the universe, so it is common to represent the vastness of time symbolically.

One common way of putting humans and their achievements in the perspective of deep time is to imagine the entire 15-billion-year history of the universe as one year, with one day equaling 42 million years, one hour equaling 1.75 million years, and one minute equaling 30,000 years. Assuming that the origins of the universe began on January 1, the first day of that imaginary year, the earliest primates arrived late in the evening on December 30; the first hominids arrived about 9:00 p.m. on December 31; the first members of our own species arrived sometime between 11:50 and 11:55 p.m.; and the earliest civilizations arose a mere ten seconds before the end of the year.

Another way to symbolize deep time is to use linear measurement. Science writer Colin Tudge (1996) suggests translating time into distance, with one millimeter (about the size of a grain of sand) equaling one year in an entire 15-billion-year history of the universe represented by 15,000 kilometers—the approximate distance from New York to Japan. Using this scale, walking a mere half-meter would take us back 500 years; 5 meters would take us to the earliest civilizations of ancient Mesopotamia and Egypt, and about another 150 meters would take us to the first members of our own species.

Geological Epochs

At a minimum, the time period of interest to archaeologists extends 2.5 million years into the past, based on unmistakable evidence of the manufacture and use of stone tools in Africa. In order to effectively manage archaeological information pertaining to this extensive period in world history, many archaeologists have borrowed frameworks of geological epochs from earth scientists (Table 7.3). Thus, it is not unusual to read about such things as Miocene ancestors, Pliocene hominids, Pleistocene sites, and

TABLE 7.3: Geological Epochs

Geological Epoch	Time Span
Holocene	10,000 years ago to the present
Pleistocene	1.7 million years ago to 10,000 years ago
Pliocene	5.0–1.7 million years ago
Miocene	24–5.0 million years ago
Oligocene	36–24 million years ago
Eocene	55–36 million years ago
Palaeocene	65–55 million years ago

Holocene events in archaeological literature. For perspective, dinosaurs became extinct about 65 million years ago, marking the end of the Mesozoic era and beginning of the Cenozoic era, which itself begins with the Palaeocene epoch.

Major Descriptive and Analytical Units in Prehistory

Archaeologists and the popular press frequently use a series of time frames to conceptualize prehistory. These typically span several distinct geographic regions and sometimes multiple continents, and range from a few thousand to hundreds of thousands of years in duration (Table 7.4). The temporal boundaries are based primarily on changes in technology, and since not all peoples and cultures make the same technological changes at the same time, the time frames should be viewed as being very general.

The Palaeolithic, Mesolithic, Neolithic, Bronze Age, and Iron Age are rarely applied outside of Africa, Asia, and Europe. The term *Palaeoindian* is used widely to describe the time period from about 12,000 to 8,000 years ago in North, Central, and South America. The term *Archaic* is used for many, but not all, areas of North and Central

TABLE 7.4: Major Time Frames in Archaeology

Time frame	Description
Lower palaeolithic	From about 2.5 million years ago to about 250,000 years ago; rarely applied outside of Africa, Asia, and Europe
Middle palaeolithic	From about 250,000 years ago to about 30,000 years ago; rarely applied outside of Africa, Asia, and Europe
Upper palaeolithic	From about 30,000 years ago to about 11,000 years ago; not commonly used outside of Europe
Mesolithic	From about 11,000 years ago to about 9,000 years ago; not commonly used outside of Europe
Neolithic	From about 9,000 years ago to about 5,000 years ago; not commonly used outside of Europe
Bronze Age	From about 5,000 years ago to about 3,000 years ago; not commonly used outside of Europe
Iron Age	From about 3,000 years ago to about 2,000 years ago; not commonly used outside of Europe
Palaeoindian	From about 12,000 years ago to 8,000 years ago; application is restricted to the Americas

America to distinguish the time period from abut 8,000 to 5,000 years ago. Because of so many regional differences, there is no comprehensive term to describe time periods throughout North and South America for the past 5,000 years.

A rough chronology for **Mesoamerica** for the past 4,500 years identifies the period from about 2,500 BC to AD 300 as Preclassic; the period from AD 300 to AD 900 as Classic; and the period from about AD 900 to AD 1519 as Postclassic.

Reconstructing culture history at a regional level requires more specific descriptive and analytical units, such as **tradition**, **horizon**, and **phase**. Some archaeologists use tradition to describe the temporal persistence of a particular technology in an area, such as a specific pottery tradition or projectile point traditions, with no restrictions (large or small) on geographic area. Most often, however, a tradition reflects a pattern of cultural continuity over a broad area (usually in the order of 40,000 square miles, or 100,000 square kilometers, or more), spanning at least a few thousand, and often several thousand years. Archaeologist Peter Peregrine (2001b: iv), who has compiled an outline of archaeological traditions around the world, defines the term as:

> a group of populations sharing similar subsistence practices, technology, and forms of socio-political organization, which are spatially contiguous over a relatively large area and which endure temporally for a relatively long period. Minimal area coverage for an archaeological tradition can be thought of as something like 100,000 square kilometers; while minimal temporal duration can be thought of as something like five centuries.

The *Outline of Archaeological Traditions*, compiled by Peregrine, attempts to summarize all the known archaeological traditions. It spans the entire prehistoric period, and covers traditions from all continents. There are currently about 300 archaeological traditions recognized.

Within a tradition, there may be moderate changes in the cultural activities of the people throughout a region, such as in the proportions of different types of foods they eat or the way they make their artifacts. Some archaeologists use the term *horizon* to distinguish these periods. A horizon encompasses the same broad region as the larger tradition, but exists for a shorter period, typically from several hundred to a few thousand years. Within each horizon, archaeologists often distinguish various phases, which are more restrictive in time and area than a horizon, and are based on relatively minor differences in culture. A tradition may be, but is not necessarily, composed of multiple horizons, which in turn may be composed of multiple phases.

The Plateau Pithouse Tradition is one example of using the analytical and descriptive units of tradition and horizon. The tradition, which comprised the last 4,000 years of prehistory in southern British Columbia is characterized, in part, by a semi-sedentary settlement pattern that included the use of **pithouses** for winter dwellings, a foraging subsistence strategy with a heavy reliance on salmon, storage technology including cache pits, anthropomorphic and zoomorphic carving in stone, and exchange with coastal groups. Within this tradition, three distinct horizons are recognized: the Shuswap Horizon, from about 4,000 to 2,400 years ago; the Plateau Horizon, from about 2,400 to 1,200 years ago; and the Kamloops Horizon, from about 1,200 to 200 years ago. Distinctions between the horizons are based on such things as differences in the size and shape of pithouses, size of cache pits, degree of exchange with coastal groups, projectile-point styles, frequency of stone sculptures, and burial practices.

Reconstructing culture history at an individual site includes identifying diagnostic markers of phase, horizon, and tradition by examining such things as artifact styles. More particularly, this includes comparing the recovered artifacts and ecofacts with the criteria of well-established phases in the region, and if they match, then the assemblage is described as a component of a particular phase, horizon, or tradition.

World Prehistory

The story of world prehistory is based on billions of pieces of evidence, including human skeletal remains, artifacts, features, and ecofacts. The sequence of events described in the following sections should be viewed as only a very basic outline of our understanding of the human past.

Human Biological Evolution

Before examining the details of world prehistory based on the cultural evidence, it is worthwhile to consider human biological evolution. The earliest widely accepted remains of hominidae are a relatively small scattering of skeletal fragments found in Africa, dated to about 4.4 million years ago and assigned to the genus *Ardipithecus.* Because of the limited number of skeletal elements, it is difficult to determine such things as height and brain size; but considering the general trends in human evolution, it is reasonable to speculate that they were similar in many respects to chimpanzees, but fully bipedal.

Beginning about 4.2 million years ago and continuing to about 1 million years ago, the genus *Australopithecus,* with several distinct species, emerged and survived in Africa. Some australopithecine species were fairly smooth-featured, while others were more rugged or robust. Some palaeoanthropologists believe the remains of the more rugged individuals are sufficient to distinguish a separate genus: *Paranthropus.* Collectively, the remains assigned to *Australopithecus* and *Paranthropus* suggest they ranged in

JUNE HUNTER

FIGURE 7.2: HOMINID SKULLS. From left to right: *Paranthropus*, *Australopithecus*, *Homo erectus*, early *Homo sapien*, modern *Homo sapien*.

height from about 3.5 to 5 feet, weighed about 50 to 100 pounds, and their brains were approximately the size of a chimpanzee's (about 400 cubic centimeters or 24 cubic inches). As with *Ardipithecus*, no remains assigned to the genus *Australopithecus* or *Paranthropus* have been found outside of Africa.

Conventional thinking indicates that one australopithecine population (i.e., one group of one species) evolved into a new genus and species about 2.5 million years ago. Groups of skeletal remains with significantly larger brains (about 700 cubic centimeters or 42 cubic inches) have been found in different areas throughout Africa and have been variously referred to as *Homo habilis* or *Homo rudolphensis*. This species appears to have existed until about 1.5 million years ago, and like the species before, has only been found in Africa.

Sometime around 1.8 million years ago, a new species or group of species evolved, probably from a population of *Homo habilis*. Compared to the earlier forms of *Homo*, these new forms, variously referred to as *Homo erectus* and *Homo ergaster*, had a brain size that overlaps the range of modern variability, with an average size of about 900 cubic centimeters (55 cubic inches), and some individuals were likely more than 6 feet tall.

The oldest finds of *Homo erectus* come from Africa, and although the termination date is difficult to determine, it appears likely that they continued to survive there until sometime between 200,000 and 100,000 years ago. The starting date of 1.8 million years applies to discoveries in Africa, but there is some suggestion that finds in Asia may be as old as 1.7 million years and that *Homo erectus* had colonized Southeast Asia by several hundred thousand years ago.

Many skeletal remains from Africa, Asia, and Europe dating between 800,000 and about 30,000 years ago have been found that indicate modern brain size (approximately 1,350 cubic centimeters or [82 cubic inches], but ranging between 1,000 and 2,000), but with the retention of more primitive characteristics like prominent ridges of bone above

ROBERT J. MUCKLE

FIGURE 7.3: KNM ER 1470. This site in East Africa is where of one of the earliest and most complete skulls classified as the genus *Homo* was discovered.

the eyes. These remains have been variously classified as *Homo antecessor, Homo heidelbergensis, Homo neanderthalensis,* and archaic *Homo sapiens.* The first remains that appear largely indistinguishable from modern humans appear about 150,000 years ago.

Early Tools in Africa

The archaeological record of world prehistory begins with stone tools in Africa. It is evident that by about 2.5 million years ago, hominids had learned how to make stone tools by chipping flakes off a cobble, producing tools from both the core of the cobble and the flakes that were taken off. The practice became widespread, and the tools have been recovered from many different areas. The earliest tools have been found in Ethiopia, and many researchers suggest the best candidate responsible for their manufacture is *Australopithecus garhi.* Another area where many early stone tools have been found is Olduvai Gorge in Tanzania, which gave rise to naming these kinds of tools the Oldowan Tool Industry. Despite the possibility that *Australopithecus* was responsible for some of the manufacture, these early tools are generally associated with

Homo habilis. The fact that they were deliberately manufactured is indisputable, but there is no consensus on what they were used for. Some have suggested they were used for butchering animals, but we do not know for certain the extent to which people were eating meat, if at all. It may have been that the stone tools were used to sharpen sticks to dig roots. Other than the fact that they made and used tools, we know very little of the culture of the earliest members of the genus *Homo.*

New Lands, New Tools

Homo erectus appears to have spread quickly through Africa shortly after their emergence 1.8 million years ago. Along with their larger brain, *Homo erectus* developed more sophisticated tool technologies known as the Acheulian Tool Industry, characterized by tear-drop shaped, cobble-sized artifacts with a sharp edge around their entire circumference. The tool is known as a hand ax. Despite the name, we don't really know the function. It was conceivably used to cut, scrape, and pierce, and some have proposed that it was indeed a multifunctional tool. Others have proposed that hand axes may have been thrown at large game animals. This throwing hypothesis would explain why there are hundreds of hand axes at single sites, such as at that of Olorgesailie in Kenya. One scenario suggests that the hand axes were thrown at game animals while they were crossing a river that went through the area hundreds of thousands of years ago. All but a few would end up in the river bottom, only to be discovered by archaeologists in the 1900s.

Early Hunting and Fire Use

By about 500,000 years ago, it is apparent the *Homo erectus* were hunting and controlling fire, although it isn't clear when precisely this began. Evidence of hunting primarily comes from butchered animal bones, and evidence of fire mainly from charcoal, ash, and burned bone in cultural context.

Deliberate Burials and Sophisticated Art

The exact date of origin for intentional human burials as a form of ritual activity and symbolic thought is subject to considerable debate among archaeologists. There is some suggestion that humans may have been deliberately discarding human remains down a shaft in a cave in Spain almost 300,000 years ago, but it is unclear if this is or should be taken as an indication of a specific form of ritual or ideology. Many archaeologists believe that by about 50,000 years ago, deliberate human burials were occurring among Neandertals, who were, according to some, simply a subgroup of *Homo sapiens*

FIGURE 7.4: OLORGESAILIE, Kenya. This is a *Homo erectus* site with an antiquity of several hundred thousand years. Thousands of hand axes and other stone tools are scattered around the site.

occupying portions of Europe and the Middle East from about 135,000 to 35,000 years ago. (Others prefer to classify them as a distinct species, *Homo neanderthalensis.*) However, due to the poor recording of many of the proposed Neandertal burial sites, some archaeologists remain unconvinced of the evidence for intentional burials, instead attributing the origins to modern *Homo sapiens* of the Upper Palaeolithic in Europe. Many archaeologists consider the deliberate burial indicative of a belief in an afterlife.

Although the dates of the earliest cave art are debated, it appears that by about 27,000 years ago, and perhaps as early as 33,000 years ago, sophisticated art was being painted on cave walls. The best-known prehistoric cave art comes from southern Europe in the time period from about 27,000 to 12,000 years ago and was painted by a particular group of modern *Homo sapiens* known as Cro-Magnon. The meaning of the art is uncertain, but because much of it is in remote parts of the caves and images are painted on top of each other, many believe they reflect an ideology-related painting by **shamans** to manipulate supernatural forces, presumably to ensure continued fertility of herd animals and successful hunts. Others beliefs include that it was ritualistic, the work of secret societies, simply art for art's sake, or a method of recording or storing information.

Colonizing Australia and the Americas

There is a general consensus that by about 50,000 years ago, humans had expanded their territory to include Australia. Because travel over significant distances of ocean was involved, one of the things archaeologists infer is the ability to make and navigate seaworthy watercraft.

There is no consensus on when humans first colonized the Americas. Conventional archaeological thought indicates that the first migrants came from Asia via the area around the present-day Bering Strait, following either an inland route or traveling along the coast during the latter stages of the last ice age, sometime between 15,000 and 12,000 years ago. Many postulate colonization occurred as long ago as 50,000 or more years ago, and others have suggested an Atlantic Ocean crossing, but these hypotheses lack convincing data to support them.

Ceramics and Pottery

The first evidence of ceramic technology comes from Europe, in the form of baked clay figurines dating to about 25,000 years ago. Pottery appears to have been first invented in eastern Asia about 12,000 years, but didn't become widespread until several thousand years ago, by which time it is found in **sedentary** communities of Asia, Africa, Europe, and the Americas.

Domesticating Plants and Animals, Settling Down, Rising Populations, and Increasing Social Complexity

There is no consensus on when people first began the process of domesticating plants and animals, but the first domesticated plants date to about 13,000 years ago. Relying on domestic plants and animals for subsistence in a significant way appears to have begun about 11,000 years ago.

Likely all correlated with the domestication of plants and animals, evidence of increasing sedentism, rising populations, and increasing social inequality appears in the archaeological record about 10,000 years ago. Domestication both requires and allows for increasing sedentism. By necessity, people depending on domestic plants and animals must be around more often to provide care, such as weeding around food-producing plants or moving animals to various grazing lands. By producing more food than it is possible to consume from wild versions, domestic plants and animals also allow people to stay in areas for longer periods without fear of depleting the resources. Rising populations result when food surpluses can support larger populations. There is considerable debate among archaeologists about the reasons for the origins of social inequality, but it is clear that it was correlated with food surpluses and increasing populations, perhaps as a way of maintaining social control.

Ancient Civilizations

There is no consensus definition of **civilization** among archaeologists, but most agree that a society has to have at least most of the following: monumental architecture, at least one city, a system of writing, an agricultural base, and a state-level political organization. Some of the best-known civilizations of the ancient world are those that were centered in the Near East, Egypt, the Indus Valley, China, the Mediterranean, Mesoamerica, and the Andes of Peru.

The Near East includes the region of the Tigris and Euphrates rivers, commonly known as Mesopotamia when referring to ancient times. The earliest civilization in both Mesopotamia and the entire world is generally considered to be that of the Sumerians, who developed the first known system of writing, called cuneiform, about 5,100 years ago. Other major civilizations of the Near East that followed in the succeeding millennia include the Akkadians, Babylonians, Assyrians, and the Persian, Roman, and Islamic empires.

Civilization in Egypt began about 5,000 years ago, with the system of writing known as hieroglyphics. As occurred in the Near East, the region was subsequently dominated first by the Roman empire and then by the Islamic empires.

ROBERT J. MUCKLE

FIGURE 7.5: EGYPTIAN PYRAMIDS. The building of pyramids symbolizes the early stages of Egyptian civilization, known as the Old Kingdom.

The first civilization of the Mediterranean region is that commonly referred to as the Minoans. Rising about 4,000 years ago and centering on the island of Crete, they had many ports in and around the Mediterranean Sea. Civilizations that followed in the region include those of the Hittites, Mycenaeans, and Etruscans, and Classical Greece and the Roman and Byzantine empires.

Civilizations have a long history in Asia. In the area of the Indus Valley in Pakistan, the first civilization emerged about 4,400 years ago. Sometimes known as the Harrapans, the people of this civilization built some of the most well-planned cities of the ancient world. In China, the Shang civilization emerged about 3,800 years ago and was subsequently followed by the Zhou and Han. In Southeast Asia, the Khmer states emerged about 1,000 years ago.

The first civilization of Mesoamerica was the Olmec, which began about 3,500 years ago. Later civilizations include those of the Maya, Teotihuacan, Toltec, Zapotec, and Aztec.

In the Andes region of South America, the first widely recognized civilization is the Chavin, which rose about 2,500 years ago and was later followed by the Moche, Tiwanaku, Nasca, and Inka. Recent research suggests that a civilization known as Caral may have arose as early as 4,600 years ago.

KEY RESOURCES AND SUGGESTED READING

The Handbook of Archaeological Sciences, edited by Brothwell and Pollard (2001) includes several contributions on dating in archaeology. The two multivolume series, *Outline of Archaeological Traditions* (Peregrine 2001b) and *Encyclopedia of Prehistory* (Peregrine and Ember 2001) are both comprehensive.

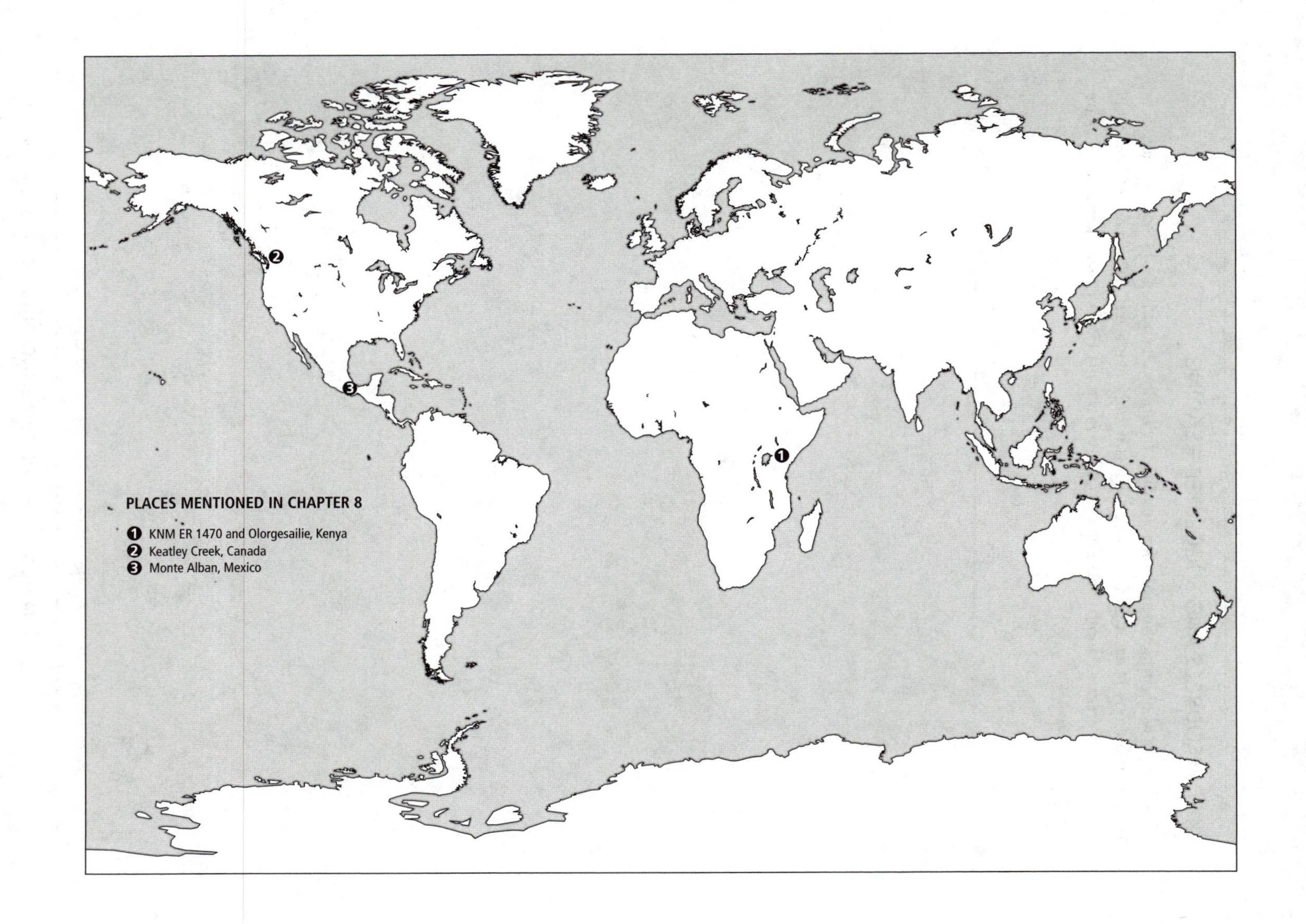
PLACES MENTIONED IN CHAPTER 8
1 KNM ER 1470 and Olorgesailie, Kenya
2 Keatley Creek, Canada
3 Monte Alban, Mexico
1
2
3

CHAPTER 8

Reconstructing Ecological Adaptations

Introduction

Studies of how people adapt to their environments have a long history in archaeology. Several important archaeological studies of an ecological nature were undertaken in the early twentieth century, and many archaeologists in the middle decades of the century were influenced by the development of **cultural ecology**—the study of the relationship between people and the natural environment—particularly through the writings of Julian Steward and Leslie White. Ecological research became a focus of processual archaeology in the 1960s and has continued to be a mainstay of archaeological projects in the early twenty-first century.

The study of the interplay between natural environments and humans in the past is widely known as ecological archaeology, with major areas of interest including reconstructing palaeoenvironments, settlement patterns, subsistence strategies, and diet. Archaeological investigations into each of these areas are outlined in this chapter.

Reconstructing Palaeoenvironments

Archaeologists reconstruct palaeoenvironments for three principal reasons: to determine what it was that people were adapting to; to discover where to look for archaeological sites; and to reconstruct site formation and disturbance processes (Table 8.1).

Determining What People Were Adapting to

Cultures are, at least in part, an adaptation to the natural environment. Knowing about past environments provides a base of information archaeologists can use to explain aspects of culture. For example, knowledge of the diversity and relative abundances of plants and animals in an area can be used to infer why people were there, what they might have been eating, and what kinds of organic materials might have been incorporated into culture in the form of tools, clothing, and shelter. Information on plants and animals can also be used

TABLE 8.1: Reasons for Reconstructing Palaeoenvironments

Reason	Examples
1. To know what people were adapting to	Availability of plants and animals, temperature, precipitation, raw materials, hazards, carrying capacity
2. To know where to look for sites	Palaeocoastlines, underwater sites, old river and stream courses
3. To reconstruct site formation and disturbance processes	Fluvial or aeolian deposition, erosion, high- or low-energy deposition

to get an idea of what hazards the people might have faced, such as sharing territory with dangerous animals and poisonous plants. Knowing about climate can provide insight into site location, housing, clothing, soils, and vegetation. Using the width of tree rings, archaeologists working in the American Southwest have been able to demonstrate that some areas underwent lengthy periods of drought before settlements were abandoned.

Archaeologists recognize that the earth is a dynamic system and environments may change substantially through time. Contrast Figure 7.3 (KNM ER 1470), on page 147, with Figure 8.1. Figure 7.3 is a photo of the site in East Africa where one of the most well known of our genera died about 1.9 million years ago. Today, the region is desolate. No people are currently living anywhere close to KNM ER 1470, and both plants and animals are sparse. It would be difficult to imagine that an early human could survive in such an environment. But palaeoenvironmental reconstruction in the area tells us that 1.9 million years ago, the environment was quite different—closer to that depicted in Figure 8.1, with plentiful streams and lakes, and fauna such as antelope, hippos, and other large mammals.

So it is as well with Figure 7.4 on page 149, which depicts the several-hundred-thousand-year-old *Homo erectus* site of Olorgesailie. Palaeoenvironmental reconstruction of this site indicates that when the hand axes and stone tools were left, the site was at the margin of a lake, and *Homo erectus* shared the environment with baboons, hippos, elephants, zebras, and giraffes. These kinds of palaeoenvironmental reconstructions provide important background to assist our understanding of past cultures.

Discovering Where to Look for Sites

When considering where to look for sites, archaeologists recognize that waterways and landforms change through time. Sea levels, for example, have been fluctuating in many

ROBERT J. MUCKLE

FIGURE 8.1: ELEPHANTS ON THE SAVANNAH. Reconstruction of many early human sites in the range of one million years and older indicates that although they are now barren, at the time of occupation they were similar to the environment depicted here.

parts of the world for thousands of years, and sites that were close to a beach while they were occupied may be many meters above or below current sea levels. Therefore, an archaeologist searching for coastal sites must rely on palaeoenvironmental evidence of ancient coastlines. Similarly, rivers and streams frequently change course, and since settlements are often alongside them, archaeologists searching for sites should be aware of where they once flowed.

Reconstructing Site Formation and Disturbance Processes

An archaeologist's interpretation of site formation and disturbance can be accepted with confidence only if he or she has some knowledge of the natural processes active during and after the creation of the site. Understanding the natural environment allows the archaeologist to judge the potential impact of myriad processes upon the archaeological record. For example, the knowledge that a river once flowed by a site may be used to support inferences of fluvial deposition or erosion of sediments.

Methods of Reconstructing Palaeoenvironments

Archaeologists reconstruct both biotic and abiotic environments using a variety of techniques and frequently relying on research from experts in the biological and earth sciences.

Reconstructing the biotic environment means identifying the species of plants and animals that were living in the area. Most plants and animals can only survive within a limited range of temperatures and levels of precipitation, so diversity also provides information on past climate.

Identifying plants is usually accomplished by examining preserved remains, including seeds, wood, nuts, bark, pollen, and phytoliths. Animals are usually identified by examining bones and teeth, but also hair, fur, antlers, claws, nails, and soft tissue. Reconstructions may also be based on animal **coprolites** and fossil impressions. Archaeologists alone are often able to identify species of plants and animals commonly found in cultural context, such as food remains. However, the identification of many other plants and animals usually requires specialists, such as palynologists (scientists who study pollen and spores) and palaeontologists.

Reconstructing the abiotic environment means determining the non-living aspects, such as topography, soil characteristics, and location of waterways, as well as the natural processes of deposition, erosion, and disturbance. The study of climate involves looking at temperature, precipitation, humidity, winds, and seasonal changes. Reconstructing the abiotic environment relies on methods developed in the earth sciences. These include geomorphic research to understand where and when features such as ancient coastlines may have existed; pedological research to distinguish soil formation processes; lithological research to determine where the sediments originated; hydrological research to determine the nature of waterways; chemical research to identify areas of significant organic activity; and sedimentological research to understand the processes that bring sediments into sites and may subsequently disturb them.

Geomorphological, pedological, lithological, and hydrological research is often performed by experts in those fields. As outlined in Chapter 6, however, chemical and sedimentological analysis is considered standard procedure in archaeology and most archaeological laboratory technicians are proficient at it.

Sedimentological analysis includes determining particle size distributions and is very useful for reconstructing the conditions under which natural sediments are deposited in archaeological sites. Layers of fine-grained sediments, such as clay and silt, are generally considered indicative of low-energy deposition, such as by a meandering river, a lake flooding, or slight winds. Coarse-grained sediments such as sand, gravel, and pebbles, on the other hand, indicate high-energy deposition, such as fast-flowing rivers, ocean tidal action, and strong winds. The reasoning is that high-energy processes pick up fine-grained sediments and hold them in suspension until the energy in the process decreases. A fast-flowing river, for example, picks up particles of clay and silt as it erodes the river bottom and banks, keeps them in suspension, and deposits them when it slows down. A river or creek bottom with little evidence of clay and silt particles indicates a fast flow.

Sediment sorting (the degree to which sediments are the same size) also indicates the transporting agent. Water, wind, and glacier meltwaters sort sediments according to size (deposits will be uniform in size), whereas glacial ice is a poor sorter (deposits of glacial till are varying sizes and shapes).

The characteristics of individual particles can also be used to indicate whether the sediments were deposited in the site by air or water. Generally, a dull or matte surface on the particles suggests deposition through by air. A polished or glossy surface on the particles suggests deposition by water.

Sediment shape can also be a useful indicator. Angular-shaped sediments have not been transported far from their source (less exposure to erosion). Rounded sediments have been transported further (more exposure to erosion). Glaciers are the exception to this. Sediments can be transported within ice for great distances without the edges being eroded.

Reconstructing Settlement Patterns

Archaeologists study settlement patterns at four different levels: individual houses, single settlements, traditional territories, and regions (Table 8.2). Estimates of population are common in all levels of study and are described separately.

Individual Houses

The study of one or a few houses in a settlement is an emerging focus of archaeological interest and is sometimes known as **household archaeology**. The physical char-

TABLE 8.2: Types of Settlement Pattern Studies in Archaeology

Level of Study	Focus
Individual houses	Physical characteristics of house; architecture; construction methods; social uses of house; defining the makeup of the household
Single settlement	Layout of settlement; variability of houses; season of occupation; site catchment area
Traditional territory	Seasonal rounds; diversity of site types; evidence of cultural continuity
Regional analysis	Relationship of sites to the natural environment; relationship of sites to each other

acteristics of houses, such as construction materials and methods, are commonly studied, along with the architecture.

Archaeologists also investigate social uses of houses, focusing on such things as the kinds of activities that were done in the house. In many societies, particularly those in warm climates, most activities were done outdoors and the houses were reserved primarily for sleeping. Examples of this are the relatively small grass houses of the Turkana and the earth-walled houses of the Masaii, both from Africa.

ROBERT J. MUCKLE

FIGURE 8.2: TURKANA VILLAGE, Africa. Research has shown that in many areas, particularly in warm climates, people spend relatively little time in houses.

In addition to estimating how many people lived in a house, archaeologists are often interested in how membership in the household was established. Archaeologists often use the number of fire hearths and identifiable internal dividing structures within the house to infer how many nuclear families or other groupings may have lived there. Stylistic similarities in artifacts and features are also examined to see if they point to family relationships. On the northwest coast of America, for example, carvings on the outside of houses, as well as artifacts found inside, often depicted the clan of the people who lived there.

In multifamily houses, differences in the status of the inhabitants are often determined by comparing the artifacts and ecofacts found in the identifiable family divisions within the house. In multifamily dwellings, it is not unusual for the higher-quality artifacts and food remains to be unequally distributed between different family areas.

Single Settlements

At the settlement level, archaeologists commonly investigate such things as variability among houses within the community, the distribution of houses, and the spatial relationship of all features within a site (e.g., middens, houses, burial grounds, and common areas).

Data on the variability and distribution of houses often supports inferences of social inequality between households (as did similar information about artifacts and ecofacts found in multifamily dwellings). Excavations at Keatley Creek, a large prehistoric village in western Canada, show that smaller houses had significantly lower proportions of foods that were ethnographically-described as better quality and had less diversity of food types overall. The smaller houses, for example, revealed substantially smaller amounts of the highly valued sockeye and spring salmon and much more of the low-quality pink salmon than the larger houses.

The patterning of houses observed in settlements is almost always planned. In the Masaii villages in Africa, for example, houses are situated around the perimeter of the village, with the large common area in the center.

ROBERT J. MUCKLE

FIGURE 8.3: MASAII VILLAGE, Africa. Houses are situated around the periphery of the site.

For archaeologists working with settlements created by non-sedentary peoples, determining the season in which the site was occupied is a common objective, and research on this is often known as **seasonality studies**. Determining the season of occupation is accomplished primarily through examining the animal and plant remains recovered from the site. The shells of some mollusk species exhibit seasonal growth rings that can be identified in cross section, which makes determining the season in which shell midden sites were occupied quite straightforward. When the remains of young animals are recovered and the birthing season is known, the level of skeletal development can sometimes be used to infer when the animal was killed. Based on the knowledge that the pigs found in some prehistoric deposits in southern England were born in springtime, archaeologists were able use immature pig bones to determine that the sites were probably created in winter. Similarly, for species that shed and regrow antlers at fixed times, the state of antler growth may be used to infer when the animal died. The presence of the remains of animals that routinely migrate through an area is another method of inferring season of occupation.

Plant remains are also often used to infer the season a site was occupied. The inference is usually based on the time of year when most or all of the plants remains found in cultural context were edible. For example, if a site has nuts that typically ripen from August to October, berries that ripen from September to November, a wild grass that is edible from April to October, and a wild root that is edible from September to November, then it can reasonably be inferred that the site was occupied in the late summer and early autumn.

Another common objective for archaeologists focusing on a single settlement is to locate the source of all the recovered remains. This includes determining the source of raw materials, such as the stone used in artifact manufacture and the clays used for making pottery. Such data is often integral to making inferences about trade, and is known as **site catchment analysis**.

Traditional Territory

In recent decades, many archaeologists have begun to focus their study of settlement patterns on areas habitually used by specific groups. The study area is known as either the **traditional territory** of the group or the **site exploitation territory**.

The focus on traditional territories is especially prevalent in indigenous archaeology, where much of the work is undertaken to prove prehistoric use and occupancy of an area. Archaeological research usually includes examining the number and diversity of site types, searching for evidence of cultural continuity within the traditional territory, and establishing the evidence of a **seasonal round**, which explains the diversity of sites.

Regional Analysis

Archaeologists study settlement patterns at the regional level in a multitude of ways. They usually examine the data from studies of individual houses, settlements, and traditional territories, and search for similarities and differences in patterns throughout a geographic region or **culture area**, encompassing multiple traditional territories.

Many archaeological studies of regional settlements adapt methods and theories from geography to examine the different ways in which humans are apt to order their settlements in relation to each other. These methods involve such things as measuring distances between settlements of various sizes and looking for geometrical patterns illustrating standard differences between cities, towns, villages, and camps. Another major method focuses on how settlements are patterned in relation to the natural environment. This includes examining the preferred locations of settlements, such as hilltops versus valley bottoms.

Estimating Population Size

Population sizes of houses, sites, territories, and regions, can be estimated in many ways, such as by looking at the number of people buried in cemeteries, the numbers of specific types of artifacts, the local or regional carrying capacity, and ethnographic and historical records. Table 8.3 lists the major types of settlement data used in most estimates.

Ecological information, burial data, and artifacts are among the least reliable sources. While ecological information may provide some measure of how many people an area could support, the estimates are usually too broad to be of value, and the carrying capacity would not necessarily have been reached. Burial information is likewise unreliable, especially for the prehistoric period. While it is not unusual to find cemeteries

TABLE 8.3: Methods to Estimate Population

Estimation Methods
Ecological information
Burials
Artifacts
Ethnographic and historic records
Covered floor space
Number of rooms, dwellings, and hearths
Volume of site deposits

when excavating sedentary communities, archaeologists would have to establish the contemporaneity of the remains and consider that some remains may have completely decomposed and others may have been buried off site. Using burials to estimate population size for non-sedentary peoples is a non-starter. Some archaeologists use artifacts, such as the number of cooking pots, to make population estimates. However, this method has its limitations in that archaeologists would need to make many assumptions about the use and discard of pots and as well recognize pots in a deposit (especially difficult considering pots are often recycled).

For recent times, historic and ethnographic records are the most reliable tool for estimating populations. However, as with all ethnographic and historic records, archaeologists must exercise caution when using observations to draw analogies to the past.

The amount of floor space; the number of rooms, dwellings, and hearths; and the volume of deposits are all commonly used as estimates of population. They are all dependant on ethnographic analogy. One study used a wide sample of ethnographies to determine that population size could be estimated by calculating 1 person for every 10 square meters (12 square yards) of floor space. Considering the variability of environments and cultures throughout the world, however, the indiscriminate use of this calculation would be naïve.

When determining population size in traditional territories and regions, archaeologists must ensure that sites being used in the calculation are contemporaneous. This includes, for example, not counting settlements whose occupants were already accounted for in another seasonal site. It also involves determining the normal patterns of behavior. During prehistoric times in some parts of the world, for example, it was common for dozens or hundreds of people to live together during some weeks or months, and spend the rest of the year traveling throughout the territory in much smaller groups.

Because the original number of sites in most regions is unlikely to be known, estimates of regional populations during prehistory are filled with assumptions and speculations. Estimates of the prehistoric population of North America prior to the arrival of Europeans, for example, range from less than one million to tens of millions.

Reconstructing Subsistence Strategies

Subsistence strategy refers to the way in which people get their food. Archaeologists recognize five basic patterns of subsistence for people living in pre-industrial times (Table 8.4).

TABLE 8.4: Major Subsistence Strategies

Strategy	Definition
Generalized foraging	Subsistence based on a wide variety of plants and animals
Complex foraging	Subsistence based on a wide variety of plants and animals, but specializing in one type
Pastoralism	Subsistence based on the herding of animals
Horticulture	Subsistence based on plant cultivation, with hand tools only
Agriculture	Intensive plant cultivation, often with the aid of animals and irrigation

Generalized Foraging

Classifying people as **generalized foragers** means that most of their food comprises a wide variety of wild plants and animals that they collect themselves. They are sometimes described as hunters and gatherers. Prior to about 15,000 years ago, all people were generalized foragers. In addition to being primarily dependant on a wide variety of wild plants and animals, generalized foragers typically live in groups of less than 50 people, are **egalitarian**, and are highly mobile, moving at least several times each year within their territory. There are few remaining generalized foraging groups today, but some can be found in the Australian outback and parts of southern Africa.

Archaeological indicators of generalized foraging include a preponderance of wild foods in cultural context; small, temporary settlements; and equal distribution of resources. Because generalized foragers move frequently, pottery, which is often bulky and relatively heavy, is rare in their settlements.

Complex Foraging

Also known as complex hunting and gathering, and probably emerging about 15,000 years ago, **complex foraging** describes a subsistence based on a wide diversity of plants and animals, but with a primary dependence on a single resource. A good example is the people of the northwest coast region of North America who for several thousands of years had a diverse diet of dozens of different plants and animals, but salmon was overwhelmingly predominant. The size of complex foraging groups was typically in the range of a few hundred to a few thousand, although they did not all reside together. Complex foragers are also characterized by semi-sedentism and marked social inequality.

Archaeological indicators of complex foraging include a great diversity of animal and botanical remains with a preponderance of one kind, semi-permanent villages, and an unequal distribution of resources.

Pastoralism

Emerging about 11,000 years ago, **pastoralism** describes subsistence based on the herding of animals such as cattle, sheep, goats, and pigs. Characteristics of pastoralism include groups of up to a few thousand spread among several villages, seasonal mobility, and slight social inequality.

Archaeological indicators of pastoralism are the preponderance of one or two species of animals in a site, with those animals showing evidence of **domestication**, seasonal movement (to graze the herds), and some social inequality in the distribution of resources.

Horticulture

Like pastoralism, **horticulture** emerged about 11,000 years ago. It describes subsistence based on plant cultivation with hand tools only (i.e., no plows or animals involved in the preparation of fields or harvesting). Horticultural groups generally range in size from the hundreds to several thousand, although they are spread among many different villages. Each village was typically occupied for several years while the nearby land was farmed. When the nutrients from the land were exhausted, the people would move to a nearby location, create new garden plots, and build new residential structures.

Archaeological indicators of horticulture include a preponderance of domestic plant remains, evidence of multiyear occupation, garden plots, and slight to moderate inequality in the distribution of resources.

Agriculture

Agriculture involves intensive plant cultivation, often (but not always) with the use of animals to assist in the preparation of fields (e.g., to pull plows) and harvesting (e.g., to transport the crops). Agriculture emerged about 6,000 years ago and was the subsistence strategy of all ancient civilizations and states. Populations supported by agriculture have very high densities (ranging from the thousands to the millions), the presence of cities, and marked social inequality. Agriculturalists often have armies, writing, and monumental architecture. All of the above are evidence of agriculture.

ROBERT J. MUCKLE

FIGURE 8.4: MONTE ALBAN, Mexico. States and cities with high population densities, such as Monte Alban, were dependent on agriculture to provide surplus food to support state-level organization and the construction of monumental architecture.

Distinguishing Wild Plants and Animals from Domestic

There is no consensus definition of domestication in archaeology. At a minimum, it is taken to mean that plants or animals are under the control of humans. At most, it means that plants and animals are dependent on humans for their survival. Many archaeologists consider plants and animals to be domestic if humans are somehow involved in the breeding. Identifying domestic versus wild plants and animals in the archaeological record is difficult, especially for those plants and animals in the early stages of domestication (Table 8.5).

Plant Domestication

There is no single attribute for distinguishing a plant as wild or domestic, and archaeologists often use a combination of morphological and cultural evidence. The principal variable used to identify domestic plants in the archaeological record is size. The part of the plant that people use is usually larger among domestic varieties than wild. A domestic cob of corn, for example, is larger than a wild cob; and a domestic squash is larger than a wild squash. It is uncertain why this is, but one possibility is that larger plants were selected for breeding, and the genes for the large sizes were passed to subsequent generations. The size increase may also have been due to human intervention in the form of watering and weeding, and in more recent times, fertilizing.

TABLE 8.5: Criteria for Distinguishing Domestic versus Wild Plants and Animals (of the same species)

Attributes of Domestic Varieties of Plants
The part of the plant that people use is usually larger
The plant may have lost its mechanism for natural dispersal
The part of the plant that people use may have become clustered
There is often a genetic change
There may be a loss of dormancy
The plants tend to ripen simultaneously
There is a tendency for less self-protection, such as thorns and toxins
Attributes of Domestic Varieties of Animals
The animals are smaller (at least in the early stages of domestication)
There is a tendency to find more complete skeletons in the faunal assemblage
There is likely to be a high percentage of young animals in the faunal assemblage
There is likely to be a high percentage of young male animals in the faunal assemblage
There is likely to be a high percentage of old female animals in the faunal assemblage

Since size is easily measured and compared, and since it is usually the edible part of the plant that is preserved in archaeological sites, it makes sense that this is the way many inferences about plant domestication are made. Generally, if archaeologists see an increase in the size of the edible parts of the plants through time, it is usually reasonable to infer that the plant was becoming domesticated.

As outlined in Table 8.5, several other attributes of plants can be used to distinguish whether they are of the domestic or wild variety. However, due to the fact that the non-edible parts of plants domesticated for food are rarely preserved, most have limited application in archaeology.

Cultural evidence of plant domestication comes in a variety of forms, including the presence of gardening artifacts such as hoes, features such as irrigation canals, and soil chemistry indicating a previous garden plot.

Animal Domestication

Ways of distinguishing domestic versus wild animals in archaeological sites include size, the completeness of the skeleton, and age and sex ratios of the slaughtered remains, as well as cultural evidence.

At least in the early stages of domestication, domestic animals were usually smaller than their wild counterparts. A domestic goat, for example, was smaller than a wild goat. The reason for the size difference is not completely understood. One popular explanation is that smaller animals were selected for domestication because they were easier to capture and control. Another possibility is that domestic animals generally would have had a worse diet than their wild counterparts, which was reflected in the stunted growth of the skeletons.

The completeness of skeletons is a good way to tell whether animals were domestic. A complete or nearly complete skeleton of a moderate-sized or large animal in a settlement suggests that it was probably domestic, likely because if the animal was hunted, some butchery would have taken place at the site of the kill. Hunters routinely discarded parts of the animal of little value to them in order to lighten the load to carry back to the settlement. For example, a hunter of a wild goat who kills an animal 15 miles (25 kilometers) from the settlement is unlikely to bring the entire skeleton back.

ROBERT J. MUCKLE

FIGURE 8.5: BUTCHERY IN A VILLAGE. The completeness of the skeleton is one way to distinguish domestic from wild varieties of animals. As depicted here in this rural Egyptian village, the entire animal is being butchered, indicating it is domestic.

Assemblages of butchered remains are also examined for age and sex ratios to make inferences about domestication. A high percentage of young adults, particularly males, is probably indicative of domestication. One reason for this is that when hunting wild animals, the young adults are typically the most difficult to kill due to their strength and speed. Also, groups who have domestic animals often preserve most females, but rely on a few males for breeding. Thus, relatively few young female remains are likely to be found in an assemblage of domestic animals.

Fencing is one type of cultural evidence of domestication, usually indicated by post holes. Large accumulations of animal dung in or near a village may also indicate domestication. In some cases, there may be some associated artifacts, such as collars.

Reconstructing Diet

Several kinds of evidence are used to determine the particular foods that people were eating. These are (i) plant and animal remains in cultural context, (ii) human skeletal remains, (iii) **human waste**, (iv) human soft tissue, and (v) residue on artifacts.

Plant and Animal Remains in Cultural Context

The most obvious indicators of diet are the plant and animal remains found in good cultural context, such as in or around middens, fire hearths, containers, cache pits, and houses. This is the most common and one of the most reliable methods of determining diet. As outlined in Chapter 6, the plant and animal remains are often quantified.

Human Skeletal Remains

Through an analysis of isotopes and trace elements in bone, human skeletal remains provide a good indication of the kinds of foods eaten. The ratio of carbon and nitrogen isotopes is different among various kinds of plants and animals, and when foods are eaten as a regular part of people's diet, those ratios are imprinted in their bones.

The ratios of isotopes can be used to make inferences about the relative amounts of protein coming from marine and terrestrial species. On the west coast of Canada, for example, the ratios of carbon 13 and carbon 12 in dozens of excavated skeletal remains have indicated that over the past 5,000 years, those living there obtained about 90 per cent of their protein from marine species (e.g., salmon). And those living in the interior along salmon-bearing rivers obtained about 50 per cent of their protein from marine species. Isotope analysis is also used to make inferences about the types of plants eaten. Root crops, nuts, and berries, for example, have different ratios than cereal grains.

The relative proportion of meat in diets can be distinguished using trace element analysis of human bone. A meat-rich diet will typically show fairly higher levels of copper and zinc and lower levels of manganese and strontium than diets with relatively little or no meat.

An analysis of human teeth can also indicate dietary preferences. Wear patterns on teeth can be used to make some broad inferences. A diet with a lot of hard, gritty foods, for example, is likely to be reflected on the surface of the teeth. Cavities are often correlated with a dependence on agricultural products.

Human Waste

Although rare in archaeological sites, human waste provides one of the best and most reliable methods of reconstructing diet, and comes in a variety of forms. Coprolites may appear in the form of cylinders, pellets, or pads, and are most commonly found in dry caves. The study of coprolites is a specialty in archaeology, and it is reported that when reconstituted, even the smell comes back sometimes. Since coprolites contain the remnants of food products, they are highly valued for reconstructing diet. It is not unusual to be able to identify plant species from partially digested seeds or leaves, as well as small bones of birds and fish. Indicators of diet also include other parts of plants, such as stalks and roots, and other parts of animals, such as hair and feathers that may have adhered to the meat, as well as fish and reptile scales.

Another type of human waste is cess, which is an accumulation of human waste including feces and urine. Cess is often used to describe the entire contents of latrines or sewers. Because it is much less likely to be preserved than coprolites, prehistoric archaeologists do not usually encounter cess.

Human Soft Tissue

The absolute best method of determining diet is from food found in the stomachs and intestines of human remains preserved through extreme environmental conditions. As with coprolites, analysis involves identifying food products. A study of the intestines of the well-preserved bog bodies from Iron Age Europe, for example, shows meals consisting of beef, pork, wheat, barley, oats, peas, bread, and blackberries.

Residue Analysis

Diet may also be reconstructed using residue analysis. As outlined in Chapter 6, foods often leave residue on artifacts. A chemical analysis of residue left in a pot, for example, can often determine the type of food stored in the pot; and blood residue on stone tools leads to inferences about the kind of animal killed and butchered, presumably for food.

KEY RESOURCES AND SUGGESTED READING

A good overview of the archaeology of households is provided by Allison (1999) in *The Archaeology of Household Activities.* The multivolume series *Advances in Archaeological Method and Theory* edited by Schiffer (1978–87) includes several contributions on reconstructing settlement and subsistence patterns. *The Handbook of Archaeological Sciences* (Brothwell and Pollard, 2001) includes multiple contributions on reconstructing subsistence and diet.

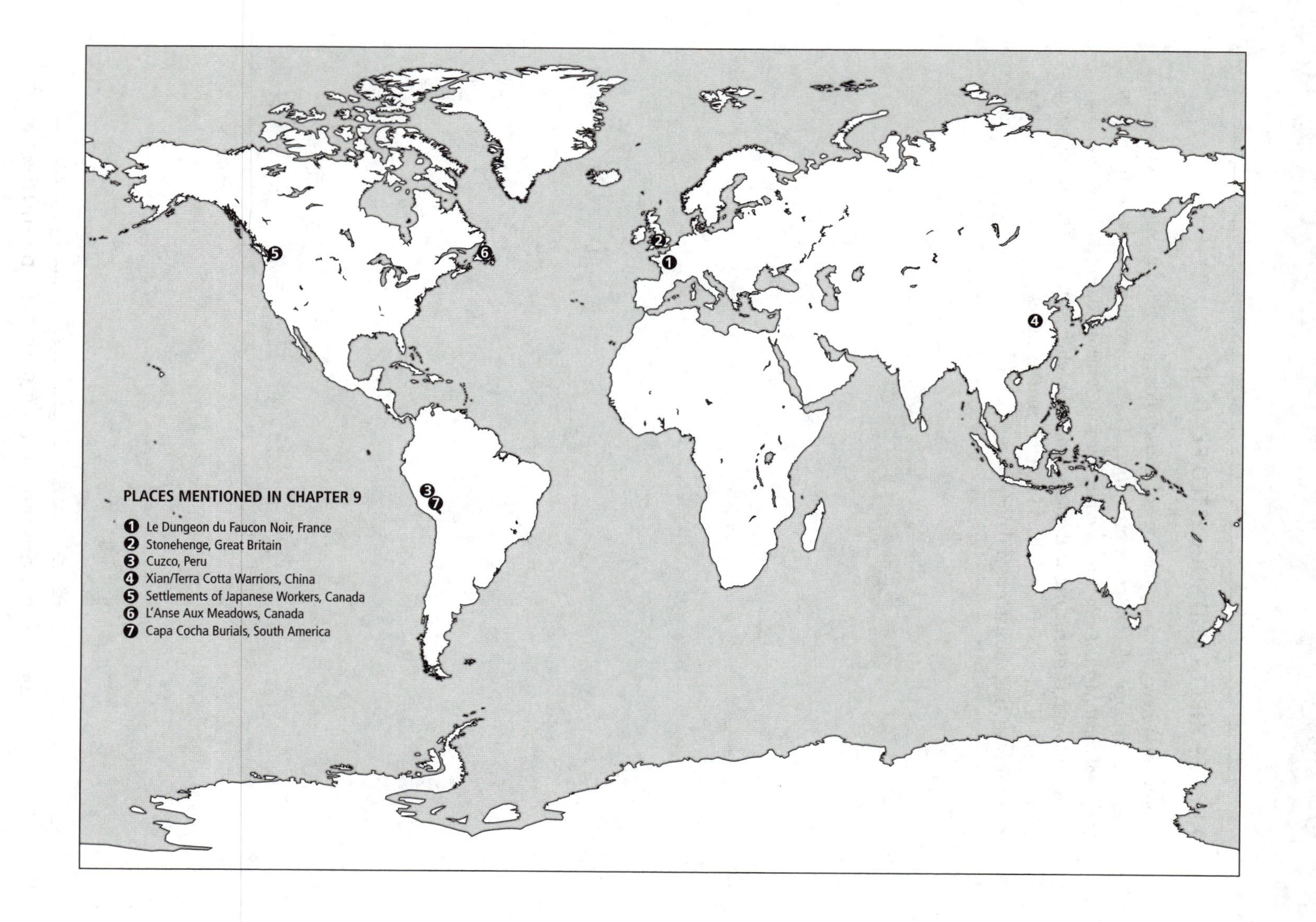
PLACES MENTIONED IN CHAPTER 9
1 Le Dungeon du Faucon Noir, France
2 Stonehenge, Great Britain
3 Cuzco, Peru
4 Xian/Terra Cotta Warriors, China
5 Settlements of Japanese Workers, Canada
6 L'Anse Aux Meadows, Canada
7 Capa Cocha Burials, South America

CHAPTER 9

Reconstructing the Social and Ideological Aspects of Culture

Introduction

Although some of the archaeological work in the early twentieth century examined the social and ideological aspects of past cultures, these types of studies have only become popular in recent decades. The new or processual archaeology that emerged in the 1960s tended to focus on ecology, but many archaeologists at this time also began to study social systems, attempting to identify social inequality and categorize societies into the classification systems developed by anthropologists. Identity and ideology emerged as a focus in the 1980s, associated with the development of post-processual archaeology.

Reconstructions of the social and ideological aspects of culture tend to be more difficult than those of culture history and ecological adaptations. Because most of what archaeologists excavate, including ecofacts and features, is directly related to ecological adaptations, it is relatively easy to make inferences about palaeoenvironments, settlement patterns, subsistence strategies, and diet. For example, inferring diet from plant and animal remains found in pots or a midden can hardly be considered a great intellectual leap.

Using those same remains, usually people's garbage, to make inferences about the social and ideological aspects of culture is clearly more difficult. It can be done; it just isn't as easy. While inferences about subsistence and diet, for example, are made by identifying the remains themselves, the patterning of those remains tends to be more important to archaeologists interested in reconstructing the social and ideological aspects of culture.

In sequence, the remainder of this chapter covers the reconstruction of (i) inequality, (ii) the type of society, (iii) identity of various sorts, and (iv) ideology.

Reconstructing Inequality

Reconstructing inequality involves determining differences of status and access to resources within a group. Groups are usually classified as being egalitarian, ranked, or stratified.

Describing a group as egalitarian means that everyone in the group has roughly equal status and access to resources. A ranked group means that everyone has a different status:

if there are 500 people in the group, then there are 500 different statuses. **Stratification** refers to a class system, in which there are typically at least three distinct classes, commonly referred to as lower, middle, and upper class. Sometimes groups exhibit ranking within classes.

Groups are not always easily categorized. In recent years, for example, archaeologists have increasingly used the word **transegalitarian** to describe groups that are transitioning between egalitarian and ranked or stratified systems. The principal evidence archaeologists use to determine levels of inequality are variability in burials and in houses.

The very fact that some members of a group were buried while others were not can be an indication of inequality. Low status people, such as slaves, may have been merely thrown out along with trash, while people with higher status were buried. Variability in grave goods also indicates differences in status: people with higher status were generally buried with more and higher quality goods. Levels of inequality may also be gauged by variability in the preparation for burial, including the building of tombs. The pyramids and tombs of the ancient Egyptian rulers and the thousands of terra

SUZANNE VILLENEUVE

FIGURE 9.1: BURIAL WITH GRAVE GOODS. Burials are one of the best ways to reconstruct levels of inequality. Differences in the amounts and kinds of grave goods (e.g., artifacts and food) reflect differences in status.

cotta warriors associated with the Emperor Qin from China (See Figure 2.4) are extreme examples of how grave goods and tombs can reflect high status.

Skeletal remains themselves may also provide indications of status. Some groups along the west coast of North America and others in Mesoamerica, for example, artificially shaped the forehead as an indication of high status. Binding a flat object to the forehead of an infant for lengthy periods produced a distinctive elongated shape.

Houses are another common way of gauging status. Settlements with highly variable houses usually indicate inequality. People with higher status typically have the largest and most costly houses. Examples of extreme differences in status as reflected in house size abound in the archaeological record, from several thousand years ago to the present. Castles in medieval Europe are an example. Figure 9.2 is a photo of a castle in France known as the Le Dungeon du Faucon Noir (the Dungeon of the Black Falcon).

JAMES MORFOPOULOS

FIGURE 9.2: CASTLE IN FRANCE. Variability in housing is used to reconstruct levels of inequality. Castles such as Le Dungeon du Faucon Noir (Dungeon of the Black Falcon) reflect the control of the powerful elite. The castle, originally constructed more than 1,000 years ago, was partially torn down by revolutionaries in the late eighteenth century to remove all traces of nobility.

Reportedly the oldest stone castle in France, dating to AD 991, it epitomized class struggles in that country. Part of it was destroyed in the late eighteenth century to remove traces of nobility.

Examining the range and variability of material remains within houses is a further way to determine social inequality. An unequal distribution of luxury items or **prestige goods** between houses or within multifamily houses likely indicates inequality. Prestige goods include raw materials in short supply, such as high quality stone for making tools or shell coming from great distances. Manufactured objects can also be classified as prestige goods, often in the form of jewelry that required a tremendous investment of labor.

Reconstructing Types of Societies

A variety of anthropological models categorize types of societies based on their economic, social, and political systems. As outlined in Chapter 2, the unilinear theory of cultural evolution, with the stages of savagery, barbarism, and civilization, was one of the first attempts to categorize people in this way.

Anthropologists created two popular models in the 1960s, and these were readily adopted by archaeologists. Despite their shortcomings, both models are still widely used in the early twenty-first century. One model, developed by Morton Fried, is primarily political in nature and categorizes societies as egalitarian, ranked, or stratified. Classification of prehistoric societies is based primarily on evidence of inequality.

Another model, developed by Elman Service, is based on a variety of criteria, including subsistence strategy, level of inequality, leadership, population, and occupational specialization. Service's model remains the most widely used, although not without some modifications over the past several decades. The categories are **bands, tribes, chiefdoms,** and **states**. Empires are another significant type, in addition to Service's model.

Bands

Bands are characterized by their small group size (usually less than 50 members), high mobility throughout their territory, egalitarianism, and subsistence strategy of generalized foraging. Each band is autonomous, but they form economic, social, and ideological alliances with neighboring bands. Marriage patterns among bands are always **exogamous**, meaning that marriage partners are found from outside one's own band. Everyone in a band has roughly equal status. Leadership is informal: the person who is recognized as being best at a specific task takes on the role of leadership for that task. There is little occupational specialization among band members (other than shamans),

TABLE 9.1: Reconstructing Categories of Societies in Archaeology

The Major Categories of Societies
Bands
Tribes
Chiefdoms
States
Empires
The Major Kinds of Evidence Archaeologists Use to Reconstruct Types of Societies
Size of population
Size of settlements
Sedentariness
Subsistence strategy
Variability among houses
Variabilty in the distribution of material remains
Monuments
Architecture
Evidence of specialization (e.g., craft areas)
Iconography
Mortuary data

with each man doing what all other men do and each woman doing what all other women do. Even the role of shaman is considered a part-time task, and he or she is still expected to do what all the other men or women in the group do. All groups prior to about 15,000 years ago were bands, and although rare, they continue to exist into the twenty-first century.

Archaeological indicators of bands are also characteristics of generalized foragers and typically include an equal distribution of resources, little variability in house size or form, relatively small settlements, seasonal occupations, temporary structures, and plant and animal remains identified as wild. Territorial boundaries are difficult to define and often overlap with neighboring bands. Because bands are mobile, pottery, which is relatively heavy and bulky, is rarely found in their sites.

Tribes

Also known as **segmentary societies**, tribes are characterized by populations typically ranging from a few hundred to a few thousand. Subsistence is usually based on pastoralism or horticulture (or both), although there are numerous examples of tribal hunting and gathering societies in resource-rich areas such as the Great Plains in North America. The level of social inequality within tribes can be described as transegalitarian. They generally have multiple villages, each with their own leader who is often described by anthropologists as a **Big Man** or **Head Man**. These leadership positions hold no authority and are usually based on the personal qualities of a person who then parlays his role into a higher status. Leadership is typically effective only at the village level. There is no central authority over the entire tribe, but the bonds between villages are maintained through kinship ties and common interest associations.

Archaeological indicators of tribes are similar to those of pastoralists and small-scale horticultural communities. Tribal societies will usually have a preponderance of plant and animal remains identified as domestic. Slight social inequality, based on the presence of a Big Man or Head Man, is likely to be reflected in a minor unequal distribution of resources and perhaps one house that is slightly larger than the others.

Considering that both pastoralists and horticulturalists spend relatively long periods of time in one area, there may also be some evidence of structures intended for long-term use.

Chiefdoms

Chiefdoms are characterized by populations ranging from a few thousand to tens of thousands, a subsistence strategy based on horticulture, and marked social inequality, including formal leadership positions. Members of a chiefdom are spread among multiple communities. Leadership extends beyond the community to the entire chiefdom. The central leader is known as the **chief**, who has authority over all members of the group. Leadership is **ascribed** and is usually based on ancestral ties with the supernatural or mythical world. The populace pays taxes to the chief and his ruling extended family. Taxation may be in the form of goods, such as a percentage of the crops harvested, or labor, such as a given number of weeks in service to the chief in subsistence or construction activities. Chiefdoms exhibit much social inequality and usually a system of ranking. One's status is typically dependent on how close one is related to the chief. Craft specialization, including artisans, is common. Although not evident in all cases, chiefdoms are also characterized by monuments. These include incised monoliths to mark territory or declare ownership, such as **stelae**, or for ritual activities, such as Stonehenge.

Archaeological indicators of chiefdoms include those associated with large-scale horticulture, such as storage facilities. Other indicators are a preponderance of food remains identified as domestic, a marked unequal distribution of resources, considerable variability in houses and burials, evidence of craft specialization areas, signs of ascribed leadership (e.g., **iconography**), and monuments.

States

States are characterized by populations ranging from about 20,000 to several million, a subsistence based on agriculture, the presence of cities, a **bureaucracy**, **monumental architecture**, and armies. States also usually have a system of writing. One of the essential differences between chiefdoms and states is that in a state, the leader's power is legitimized or at least supported by an army. In states, leadership can be either achieved or ascribed. The surplus created by agriculture is used to support not only artisans, crafts specialists, and armies, but also a bureaucracy, which is primarily responsible for carrying out the wishes of the leadership, including enforcing laws and collecting taxes. States invariably are associated with civilization.

Archaeological indicators of states correlate with those of agriculturalists and civilizations. Evidence of a system of writing is perhaps the easiest way to distinguish a state from a chiefdom, although it is understood that some states, such as the Inka, lacked writing. Monumental architecture, cities, unequal distribution of resources, and domestic foods are other types of evidence that are commonly associated with states, but these characteristics are also common among chiefdoms.

Empires

Although not considered a category in Service's classification system, an **empire** is a special kind of political system that is territorially expansive, with one state exercising control over other states, chiefdoms, tribes, or bands. Territorial expansion is supported by the actual or potential threat of military power. Archaeological indicators of empires include the commingling of cultural traditions, such as architecture, and the creation of elaborate road systems linking the territories.

The most well-known empires of the past include the Aztec, Inka, and Roman. The dominance of the many distinct societies throughout Mesoamerica by the Aztec peoples of northern Mexico from the fourteenth to the early sixteenth centuries is referred to as the Aztec empire. The Spaniard Hernando Cortez was able to conquer the empire with relative ease in part because he enlisted many volunteers from cultures under Aztec domination.

During the Inka empire, millions of people in dozens of different cultures were dominated by one group originally based in Cuzco, Peru, beginning in the early fifteenth century and ending with conquest by Spanish forces led by Francisco Pizzaro in the early sixteenth century. At its height, the Inka empire controlled much of the western coastal region of South America, including areas now recognized as Peru, Bolivia, Ecuador, and portions of Argentina, Chile, and Columbia. The Inka legacy includes a reported 12,000 or more miles of roads, used in part to exert military control over those living throughout the empire. As with the conquest of the Aztec, the Spanish forces were able to enlist the aid of subjected peoples in their fight against the Inka.

The Roman Empire, which existed from about the third century BC to the fifth century AD, included domination of much of Europe, northern Africa, and western Asia.

The Roman Empire's presence in the archaeological record can be seen throughout the region, including its trademark roads and architecture.

Reconstructing Identity

Archaeologists attempt to reconstruct several kinds of identities, primarily using artifacts, symbols, and mortuary remains (Table 9.2).

TABLE 9.2: Reconstructing Identity in Archaeology

The Major Kinds of Identity Archaeologists Attempt to Reconstruct
Ethnic identity
Descent group
Gender
Children
Specific individuals
The Major Kinds of Evidence Archaeologists Use to Reconstruct Identity
Artifacts
Symbols
Mortuary data

Ethnic Identity

An **ethnic group** is defined as a group of people who share a common language, culture, history, and territory, with members consciously identifying with the group.

Reconstructing ethnicity in archaeology, particularly for the prehistoric period, is

CARMEN WHITE

FIGURE 9.3: ROMAN COLISEUM. Similarities in architecture, such as that of the Roman Coliseum, is one way of identifying empires.

notoriously difficult and controversial. There is much debate about the reliability of inferring ethnicity from material remains, especially considering that neighboring groups frequently shared many cultural attributes and that cultures continually change. Many people have attempted to reconstruct ethnicity for political reasons, including those who work in the field of indigenous archaeology and who aim to support claims of aboriginal rights and territory.

Reconstructing ethnicity is often based on **ethnic markers**. Examining evidence of African-American ethnicity in the archaeological record of the New World, archaeologist Timothy Baumann (2004) describes three forms of ethnic markers: (i) artifacts that were made in or are indigenous to Africa, such as a clay pipe from Ghana found in a New World cemetery, (ii) artifacts made in the New World that exhibit African styles, such as a pipe made in a European form but exhibiting West African decorative motifs, and (iii) non-African materials used in African ways, such as European-made bowls (which were found in greater proportion to plates) that were used for gumbos and stews. Ethnic markers such as those listed above are commonly used to identify Asian ethnicity in late nineteenth and early twentieth century sites in western North America. The ethnic markers are most frequently artifacts that have been manufactured in China or Japan, such as rice bowls and bottles, but they can also include features. Excavations at a historic logging camp on the west coast of Canada, for example, revealed a Japanese-style bathhouse known as an **ofuro** (Muckle 2004).

Chapter 3 briefly discussed the site of L'Anse aux Meadows, which achieved UNESCO World Heritage Site status largely based on the fact that it provides the earliest reliably dated evidence of Europeans in the Americas. The ethnic markers used to identify Viking ethnicity included characteristic iron nails and rivets, soapstone spindle whorls, and distinctive boatsheds.

Ethnicity may also be identified through rock art. It has been suggested that, in at least some situations, people new to an area may create distinctive rock art as a means of establishing their presence (Quinlan and Woody 2003).

Descent Groups

A **descent group** is defined as a group in which all members can trace lineal descent to a single ancestor. The ancestor may be mythical or real. Lineage is one kind of descent group in which all the links to the ancestor are known. Groups of lineages often form clans, in which all members assume common ancestry, but only some of the links are known.

Clans typically number in the hundreds and thousands, with members spread out over expansive territories. Symbols are frequently used to identify clan membership, and it is these symbols that archaeologists often use to reconstruct descent groups. On

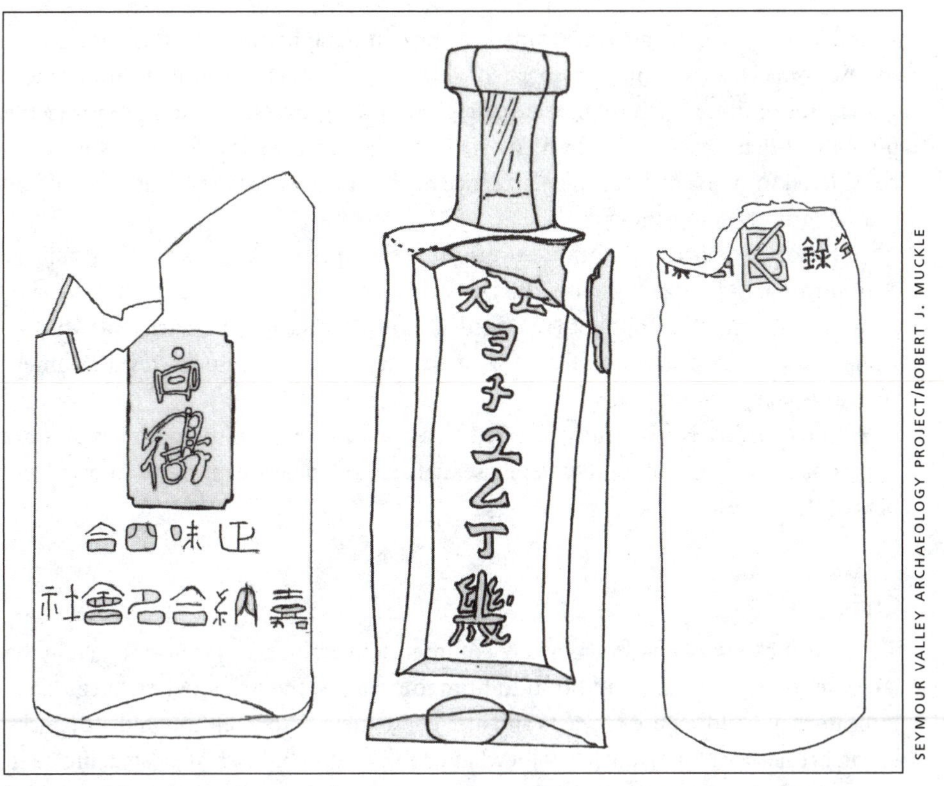

SEYMOUR VALLEY ARCHAEOLOGY PROJECT/ROBERT J. MUCKLE

FIGURE 9.4: JAPANESE ARTIFACTS IN A CANADIAN LOGGING CAMP. One way of reconstructing ethnicity is to find ethnic markers. These bottles were all made in Japan. Along with many other artifacts of Japanese origin and features built in a Japanese style, these bottles contribute to the conclusion that the camp was occupied by Japanese workers almost 100 years ago.

the northwest coast of North America, for example, carvings and paintings on houses and grave markers can be used to infer clan membership.

Sex and Gender

As outlined in Chapter 6, skeletal remains can determine whether an individual was male or female. Gender, however, is a cultural construct and encompasses the way people are perceived and expected to behave, including the traditional female and male roles, as well as other categories for hermaphrodites, androgynous people, homosexuals, and transsexuals, depending on the society

Inferences of gender are usually made using ethnographic analogy. It is not unusual to have some types of artifacts associated with men and others associated with women, with ratios of these taken to indicate gender. Among foragers, for example, projectile points are often considered to be men's artifacts, and digging sticks or baskets are often considered women's artifacts. The presence of either artifact as grave goods would be a good indication of gender.

In historic resource utilization camps in North America, such as those associated with mining and logging during the late nineteenth and early twentieth centuries, men-only and mixed camps both operated. One way archaeologists determine whether women were in the camps is by the ratios of artifacts commonly associated with women, such as jewelry and fancy dishes.

Homosexuality is frequently inferred based on art. Pictographs and portable art (e.g., small carvings) sometimes depict sexual acts, often between two or more members of the same sex.

Children

The identification of children is an area of interest in archaeology that emerged in the late-twentieth century. In addition to human remains, the principal archaeological indicators of children are artifacts and art. These include toys, although distinguishing an artifact as a toy is in itself somewhat problematic. Children are also depicted in art, and in some cases, the art itself is interpreted as having been created by children because of its simple qualities. Experiments have shown that fingerprints found on ceramics and wall surfaces can be used to estimate the age of the maker.

Specific Individuals

Many individuals of the past, including some rulers of the ancient civilizations of Egypt and China, have been identified, primarily by analyzing written records that accompany the burials. In recent years, archaeologists have expanded their interest to include identifying individuals of the prehistoric past. Rather than focusing on the names and positions of leaders, current research concentrates on identifying characteristics of individual commoners, craftspeople, or artisans. This includes, for example, determining physical stress on the body by examining skeletal remains, which could provide an indication of occupation; examining special characteristics of artifacts that may indicate the work of a particular craftsperson (e.g., the way lithic tools or pots were finished); observing the wear on tools to determine if an individual was right- or left-handed; and the looking at characteristics of art to determine whether multiple pieces were created by the same or different artists.

Reconstructing Ideology

Reconstructing ideology involves making inferences about what people thought, including worldviews, beliefs, intellectual frameworks, and values. Although the material remains of ideology form an obvious part of the archaeological record, there have been relatively few attempts until recent times to establish a body of archaeological method and theory to deal with it. Inferring ideology from material remains has long been considered the most difficult of all archaeological inferences. As a major theme of archaeological research, it emerged in the late twentieth century and is often known as **cognitive archaeology**. The research primarily focuses on evidence of **sacred sites** and **religious ritual**; mortuary practices; and art. Although not routinely encountered in the archaeological record, cannibalism and trepanation are also often considered in the framework of ideology.

Sacred Sites and Religious Ritual

Sacred sites are those presumed to have religious significance. For the purpose of archaeology, religion is defined as a shared belief about supernatural powers. Religious rituals are formalized, repetitive acts associated with religious beliefs, and often take place at sacred sites.

In a seminal paper on archaeology and religion, Colin Renfrew (1994) suggests that religious ritual can be identified by material evidence that focuses attention; reflects boundary zones between this world and the next; represents images or symbols of a **deity**; and demonstrates participation and offering (Table 9.3). Site location, features, and artifacts may serve to focus attention. Mountaintops and caves are particularly common ritual sites, which in addition to providing a focus, can also represent the interface between worlds. Features such as altars, artifacts such as figurines, and repeated symbols also function to focus attention.

The boundary zones between this world and the next may also be reflected in the presence of water, such as in basins or pools. Evidence of deities may come in a variety of forms, including carved figurines, painted images, and **frescoes**, all of which may be abstract or realistic.

Evidence of participation and offering may be reflected in many ways, including art and iconography representing prayer or worship. The presence of drugs or musical instruments may represent induced religious experiences. Offerings of various kinds may also be interpreted as evidence of ritual. These include both human and animal sacrifice as well as offerings of food, drink, and artifacts.

One example of ritual that is reflected in material evidence is the practice of **capa cocha**, an Inka ritual involving the sacrifice of children to the gods on mountaintops. Pilgrimages

TABLE 9.3: Archaeological Indicators of Ritual (based on Renfrew, 1994)

Evidence that focuses attention	Special, natural locations, such as a mountaintop or cave Special building designed for religious functions, such as a church or temple Features and artifacts that focus attention, such as an altar The repetition of symbols
Evidence that suggests a boundary zone between this world and the next	Features and artifacts that promote concepts of pollution, such as pools and basins of water Architecture that may reflect both public displays and hidden mysteries
Evidence that suggests the presence of a diety	Images of the deity Animal symbolism relating to specific powers Symbols also seen in other ritual contexts, such as funerary
Evidence of participation and offering	Art and iconography reflecting prayer and worship Devices for inducing religious experiences, such as music and drugs Animal or human sacrifice Offerings of food, drink, and other material objects Great investment of wealth in the offerings and the facilities

through Inka territory, some of which took months to complete, climaxed with the sacrifice of a child on high altitude sites in the Andes. In addition to the sacrifice, a wealth of goods was offered, including figurines made of gold, silver, and exotic shell.

At least four archaeological indicators of ritual are evident in the capa cocha sites: the mountaintop locations, which represent both a place for focusing attention and a boundary zone between this world and the next; the sacrifice of children; the presence of figurines; and a great investment in time (trekking to the very high altitudes of the Andes).

Mortuary Practices

The deliberate and ritualistic postmortem treatment and disposition of the body is usually taken to indicate a belief in an afterlife. While some have suggested that disposing of bodies by burial is simply a way to remove rotting corpses, this can easily be countered with arguments that burial is far more time consuming than other means of disposition, such as simply dragging the corpse to a midden. Although not all archaeologists accept that burial indicates a belief in an afterlife, at a minimum it is taken to represent a reverence for the dead.

The presence of grave goods usually strengthens inferences about a belief in an afterlife. When the grave goods include food, this is almost always taken to affirm a belief in an afterlife. When the grave goods consist of personal artifacts, however, some archaeologists may counter that this simply represents further reverence for the dead and perhaps a belief in bad luck (from using artifacts associated with a deceased individual).

The positioning of a body may provide some indication of belief systems. It is not unusual for archaeologists to find bodies laid out in cardinal directions, such as an east-west alignment correlated with the rising and setting of the sun. The alignment of the body may even be used to make inferences about specific religions. For example, in some cemeteries that have been excavated, the individuals were buried on their side and aligned towards Mecca, suggesting the individuals were Muslim. In a study of almost 500 Inuit burials from Siberia, Alaska, and Canada, Barbara Crass (1999) identified distinctive alignments in directional orientations that she suggests can be correlated with Inuit ideology about different realms of the afterlife, with the positioning of the body directing the soul to the proper realm.

It is not uncommon for archaeologists to discover human remains buried in the fetal position, which provides an indication of people's thoughts about the life cycle. It is also not uncommon to discover **ochre** sprinkled around or painted on bodies, which also suggests belief systems strongly tied to the earth. Usually red and powdery, ochre is roughly translated in many languages as "blood of the earth."

Whether burials were individual or collective can be used to make inferences about the values of the society. When a collection of individuals buried together are identified as a family, for example, it may be inferred that the sense of family was highly valued.

Similarly, it is not uncommon for individuals to have undergone a primary burial followed by a secondary burial. In this case, individuals who were buried shortly after death would be exhumed after a number of years so that all the individuals of a group (e.g., a lineage) could then be interred together, providing evidence of the value placed on descent group.

The Meaning of Art

Both visual and performing arts are recognizable in the archaeological record, but the visual arts receive most attention. Some of the major areas of archaeological interest in art are outlined in Table 9.4.

TABLE 9.4: Major Areas of Archaeological Interest in Art (based on Corbey, Layton, and Tanner, 2004)

Iconography	Investigating the meaning of motifs
Formal	Focusing on the style of art and attempting to determine the tradition to which it belongs
Semiotic	Studying the meaning of symbols
Functionalist	Looking at the purpose of the art, such as strengthening group identity
Aesthetic	Examining how, why, and to whom the art is attractive
Structuralist	Investigating the combinations of elements of the art and the underlying thoughts they represent
Deconstructionist	Stressing the elusiveness of meaning and subjectivity of the analyst
Critical	Examining how the art reflects, legitimizes, or criticizes power
Hermeneutic	Interpreting the artist's intention through empathy and context
Processual	Studying how art contributes to how humans adapt to their environment

Pictographs and petroglyphs are often considered to be the work of shamans attempting to influence supernatural powers. This interpretation primarily comes from the fact that pictographs and petroglyphs are often located in remote and difficult-to-access locations, such as cliff faces and deep recesses of caves. Also, the style of rock art is often distinct from other art associated with the community, suggesting a different purpose. Further, pictograph images are often superimposed over each other, suggesting that it is the process of doing art, rather than the final product, that is most important.

Non-shamanistic explanations of rock art include those tied to economics and social life. Art is often seen as a mechanism of recording and measuring, which is also often seen as a component of ideology. Similarly, art is often perceived to be a reflection of gender, sexuality, and power, which are both social and ideological.

Most studies of art in the context of reconstructing ideology focus on two-dimensional artistic depictions (such as painting) as well as three-dimensional sculptures manufactured from wood, stone, clay, antler, bone, and metal. Sculptures, both large and small, are represented around the world. The **venus figurines** are one well-known type found in many sites in Europe dating between about 30,000 and 20,000 years ago. The figurines, averaging about 4.4 inches (11 centimeters) in height and made from a variety of materials, generally portray women, often with large buttocks and breasts, and explicit genitalia. Features of the face are often simple or nonexistent. There is no consensus on what these figures mean, but they are usually correlated with ideology. The figures have been variously interpreted as symbols of fertility, goddesses, or matriarchies; self-portraits by women artists; educational tools; and prehistoric pornography.

Cannibalism and Trepanation

Although not common, evidence of cannibalism does exist in the archaeological record. It isn't likely, however, that cannibalism has ever been a regular component of any group's subsistence strategy. The major types of cannibalism and its archaeological indicators are listed in Table 9.5.

Considering the amount of meat returned for the effort and risk, hunting, killing, and butchering humans does not make economic sense. Hunting deer, for example, is less dangerous (a deer isn't typically going to have a weapon to fight back), and provides more meat per individual than most humans.

Where cannibalism does occur, it is often interpreted as being opportunistic, such as when killing enemies, which is a form of both exocannibalism and vengeance can-

TABLE 9.5: Types and Archaeological Indicators of Cannibalism

Types Of Cannibalism	Definitions
Exocannibalism	Eating non-group members
Endocannibalism	Eating group members
Ritual cannibalism	Eating people, usually in very small or symbolic portions, as part of a ritual
Vengeance cannibalism	Eating your enemies
Aberrant behavior	Deranged individuals eating people
Archaeological Indicators Of Cannibalism	**Examples**
Modification to human bone	Butchery marks on human bone Artificially enlarged foramen magnum Charring or burning of human bone
Coprolites	Human coprolites containing human remains
Context	Human bone found mixed with food refuse

nibalism. This may explain why some archaeological sites exhibit some human remains that have been obviously cannibalized, while some other individuals have been buried.

Based on ethnographic observations, some evidence of cannibalism can be inferred to be ritualistic in nature. Ethnographic observations of cannibalism in recent times suggest that cannibalism usually demonstrates a reverence for the dead. When a prominent person of a particular lineage dies, for example, parts of that individual may be cannibalized by other members of the lineage in a show of respect and perhaps in the belief that they may obtain some of that person's qualities and abilities. These are examples of both endocannibalism and ritual cannibalism.

Archaeological indicators of cannibalism include bones that have been cooked, bones that have been broken in a particular fashion to get marrow, butchery marks on the bone, and disposal with other trash. These indicators are most likely to suggest that food was the primary reason for the cannibalism. Another indicator of cannibalism, particularly ritualistic cannibalism, is an artificially enlarged **foramen magnum**. A common method of extracting the brain was to extract it through the foramen magnum, which was enlarged by removing some of bone around the edges of the hole. Ethnographic observations suggest that with ritualistic cannibalism, the brain was a favored part of the body, perhaps because it was perceived to be the most likely location of person's essence.

Trepanation, also known as **trephination**, is the removal of a piece of bone from the skull. Trepanation is known to have occurred in prehistoric times in Europe, Africa, Asia, and the Americas, with more than one thousand known cases in total. Bone was typically removed by incising or drilling.

Trepanation is often considered in the context of ideology because a common explanation for the phenomena is that the procedure was done on people who may have been thought to be possessed by evil spirits, with the removal of bone providing a route for them to escape. It is also often thought to be ritualistic and maybe a medical procedure to relieve perceived pressure on the skull and perhaps some conditions like epilepsy.

Because many trepanned skulls show no signs of healing around the edges of the incised or drilled hole, it is assumed that death was not an unlikely consequence of the procedure, presumably by infection setting into the brain. Evidence of healing around the edges of the hole on many others, however, indicate that the procedure wasn't always fatal. Some individuals evidently went through the procedure up to several different times during their lifetime.

KEY RESOURCES AND SUGGESTED READING

Major works on reconstructing identity include *The Archaeology of Ethnicity: Constructing Identities in the Past and Present* by Jones (1999) and *Archaeological Approaches to Cultural Identity* by Shennan (1989). Two special thematic issues of the *SAA Archaeological Record* in 2004 focused on ethnicity. The subject of children in the archaeological record is covered in *The Archaeology of Childhood* by Baxter (2005) and an entire issue of *World Archaeology* (volume 32, no. 2, 2000) is devoted to queer archaeology. The archaeology of religion, including ritual is covered in *The Ancient Mind: Elements of Cognitive Archaeology* by Renfew and Zubrow (1994).

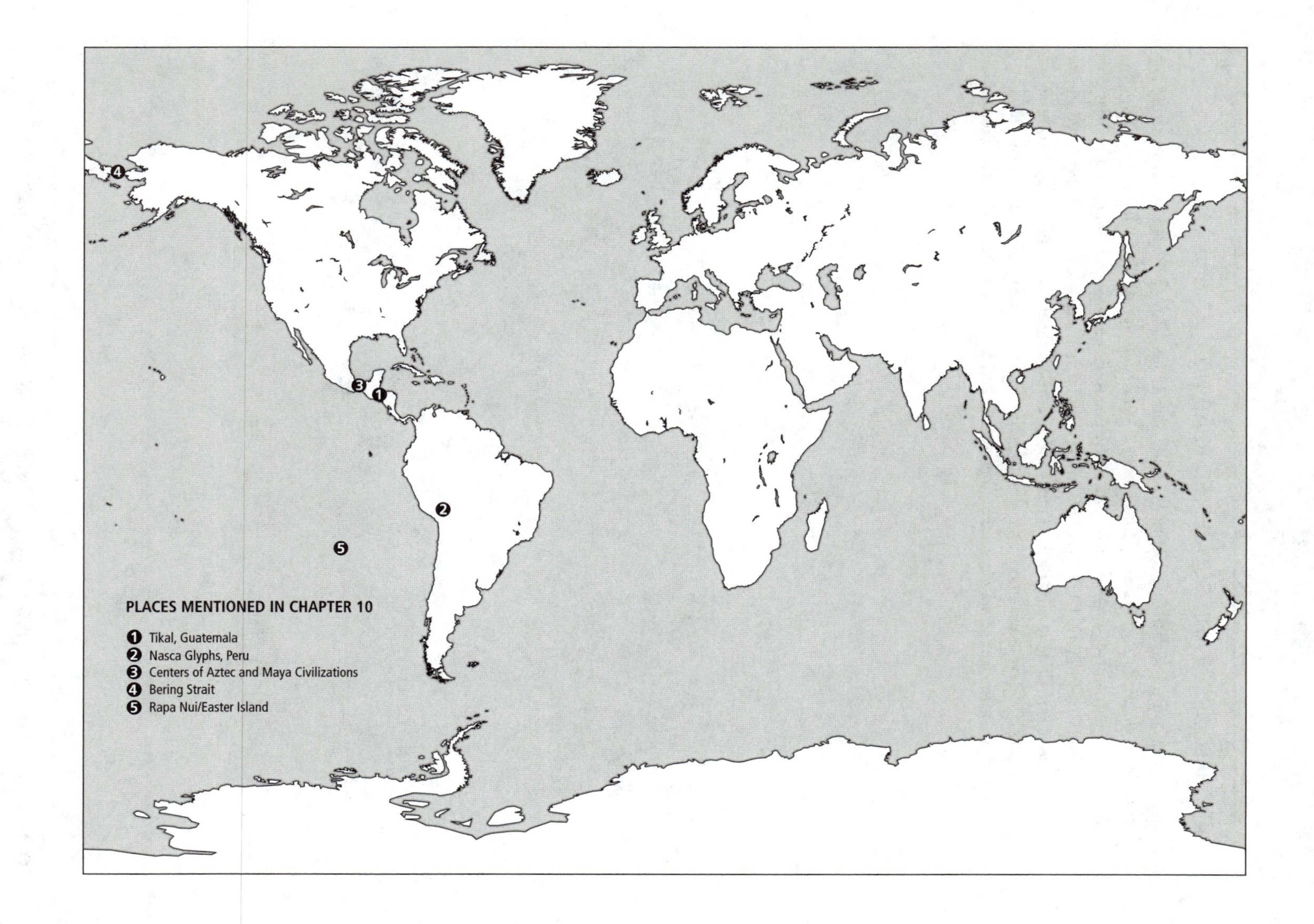
PLACES MENTIONED IN CHAPTER 10
1 Tikal, Guatemala
2 Nasca Glyphs, Peru
3 Centers of Aztec and Maya Civilizations
4 Bering Strait
5 Rapa Nui/Easter Island

CHAPTER 10

Explaining Things of Archaeological Interest

Introduction

This chapter focuses on explaining how and why things change. To situate the kinds of things that archaeologists need to explain, it begins with an overview of three levels of archaeological research. It then focuses on culture change, covering its mechanisms and conceptual frameworks, and explanations for the rise of food production and the collapse of civilizations. The final sections examine bias in archaeological explanations and how archaeologists evaluate competing hypotheses.

Three Levels of Archaeological Research

Archaeological work usually falls within one of three levels (Table 10.1) **Low-level research**, also known as low-range research, constitutes most types of field and laboratory work. It involves such things as finding, recording, and excavating sites as well as basic laboratory analysis. Although ultimately governed by some theoretical considerations in the research design, low-level research is the least explicitly theoretical aspect of archaeology. Reconstruction of culture history may also be thought of as low-level research. Matthew Johnson (1999: 4–7) describes the theoretical aspect of low-level research as follows:

> In practice, every day of our working lives as archaeologists, *we decide on which order to put our facts in*, what degree of importance to place on different pieces of evidence. When we do this, we use theoretical criteria to decide which facts are important and which are not worth bothering with.... What makes us archaeologists as opposed to mindless collectors of old junk is *the set of rules we use to translate those facts into meaningful accounts of the past*, accounts that "make sense" to us as archaeologists and (it is hoped) to our general audience. And those rules, whether they are implicit or explicit, are theoretical in nature. Facts are important, but without theory they remain utterly silent.

TABLE 10.1: Three Levels of Archaeological Research

Low-level research	The least explicitly theoretical aspect of archaeology Includes most kinds of field and laboratory work and the reconstruction of culture history Includes such things as recording sites and describing artifacts
Middle-level research	Attempts to understand the patterning of material remains, primarily through ethnoarchaeology, experimental archaeology, and studies of taphonomy
High-level research	Focuses on explaining significant events in the human past and understanding how various parts of cultures influence each other and why cultures change

Middle-level research, also known as middle-range research or **middle-range theory**, is most often identified with ethnoarchaeology, experimental archaeology, and taphonomy. The study of site formation and disturbance processes clearly falls within the realm of middle-range research. Middle-range research provides the links between the material remains observed by the archaeologist and human behavior. It can then be used to make broader inferences about cultures and culture change.

High-level research, also known as **grand theory** or **general theory,** attempts to explain significant events in the human past and the basic nature of cultures, including how the various parts of cultures influence each other and why cultures change. Research at this level is the most explicitly theoretical, and includes studies of what are commonly referred to as revolutionary developments or big events in the history of humankind (Table 10.2).

The production of food and the collapse of civilizations are perhaps the two types

TABLE 10.2: Major Areas of Grand Theoretical Interest in Archaeology

The rise of social complexity
The collapse of civilizations
The origins of tool use and tool making
The development of home bases and division of labor
The origins of abstract thought
Migrations and expansions of territory in prehistory
The origins of food production

of major events that have both academic and popular appeal. The conditions under which these events occur are discussed in more detail later in this chapter.

Many other types of archaeological work fall under the category of high-level research. Studying the use and production of tools involves determining the antiquity of the establishment of tool making (currently reliably dated to about 2.5 million years ago) and the conditions under which the spread of new technologies throughout prehistory occurred—including stone tools, fire, spears, **atlatls**, and bows and arrows. Biological anthropologists and archaeologists are both interested in the development of home bases and the division of labor, and study in this area involves determining the antiquity of these events and the conditions under which they occurred. Archaeological interest in the origins of abstract thought includes examining the development of and evidence for speech, art, and beliefs. Studies of migration and territorial expansion focus on the initial spread of the genus *Homo* out of Africa close to 2 million years ago, the expansion of modern *Homo sapiens* throughout Africa, Asia, and Europe beginning about 100,000 years ago, and migrations to Australia about 50,000 years ago and to the Americas at least 12,000 years ago. Studies of the rise of social complexity focus on understanding the conditions that lead to different forms of inequality and types of societies, including the emergence of states and civilizations.

Mechanisms of Culture Change

There are two basic kinds of culture change: **synchronic change**, meaning change through space, and **diachronic change**, meaning change through time. The major mechanisms of cultural change include *in situ* evolution, diffusion, trade, and migration.

Studies of synchronic change usually focus on the mechanisms under which ideas and materials spread relatively quickly through broad areas, such as continents or hemispheres. Diffusion, trade, and migration are the usual explanations for synchronic change.

Studies of diachronic change also examine expansive geographic areas, but focus as well on explaining change in specific sites. *In situ* evolution in specific sites or regions can be established by observing the same basic pattern of culture persisting through time, although a few major changes and many minor ones may occur. Sometimes major and relatively sudden changes, in settlement patterns or subsistence strategies for example, are thought to be indicative of population movements, but they are often *in situ* adaptations to changes in the environment. Changes in house size during prehistoric times in some areas of North America, for example, are strongly correlated with significant alterations in temperature. The incorporation of certain types of fish and shellfish in diets is correlated with the stabilization of rivers and sea levels (which is assumed to have led to increased productivity of these resources).

Invention is the primary mechanism of *in situ* technological change. Generally defined as the creation of a new artifact type, invention is identified in the archaeological record by the discovery of prototypes. Much like mutations are the ultimate source of change in biological evolution, invention may be seen as the ultimate source of change in technology. Archaeologists also often refer to innovation, which is usually taken to mean the application of an existing technology in a new way. For example, the technology of firing clay to make ceramic figurines (evident about 25,000 years ago) was later applied to the making of pottery (beginning about 12,000 years ago).

Diffusion (the spread of ideas) is undeniably the principal source of cultural change. It is widely agreed that more than 90 per cent of the traits of any one culture, past and present, have spread through diffusion. The notion that good ideas spread quickly is not new, and applies to the simplest stone tools dating to more than two million years ago and electronic technology in contemporary times. It is not necessary to find evidence of the physical movement of material technology, whether through trade or changing populations, to explain why new technologies appear suddenly in a culture. But because diffusion deals with the spread of ideas rather than material objects, it is somewhat difficult to identify with certainty in the archaeological record. Inferences about diffusion are often based on the relatively sudden incorporation of a technology, with no apparent prototypes in the area. Examples include the spread of atlatls and bows and arrows around the world during prehistory.

Trace-element analysis of raw material often indicates an artifact was acquired through trade. Many types of stone, such as obsidian, exhibit trace elements that are unique to the original source. Trade routes and spheres of interaction are often established by linking sites with specific raw materials to their original source. Chemical fingerprinting of obsidian, for example, indicates that it has been traded over the past 10,000 years though various linguistic and ethnic areas of the Pacific Northwest.

Specific kinds of seashells are also often used to infer trade. Shells studies have demonstrated that shells were a part of extensive trade networks extending thousands of miles in both North and South America. Conch shells from the Gulf of Mexico, for example, have been found in archaeological sites in Ohio and Manitoba.

Migration, which infers the replacement of one ethnic population with another, is commonly used to explain cultural change. Archaeological indicators of migration include the relatively sudden occurrence of multiple cultural traits, including new settlement patterns, subsistence strategies, diet, artifact types, art, and burial practices. This includes the use of local raw materials in new ways, such as obsidian suddenly being used for making jewelry instead of for arrowheads. Inferences about migration are more credible if they are supported by significant and sudden differences in skeletal remains and if the homeland of the migrant population can be identified, based on the similarities of cultural traits.

Conceptual Frameworks

Archaeologists seeking to explain cultural change usually identify with a particular **conceptual framework**, also commonly known as a **paradigm**, research strategy, grand theory, or **heuristic theory**. These frameworks provide starting points and guides for archaeologists in their research.

Describing the nature of such frameworks, Philip Salzman (2004: 30–32) defines and describes heuristic theories as:

> [those] that guide our inquiries. Heuristic theories are very general in the sense that they are very abstract and purport to cover myriad facts from many times and places.... Heuristic theories guide anthropological thought by offering a vision of social and cultural reality and directing attention to what it deems important. Each heuristic theory proposes a way of looking at the world, a way of carrying out research, and a way of understanding research findings.... Heuristic theories cannot really be tested to see whether they are true of false but instead are generally judged to be useful or not useful, fruitful or not fruitful in generating interesting results.

Table 10.3 lists a sample of conceptual frameworks used in archaeology. Unilinear cultural evolution is of historical use only, and many others (e.g., annales school, catastrophe and chaos theories, environmental determinism, Darwinian archaeology, and sociobiology) are not commonly used. The dominant frameworks used in archaeology in the early twenty-first century fall into the broader categories of materialist, social, and ideological.

Materialist Frameworks

Materialist frameworks assume that the driving force of cultural change lies within the sphere of ecology, including changes in the environment, economy, technology, or demography. Cultural ecology and cultural materialism are materialist frameworks, and they have been the dominant conceptual frameworks in archaeology for the past several decades. The basic idea is that all, or almost all, cultural change is triggered by something that initially occurred within the ecological sphere. Archaeologists using materialist frameworks tend to consider the ecological sphere of culture as the most important, and view aspects of culture change in the social and ideological spheres as primarily reflections of or repercussions from occurrences in the ecological sphere. Religion, values, patterns of social inequality, and type of society can be all explained by an initial change in environment, technology, economy, or demography.

TABLE 10.3: Conceptual Frameworks in Archaeology

Agency theory	Focuses on intentional actions of individuals in creating change
Annales school	Stresses the interrelationship of short- and long-term events
Catastrophe theory	Views culture change as a buildup of minor factors that suddenly overload a cultural system, causing major changes
Chaos theory	Views culture change as being caused by small-scale and apparently random phenomena
Cognitive idealism	Views ideology as the driving force of culture change
Conflict theory	Focuses on social conflict within and between cultures
Critical theory	Focuses on the inner, hidden workings of societies (Also known as the Frankfurt School)
Cultural ecology	Focuses on the interrelationship between humans and the natural environment
Cultural materialism	Focuses on the environment, economy, technology, and demography as the driving force of culture change
Darwinian archaeology	Modeled after Charles Darwin's theory of biological evolution, but with "cultural," rather than biological traits being subject to selection processes
Diffusionism	Focuses on the spread of ideas
Environmental determinism	Views culture as primarily an adaptation to natural environments
Feminist archaeology	Focuses on females in the archaeological record
Functionalism	Focuses on the interrelationship of the various components of a culture
Historical particularism	Views the evolution of each culture as being unique
Marxist archaeology	Focuses on the economy and conflict between classes
Sociobiology	Views cultural behavior as driven by biology
Structuralism	Focusing on social systems and institutions
Unilinear cultural evolution	Views cultural evolution as following a singular, predetermined course. Of historical interest only. No longer considered valid.

Social Frameworks

Social frameworks begin by assuming that cultural change may be initiated in the social sphere of culture. Archaeologists using social frameworks look first to social phenomena as a cause of change in all aspects of culture, including the ecological and ideological spheres. Common social frameworks in archaeology are conflict theory, feminist archaeology, and Marxist archaeology.

Ideological Frameworks

Ideological frameworks start with the basic assumption that the ideological sphere of culture initiates culture change, with repercussions in the social and ecological spheres. Agency theory and cognitive idealism (also known as cognitivism) are considered ideological frameworks.

The conceptual framework an archaeologist uses usually reflects the way she or he thinks cultures work. Most people have some ideas about what the most important parts of culture are, although outside of academia, labels such as "conceptual frameworks" and "paradigms" are rarely used.

Consider, for example, aid agencies seeking assistance for an impoverished people. Change may be initiated in different ways for the overall betterment of the people. Some groups may wish to send tractors or new varieties of high-producing crops to the area, reasoning that once the economy is taken care of, everything else will fall into place. These groups are working within a materialist framework. Other groups, also claiming to be working for the betterment of all in the region, may wish to replace a particular leader or overthrow the government—clearly working within a social framework. Others may wish to instigate change in the ideological sphere, reasoning that if you can change people's beliefs and values, then everything else will fall into place.

Another example can also serve to illustrate the different frameworks. Imagine three different experts attempting explain the rise of youth violence. One expert, using a materialist framework, suggests that it has been caused by lack of permanent, well-paying jobs for youth. Another expert, using a social framework, may believe the root cause of youth violence lies in the breakdown of the nuclear family. The final expert, using an ideological framework, may attribute the cause to the decreasing participation of youth in church activities and subsequent loss of moral guidance.

Although both examples above (i.e., aid for impoverished people and youth violence) provide materialist, social, and ideological views, no one view is necessarily better than the other. Each view is based on the sphere of a culture the people involved believe is most important to initiating or explaining change.

The fact that conceptual frameworks are neither right nor wrong, true or false, means that there will always be disagreements among archaeologists about why cultures change. Choosing a conceptual framework to guide research is an archaeologist's personal choice, based on a plethora of factors, including but certainly not limited to his or her own evaluations, experience, and belief systems.

The need for choosing a conceptual framework to guide research is perplexing for many newcomers to archaeology. Those who have studied or practiced archaeology for a period of time, however, usually understand the necessity. Archaeologists recognize that facts do not speak for themselves, and there is no objective truth. At a very elementary level, conceptual frameworks narrow down the types of facts that are collected. The types of data that can be collected to explain any phenomena are almost infinite. Conceptual frameworks serve to organize thoughts and define the methods of research.

Because there is no agreement on a universal research strategy, and never will be, debates will always be a part of archaeology. It is unlikely, for example, that consensus on the conditions underlying the origins of food production and the collapse of civilizations will ever exist.

Explaining the Transition to Food Production

Food production is the term used to describe the advent of plant and animal domestication, which led to pastoralism, horticulture, and agriculture. Early theorists postulated that a solitary genius had come up with the idea for food production or that plants were accidentally discovered growing in middens. They then invoked diffusion to explain the relatively widespread adoption of food production around the world. Food production has long been considered a milestone in human development, and prior to the 1960s, most assumed that it made life better overall for those who made the transition, by creating more leisure time and better health.

In the mid-twentieth century, as ethnographers and ethnoarchaeologists began research on various groups of food producers (pastoralists, horticulturalists, and agriculturalists), and non-food producers (generalized foragers) in the contemporary world, and as bioarchaeologists studied the activity of those groups in the past, it became clear that life for the earliest food producers was probably more difficult than for foragers. In particular, ethnographic research showed that food producers work longer in subsistence activities than non-food producers. Thus, foragers have more leisure time than food producers. Research from bioarchaeology showed that early food producers suffered worse nutrition and health than foragers.

Once archaeologists realized that food production did not immediately lead to a better life overall, they discounted all the early hypotheses that saw only the benefits

ROBERT J. MUCKLE

FIGURE 10.1: AGRICULTURE IN EGYPT. A primary area of interest in archaeological research is to understand the conditions that led to the transition to reliance on domestic foods. This photo illustrates a water buffalo rigged to a wheel mechanism designed to enable the irrigation of fields

and none of the ill effects of relying on domestic foods. In recent decades, archaeologists have been examining other potential benefits that may have been viewed as a worthy trade-off to increased work and worse health.

One of the most oft-cited benefits of food production is that it supports larger populations and allows increased sedentism. The debate, however, is whether these are really advantages. There is no doubt that domestication, because of the increased productivity of plants and animals, supports higher populations, but many people would argue that higher populations, with all that they bring in the form of conflict and transmission of disease, may be at least as much a disadvantage. While domestication also clearly allows increased sedentism, not all view that as an advantage either. Many foragers, for example, place a high value on mobility and resist efforts to become sedentary. However, sedentism allows for the accumulation of material things, and some perceive this to be an acceptable trade-off for more work and worse health. In Western industrialized nations, it is not uncommon for people to work very long hours, often leading to deteriorating health, so that they can drive nice cars, live in nice houses, and have an array of electronic gadgets.

Many archaeologists focus on the fact that increased productivity of plants and animals can provide a surplus of food to be used in times of stress on the natural resources.

Others argue, however, that since food production tends to focus on considerably fewer plants and animals than a foraging way of life, it is actually riskier. They reason that if a particular disease decimates one or two wild plant or animal species in a region, foragers can still rely on the dozens of others they normally use. But if a disease were to hit one or two of the crops or animal species upon which food producers rely, the results would be catastrophic for the people.

Few archaeologists would dispute that people were aware of their ability to increase the productivity of plants and animals. People likely did some occasional weeding and watering of plants and perhaps ensured supplies of food and water for animals long before these activities emerged in the forms we recognize as pastoralism and horticulture. Research by archaeologists, ethnobotanists, geographers, and others shows that prior to the arrival of Europeans, the indigenous peoples of the northwest coast of North America managed their landscapes, plants, and animals in a variety of ways to increase productivity, without reaching the stage known as domestication. These management techniques included weeding, burning, transplanting, removing rocks from clam beds, and introducing some types of fish into waterways in which little or no productivity of those species previously existed.

Contemporary archaeological explanations of the transition to food production can be considered in the context of materialist, social, and ideological frameworks.

Materialist explanations often invoke **population pressure** as the trigger for food production, reasoning that there was no longer enough food to support the extant population numbers. In other words, the carrying capacity of the region was no longer large enough to support the population. This may have been caused by environmental changes. For example, the wild plants and animals in a local area may have supported a population of about one thousand for many thousands of years. Then, due to any of a number of environmental changes, the wild resources were only sufficient to support about nine hundred. This reduction in food availability led to population pressure, and the people eventually had to spend more time in food production or reduce their population size. They chose food production.

Explanations within social frameworks suggest that the trigger for the transition lay in the social sphere of cultures. Some adherents of this view suggest that it was the acquisition of increased social status that led to food production. For example, leaders who wished to raise their status may have put pressure on their kin groups to create food surpluses for feasting or trade, further elevating their status and wealth. Another social explanation is that domestication originated as a way to use the marginal members of societies, such as children and the elderly.

Ideological frameworks provide various explanations for food production, and most consider the domestication of plants and animals for subsistence to be a by-product of ideology. One such explanation is that domestication is a by-product of shamanism, reasoning that the first domesticates may have been pharmaceuticals. James Pearson (2002) suggests that shamanism might have been an underlying factor in the origin of agriculture because the experience with pharmaceutical plants may have been transferred to food plants. Others reason that food production was a by-product of producing plants for alcohol, leading humorist Dan Murphy (2002) to write, "There are academics who now think that we gave up our nomadic ways and started tilling the soil mostly so we could get the hops and rye and grapes with which to concoct drinks. If they're right, it means that the cocktail is the basis of civilization. And we settled in towns and cities primarily so our waiters could find us."

It is worth considering that people making the transition to food production did not necessarily know the disadvantages. However, once started, it is near impossible to revert to a foraging way of life without significant reductions in population. Both archaeology and history have demonstrated that as carrying capacity increases, human populations invariably also increase to catch up.

In his article titled "The Worst Mistake in the History of the Human Race," science writer Jared Diamond (1987) considers all the disadvantages of domestication and concludes that "forced to choose between limiting population or trying to increase food production, we chose the latter and ended up with starvation, warfare, and tyranny."

Explaining the Collapse of Civilizations

All civilizations collapse, eventually. The collapse of individual civilizations and of civilizations in general is a topic of much interest and debate in archaeology. Table 10.4 lists some of the explanations for collapse, within materialist, social, and ideological frameworks.

The most common materialist explanations for the collapse of civilizations, both in particular and in general, tend to focus on the degradation of soils used for growing crops and ever-increasing populations. One common explanation is that with growing populations and the correlated need for larger amounts of food, fields were not left fallow long enough to replenish the nutrients for productive crops. Consequently, the amount of food that was produced began a continual decline until the population could no longer be supported. Other materialist explanations suggest the following reasons: population growth increased faster than crop yields could keep up, salts left by irrigation water rendered the soils unsuitable, climate change caused droughts, and epidemic diseases damaged crops.

Social explanations for the collapse of civilizations include internal conflict, warfare, and failure to maintain trading alliances. Explanations involving internal conflict

TABLE 10.4: Explanations for the Collapse of Civilizations

Materialist	Ecological catastrophe (e.g., earthquakes, volcanic eruptions) Climatic change (e.g., drought) Epidemic diseases to crops Depletion of soil nutrients through overuse Rendering the land useless through irrigation, leading to increased salinity of soil Overpopulation
Social	Collapse of trading networks Warfare with other groups Peasant revolts and other forms of internal conflict
Ideological	Too much effort spent on religious activities, drawing people away from the agricultural labor force Fatalism, stemming from religious prophecy forecasting doom

usually suggest a class revolt of some kind or ethnic rebellions within empires, which require that resources normally allocated to agriculture be redirected to the conflict, leading to the collapse of the economic system.

Ideological explanations often suggest that excessive resources were expended in religious activities. For example, the construction of religious monuments may have drawn people away from the agricultural labor pool, and that may have started a chain reaction of events. In the first year of construction, the reasoning goes, crop production may have been reduced, and this reduction was then interpreted as evidence that the gods were unsatisfied. Therefore, people may have further increased their religious activity in the next year, making that year's crop even worse, and so on.

Another ideological explanation suggests that collapses resulted from a degree of fatalism, reasoning that religious prophecies predicted doom, and people simply accepted it. It has been suggested, for example, that when the Spanish became a threat to the Aztecs about 500 years ago, the Aztec emperor was a fatalist who believed in omens of disaster. To the emperor, overthrow by aliens was inevitable, and the Aztec strategies for dealing with the Spanish were formulated with this assumption in mind.

Understanding Bias in Archaeological Explanations

Table 10.5 lists some of the types of bias in archaeological explanation. Some kinds of bias are obvious and others are not. One of the most obvious is the inherent bias of

SUZANNE VILLENEUVE

FIGURE 10.2: TIKAL, Guatemala. A major Mayan site, with population estimates ranging up to 200,000, Tikal (like many other Mayan sites) was abandoned relatively suddenly about 1,000 years ago. Understanding the conditions leading to the collapse of civilizations is a primary area of interest in archaeology.

TABLE 10.5: Major Kinds of Bias in Archaeological Explanations

Inherent bias of the archaeological record
Bias of conceptual frameworks
Bias of age
Bias of sex
Bias of nationality
Bias of ethnicity
Bias of training and education
Bias of time and place

the archaeological record. As outlined in Chapter 4, this includes the bias the original inhabitants showed when they chose what to abandon or discard and what to recycle or keep. It also includes preservation bias, such as the fact that stone and clay are more likely to preserve than metal and organic remains.

The bias of conceptual frameworks should be at least equally obvious. As outlined earlier in this chapter, the conceptual framework an archaeologist chooses usually reflects what he or she perceives to be the most important sphere of culture and the driving force of cultural change. This kind of conceptual bias can usually be seen in the introductory sections of research articles. The bias is rarely explicitly stated, but after reading the first few paragraphs of an article, the basic assumptions of the author usually become obvious. Materialist frameworks are the ones most commonly used by archaeologists over the past several decades. The bias towards materialist frameworks may stem from the fact that archaeologists deal mostly with remains that are directly related to the ecological sphere of culture (e.g., physical remains of environments, settlement patterns, subsistence, and diet), leading to a tendency to overemphasize their importance.

Biases of age, sex, nationality, and ethnicity may also be obvious. Our perspectives are colored by who we are. People of different ages, sexes, nationalities, and ethnic groups have different experiences and agendas. Like many academic disciplines, the history of archaeology has been shadowed with heavy male bias, although this has begun to change significantly in recent decades. One example of this bias is the focus in the archaeological record on what are generally perceived to be male activities, such as hunting and warfare. Similarly, throughout most of its history, archaeological research could fairly be called **Eurocentric**. A study of atlases of "world prehistory" by Chris Scarre (1990) showed an extreme bias towards European prehistory. In a sample of archaeological atlases produced by European publishers, Scarre found that despite purporting to be about world prehistory, they devoted about 30 per cent of their space to Europe and more than 20 per cent to the Near East. The UNESCO list of World Heritage Sites is similarly biased in that Europe is over-represented. Post-processual archaeologists often make biases of age, sex, nationality, and ethnicity explicit. Most others do not.

The bias of training and education may not be so obvious, but is nevertheless important to understand. Students are usually heavily influenced by their professors. One of the reasons it is usually considered preferable for professional archaeologists to receive their degrees (B.A., M.A., and Ph.D.) at different universities is that it exposes them to a variety of frameworks, ideas, and experiences.

The biases of time and place are among the least obvious, but perhaps most important, to understand. It has become increasingly apparent in recent years that whether consciously or not, archaeologists are strongly influenced by current events. Examples include explanations of European cave art and the collapse of the Mayan civilization.

Paul Bahn (2000) shows how explanations of European cave art reflect obsessions and prejudices of the times. In the late nineteenth and early twentieth centuries, simplistic notions about "primitive" people correlated with the idea that the cave art must have been mindless graffiti, play activity, or associated with magic. The sexual revolution of the 1960s is correlated with a plethora of studies examining the sexuality depicted in the cave art; the general interest in space exploration is correlated with interpretations of cave art as astronomical in nature; the burgeoning use of computers led to descriptions of the art as "a series of giant floppy disks or CD-ROMs"; and the legacy of drug culture and its associated hallucinogens and altered states of consciousness is correlated with explanations that the art reflects trance imagery.

In the article, "The Ancient Maya and the Political Present," Richard Wilk (1985) examined explanations for the collapse of the Maya in the context of American history, suggesting that archaeological explanations by Americans are influenced by informal and often hidden philosophical and political debates. Explanations pointing to warfare, most prominent in the 1960s, are strongly correlated with American military involvement in Vietnam. Ecological explanations, gaining prominence in the 1970s, are strongly correlated with environmental movements of the time; and ideological explanations parallel the rise of religious fundamentalism, also in the 1970s. This trend has continued, with researchers observing that the rise of economic explanations in the 1990s occurred in tandem with economic globalization during that time, and the recent shift back to explanations of warfare correlate with American concerns with terrorism and war. The implication is that the current events surrounding archaeologists on a daily basis through popular media are likely to affect the way they think about the past.

Evaluating Competing Explanations

Table 10.6 outlines criteria for evaluating explanations in archaeology. These criteria are a guide, part of the package called critical thinking skills.

TABLE 10.6: Criteria for Evaluating Archaeological Explanations

Is the hypothesis testable?	If not, consider it no further
Is the hypothesis compatible with our general understanding of the archaeological record?	If not, be cautious
Can the hypothesis be used to explain more phenomena than competing explanations?	In general, the more phenomena a hypothesis can explain, the better
Occam's Razor	The simplest explanation is usually the best
Have all competing explanations been considered equally?	Do not accept one hypothesis by merely rejecting the others

The idea that explanations are testable is fundamental to all scientific inquiry. Quite simply, if the hypothesis cannot be tested empirically, then it should be considered no further. Gods and extraterrestrial aliens may exist, but there is no empirical evidence of their presence. Therefore, explanations relying on god(s), aliens, or other supernatural phenomena are simply not acceptable in archaeology. When faced with a hypothesis, archaeologists should first ask if there is a way of testing it with material remains.

In general, hypotheses that are compatible with our general understanding of the archaeological record are more likely to be accepted than those that are not compatible. Despite recent claims that the first migrants to the Americas may have come via the North Atlantic Ocean or the South Pacific, the hypothesis that they came from northeast Asia via the area around the Bering Strait remains the most plausible explanation for most archaeologists. The Bering Strait route is most compatible with our understanding of world prehistory, which places people in northeast Asia prior to the Americas, and provides evidence of similarities in culture.

Hypotheses that can explain several phenomena are usually considered to be better than others. This is often referred to as the explanatory power of the hypothesis. A hypothesis that explains the collapse of all or many civilizations, for example, is usually considered better than one that explains the collapse of a single civilization.

Occam's Razor, also known as Occam's Rule, is based on the notion that the simplest explanation is usually the best, and the simplest explanation is the one requiring the fewest assumptions. It is named after William of Occam, the thirteenth-century philosopher who developed it.

It is good practice to consider all explanations equally. A common mistake is to begin with a series of possible explanations and then systematically eliminate them one by one until there is only one remaining, and then declare that hypothesis the best.

Almost all explanations invoking gods or aliens use this approach, ruling out all sorts of explanations that can be empirically tested and then concluding the phenomena must be attributable to a god, extraterrestrials, or some other supernatural phenomena.

Figure 10.3 illustrates the image of a hummingbird in the Nasca desert of Peru. It is one of the dozens of animal figures that, along with hundreds of miles of straight lines, concentric circles, and geometric shapes, collectively are known as the Nasca glyphs. They were evidently created by sweeping the top layers of pebbles on the desert to expose the lighter soil underneath, and research indicates that they were created about 1,000 years ago.

Many people have proposed explanations for the glyphs. One common archaeological explanation suggests they served as sacred pathways and symbols.

Competing explanations by non-archaeologists often invoke the influence of extraterrestrial aliens. The leading proponent of the extraterrestrial influence is Erich von Daniken, author of several books promoting supposed evidence of extraterrestrial aliens on Earth and currently associated with Mystery Park, an archaeological theme park in Switzerland (see Figure 1.3, page 10). According to von Daniken, the straight lines may have been landing strips for alien spacecraft, and the images may have been created by earthlings based on instructions from the aliens.

When we go through the criteria for evaluating competing explanations for the glyphs, we need look no further than testablility. The hypothesis that they were landing strips for alien spaceships or were created under instructions by aliens is simply not testable. But it is certainly easy enough to empirically test the hypothesis that they are sacred pathways. In fact, data has been collected depicting similar images on the pottery of the Nasca people of the time, and ethnographic and historic research shows numerous examples of people walking straight lines as part of religious rituals.

The sacred pathway and symbol hypothesis also wins as the most compatible with our current understanding of the archaeological record. The lines and images are both compatible with Nasca culture. The alien hypothesis is not compatible at all. The application of Occam's Razor suggests a clear preference for the archaeological hypothesis of sacred pathways as well. The only assumption that has to be accepted for the sacred pathway and symbol hypothesis is that the Nasca people had the capability to create the lines (which experiments have demonstrated to be quite simple). Supporting the

CORBIS

FIGURE 10.3: HUMMINGBIRD GLYPH ON THE NASCA DESERT. Dozens of animal forms and several hundred miles of straight lines are found in the Nasca desert. Archaeologists have no problem correlating them with the Nasca peoples living in the area 1,000 years ago, although some other people prefer to believe they are associated with extraterrestrial aliens.

alien hypothesis, on the other hand, requires assumptions that extraterrestrials exist, have come to Earth and landed their craft, and have had successful communication with earthlings who have then followed instructions in creating the animal images.

The Nasca glyphs are among hundreds of sites and features throughout the world for which popular, non-scientific explanations invoking lost civilizations, extraterrestrials, and supernatural forces abound. Other well-known examples include Stonehenge, the statues of Easter Island (Rapa Nui), and purported evidence of Atlantis. As with the Nasca glyphs, it is difficult to accept the non-scientific explanations when pitted against archaeological explanations and evaluated against the stated criteria. Proponents of the non-archaeological explanations often prey upon the fallacy that people without a European heritage were not smart enough or did not have the intrinsic cultural imperatives to construct monumental architecture and other large-scale features. Research in archaeology and anthropology suggests the opposite is quite true—people throughout the world in prehistoric and recent times had both the ability and the imperative.

KEY RESOURCES AND SUGGESTED READING

Conceptual frameworks are covered in *Theoretical Archaeology* by Dark (1995), *Archaeological Theory: An Introduction*, by Johnson (1999), and *A History of Archaeological Thought* by Trigger (1989). Research on the management of wild plants and animals by foragers is covered in *Keeping it Living: Traditions of Plant Use and Cultivation on the Northwest Coast of North America*, by Deur and Turner (2005). The collapse of civilizations has received considerable recent attention. *The Collapse of Ancient States and Civilizations* by Yoffee and Cowgill (2001) is an academic treatment while Jared Diamond's (2005) *Collapse: How Societies Choose to Fail or Succeed* and Ronald Wright's (2004) *A Short History of Progress* are geared for the general reader. Debunking popular, non-archaeological ideas about the past is the subject of *Frauds, Myths, and Mysteries: Science and Pseudoscience in Archaeology, 5th ed* by Feder (2006).

Epilogue

The Current State of Archaeology

In addition to summarizing some of the key points in the book, this section provides some additional information on job prospects in archaeology and the principal issues within the discipline today.

Some years ago, archaeologist Patty Jo Watson identified five historical uses of archaeological data: (i) to supply information about collectors' items and museum objects, (ii) to furnish documentation for art history and the history of architecture, (iii) to comprehend sequences of events and chronologies in the absence of written documents, (iv) to help support much fuller historical studies in order to make particular events better known, and (v) to furnish independent data for testing hypotheses about culture process geared to discovering rules about how cultures change. We can now add several more uses of archaeological data to this list: (i) to contextualize current events, such as warfare, (ii) to support global social movements, such as feminism, conservation, and indigenous empowerment, (iii) to demonstrate the importance of heritage, (iv) to evaluate ideas about the past, (v) to contribute to the economy through the heritage industry, and (vi) to bring awareness and offer solutions to some important problems of living in the twenty-first century.

The current state of archaeology, at least as it exists in North America, is perhaps best summed up by Geoffrey Clarke in the article "American Archaeology's Uncertain Future" (2003: 61):

> In sum, American archaeology at the beginning of the twenty-first century is many things. At a minimum, it is a science-like endeavor, an industry (the "heritage industry"), a platform for promoting various political agendas, a medium for educating the public, and an exercise in public relations. As before, it has academic, private, museum, and government aspects, but these different constituents coexist in an uneasy alliance with each other brought about by very real differences in interests, attitudes, and objectives.

It is tough to make a decent living in archaeology without obtaining at least a master's degree. A 2005 salary survey initiated by the Society for American Archaeology in cooperation with the Society for Historical Archaeology received more than 2,000 respondents (Association Research Inc. 2005) Of these, 93 per cent had an M.A. or Ph.D., and about 7 per cent had a B.A. only. The results also showed that individual salaries often depended on education, experience, and location. The median salary of archaeologists was $50,000. The average salary for those with a bachelor's degree was a little more than $40,000, and for those with a Ph.D., it was a little more than $61,000. Not surprisingly, university professors and owners of archaeology contracting firms were among the highest paid. A few short decades ago, almost everyone in archaeology worked for academic institutions, museums, or government. In the early twenty-first century, most archaeologists work within the field of cultural resource management.

There are many issues and debates in archaeology today. Some of these are of purely academic or scholarly interest, such as the issue of competing explanations of past events in prehistory or the pros and cons of various conceptual frameworks. For those working in academic institutions within North America, the issue of whether archaeology should continue to operate within the umbrella of anthropology is significant. Other issues, such as enforcement of heritage legislation, pay equity, and working conditions are most dominant in the areas of cultural resource management. Curation is an issue facing almost every archaeologist who engages in fieldwork, especially the question of how to deal with the ever-increasing numbers of collections and the rising costs of storage space.

Predicting the Future of Archaeology

In the article "A Forecast for American Archaeology," Lawrence Moore (2005) outlines some of the changes that archaeologists can expect from American society as it transforms over the next few decades, based in part on demographics and economic forecasts. Moore suggests that public archaeology in particular is an industry that needs to be successfully developed to take advantage of the changes in society. Demand for those doing public outreach will increase. In the event of an economic depression, archaeology may manage quite well, at least if what happened during past depressions is considered. For example, Moore notes that during the 1930s, archaeological associations such as the SAA were created, archaeology departments at big universities were built, and fieldwork was federally funded.

The use of sophisticated technologies is likely to increase in field and laboratory work. Despite the potential application of high-tech field and laboratory methods in some research projects, the fact remains that most projects are still relatively low-tech due to budget constraints. Many archaeological projects are quite small in scale and operate with minimal budgets. But continued decreases in costs for many of the once-prohibitive technologies, such as remote sensing techniques and total stations, will make the application of these technologies routine.

Archaeologists will continue to explore new avenues of research. Recently emergent areas of interest, such as indigenous archaeology, the archaeology of childhood, the archaeology of the very recent past and contemporary life, and community archaeology, are likely to flourish. Perhaps one of the most enlightening areas will be in the use of DNA research in archaeology.

Archaeological issues, research, and practitioners will become increasingly connected on a global scale. This has already started with popularity of archaeological list serves and the activities of the World Archaeological Congress.

Archaeologists will also continue to find and record many thousands of archaeological sites each year, lament the destruction of sites, and work towards the preservation of the archaeological record.

Final Comments

Introductory archaeology texts are meant to do many things, including familiarize students with the basic objectives, vocabulary, concepts, history, and methods of the discipline. All this information is a lot to remember. At a minimum, here is what I hope all readers retain for years to come, and perhaps pass on to others.

1. *Archaeology is important and relevant to everyday life.* This includes its role in providing the following: (i) contexts for current events, (ii) methodological and theoretical frameworks for collecting and interpreting data, (iii) expertise to support, refute, or assess claims and ideas about the past from diverse people and groups, (iv) an economic base for many people and nations, and (v) ways to understand and cope with contemporary refuse.
2. *The archaeological record is vast.* It includes the material remains of human activity for at least 2.5 million years and from every continent. There are hundreds of thousands of recorded sites and probably billions of recorded artifacts. Tens of thousands of sites and their associated artifacts are added each year.
3. *Archaeology is firmly grounded in scientific method and theory.* This is not usually obvious from the popular press and media, but archaeologists are not treasure hunters.
4. *Archaeological sites are being destroyed at an alarming rate.* Natural processes are agents of destruction, but the loss of sites from industrial development and looting is of greater concern.

5. *Archaeology is filled with bias.* This includes the bias of the archaeological record itself (e.g., inorganic materials are overrepresented), the bias of conceptual frameworks used to investigate the past, and the bias of individuals. The recognition of bias is not necessarily a bad thing. Research in all disciplines is inevitably biased in some way. It is important to understand that alternative explanations almost always exist. There is little certainty about anything in archaeology.
6. *People have been smart for a very long time.* Tool technologies have been around for more than 2 million years; people have been controlling fire for hundreds of thousands of years; sophisticated art has been in evidence for more than 20,000 years; plants and animals were manipulated to the point of domestication more than 10,000 years ago; and civilizations began rising more than 5,000 years ago.

Over the past few decades, the world of archaeology has changed substantially. It is likely to continue changing in all aspects of the discipline. For anyone involved with archaeology as a career or as a mere observer, interesting times are ahead.

Glossary

Absolute dating: Dating that provides specific dates or range of dates, in years. Examples of absolute dating techniques include dendrochronology, radiocarbon, and potassium/argon dating.

Academic archaeology: Archaeology undertaken for intellectual or scholarly reasons and based primarily in colleges, universities, and research museums and institutes.

Agriculture: A subsistence strategy characterized by the intensive cultivation of food plants, often involving the use of plows, draft animals, and irrigation.

Analogy: A form of reasoning based on the premise that if two things are alike in some respects, they may be alike in other respects as well. Many explanations in archaeology, particularly about how sites were created and the function of artifacts, are based on analogy. Analogies in archaeology are commonly drawn from existing ethnographies, ethnoarchaeology, and experimental archaeology.

Anthropology: The evolutionary, holistic, and comparative study of humans. In North America, archaeology is usually considered to be a branch of anthropology.

Antiquarians: Hobby collectors of ancient art and antiquities, particularly from ancient Greece and Rome.

Archaeobiology: A subfield of archaeology focusing on animal and botanical remains recovered from archaeological sites. Archaeobiology includes both archaeobotany and zooarchaeology.

Archaeobotany: A subfield of archaeology focusing on plant remains recovered from archaeological sites; also known as palaeoethnobotany.

Archaeological record: Minimally includes all the material remains documented by archaeologists. More comprehensive definitions also include the record of culture history and everything written about the past by archaeologists.

Archaeological site: Any location where there is physical evidence of human activity. To be defined as an archaeological site, a location need not meet minimum requirements for age or contents, although some government jurisdictions may dictate minimum criteria for inventory purposes.

Archaeological theme park: Extreme versions of heritage tourism, consisting of heritage-related theme parks where entertainment appears to take precedence over archaeological data and interpretations.

Archaeology: The study of humans through their material remains. Most archaeology focuses on the human past and is undertaken within the framework of science.

Archaeomagnetism: An absolute dating technique based on the knowledge that when heated to high temperatures, magnetic particles in clays and other sediments align themselves towards the North Magnetic Pole. *In situ* measurements of particle alignments are correlated with historical records of the location of the North Magnetic Pole.

Archaeometry: Archaeology associated with the methods of natural sciences, such as math and physics, usually used in the analysis of materials.

Argon dating: Absolute dating techniques (potassium/argon and argon/argon) based on the rate at which potassium and radioactive argon change into stable argon gas.

Armchair archaeology: A phrase used to describe both professionals and amateurs who focus on describing or explaining what others have done, without participating in fieldwork themselves.

Artifact: Any object that shows evidence of being manufactured, modified, or used by people. Most archaeologists also restrict the term artifact to items that are portable.

Ascribed: Predetermined by birth.

Atlatl: A spear-thrower usually about a meter long, upon which the spear was laid to effectively increase the length of the arm to power the spear.

Band: A type of society characterized by relatively small groups (usually less than 50) that act autonomously, are egalitarian, and have a subsistence based on generalized foraging.

Behavioral disturbance processes: Human processes such as trampling, scavenging, construction, and looting that affect the original patterning of archaeological remains; also known as cultural disturbance processes and C-transforms.

Behavioral formation processes: Human processes that lead to the creation of archaeological sites, such as deliberate discard, loss, and abandonment; also known as cultural formation processes.

Biblical archaeology: Archaeology that focuses on peoples, places, and events mentioned in the Bible.

Biface: Tools, usually stone, that have been modified on both of the major surfaces.

Big Man: One kind of village leader in tribal societies, with no real power or authority. Also called Head Man.

Bioarchaeology: The study of human remains from archaeological sites.

Bioturbation: Disturbance of archaeological sites by plants and animals.

Blade: A stone tool that is at least twice as long as it is wide, and has at least roughly parallel sides.

Bog men: Dozens of human bodies preserved in the bogs of northern European countries, especially Denmark. Also known as bog people.

bp or **BP**: Abbreviation for *before present*, which is taken to mean AD 1950; used to indicate dates in years before present when materials are dated by radiocarbon dating only.

Bureaucracy: Full-time government workers, characteristic of state-level societies.

C 14 dating: An absolute dating technique based on the known rate of the decay of carbon in organisms, beginning at the instant of death. Also known as carbon 14 and radiocarbon dating.

Cache: A stored quantity of something, usually food or artifacts.

Cache pit: A pit dug into the ground to store something, usually food.

Calibrated relative dating: A category of dating techniques that is a hybrid of absolute and relative techniques.

Capa cocha: An Inka religious ritual involving child sacrifice at high altitudes.

Carbon 14 dating: An absolute dating technique based on the known rate of decay of carbon in organisms, beginning at the instant of death. Also known as C 14 dating and radiocarbon dating.

Ceramic: Baked clay.

Chief: The leader of a chiefdom, with real power and authority.

Chiefdom: A type of society characterized by populations ranging from a few thousand to tens of thousands, marked social inequality, subsistence based on horticulture, and formal positions of leadership.

China: A category of ceramics based on the type of clay and its porosity, and requiring a firing temperature between 1,100 and 1,200 degrees.

Chronological sequencing: A category of relative dating methods that puts sites and objects in sequence. Includes stratigraphic dating, seriation, and *terminus quem.*

Civilization: There is no consensus definition of civilization, but most archaeologists agree a society must have most of the following: monumental architecture, at least one city, a system of writing, an agricultural base, and state-level political organization.

Classical archaeology: Archaeology focusing on the empires of ancient Greece and Rome.

Cognitive archaeology: Archaeology that focuses on ideology; also known as archaeology of the mind.

Collateral damage: Unintended damage. Used primarily in archaeology to describe the impact of military actions on archaeological sites.

Colonial archaeology: Archaeology focusing on the time periods and places under European colonial rule, especially in Australia, Canada, and the United States.

Complex foraging: A subsistence strategy based on gathering and hunting a wide variety of plants and animals, but with a specialization in one type, leading to increasing social complexity.

Conceptual framework: A theoretical framework that guides research; also known as a paradigm, research strategy, research approach, grand theory, and heuristic theory.

Coprolite: Human feces and other animal waste, preserved through drying or mineralization.

Core tools: Stone tools that are produced by removing flakes from the original cobble, with the remaining core of the cobble becoming the tool.

CRM: An acronym for cultural resource management.

C-transforms: Also known as cultural disturbance processes or behavioral disturbance processes, these are human activities that alter the original patterning of archaeological remains, including trampling and construction activities. The term *c-transforms* was widely used in the 1970s and 1980s but is rarely used in the twenty-first century.

Cultural ecology: Focuses on the relationship between people and the natural environment.

Cultural formation processes: The human processes that lead to the creation of archaeological sites, such as deliberate discard, abandonment, and loss; also known as behavioral formation processes.

Cultural landscape: A distinctive geographic area with cultural significance.

Cultural resource management: Archaeology undertaken within the context of the heritage industry, often because archaeological assessments are required by legislation, to be completed in advance of potential disturbance to areas where sites are known or suspected to exist. Often abbreviated as CRM.

Culture: The learned and shared things that people have, do, and think.

Culture area: Broad geographic area in which there are general similarities in cultures. There are ten culture areas in North and Central America (Arctic, Subarctic, Northwest Coast, Interior Plateau, Great Basin, Plains, California, Southwest, Eastern Woodlands, and Mesoamerica).

Culture history: A description of the archaeological record and the chronological sequence of events in an area.

Culture process: How cultures work, including how and why they change.

Culture reconstruction: An interpretation of past lifeways, including subsistence and settlement patterns, social and political strategies, and ideology.

Cuneiform: An early form of writing found in Mesopotamia.

Curation: The process of cataloging, labeling, conserving, and storing artifacts and other material remains.

Dating by association: Dating artifacts and sites by their association with other artifacts, ecofacts, or geological features of known age; a subcategory of relative dating.

Debitage: Waste from the manufacture of artifacts, usually stone. Also known as detritus.

Deep antiquity: A phrase used to convey the long history of humankind, including the 2.5-million-year record of human culture.

Deep time: A phrase used to convey the 15-billion-year history of the universe.

Deity: A god.

Dendrochronology: Tree-ring dating.

Descendant community: A group of people who can trace their ancestry to others who lived in an area. In archaeology, descendant community usually refers to the indigenous peoples of a region.

Descent group: People who trace their common lineal descent from a real or mythological ancestor, including lineages and clans.

Detritus: Waste from the manufacture of artifacts, usually stone. Also known as debitage.

Diachronic change: Change through time.

Diagnostic artifact: An artifact that is characteristic of a particular time, group, or culture.

Diffusion: The spread of ideas.

Dirt archaeology: Fieldwork, including looking for and excavating archaeological sites.

Domestication: There is no consensus definition of domestication in archaeology, but at a minimum it means that plants and/or animals are under the control of humans.

Earthenware: A category of ceramics based on the type of clay and its porosity, and requiring a firing temperature between 900 and 1,200 degrees.

Ecofact: Items from archaeological sites, not recorded as artifacts or features, but that are relevant to archaeological interpretations. Includes animal remains, botanical remains, and sediments.

Ecological archaeology: Archaeology focusing on the relationships between people and natural environments.

Egalitarian: A level of equality where everyone has roughly equal status and access to resources.

Egyptology: A multidisciplinary field of study focusing on ancient Egyptian civilization. Prominent specialties within Egyptology include archaeology, history, and art.

Empire: A special kind of political system that is territorially expansive, with one state exerting control over other states, chiefdoms, tribes, and bands.

Ethnic group: People who share, or once shared, a common language, history, and territory, with members who have a self-conscious identification with the group.

Ethnic marker: Artifacts, features, or other material remains that are indicative of particular ethnic groups.

Ethnoarchaeology: A subfield of archaeology that involves making observations of contemporary people in order to better understand the archaeological record.

Ethnographic analogy: When archaeologists make interpretations of the archaeological record based on similarities observed in ethnographically described cultures.

Ethnography: A written description of a culture, based on first-hand observation by a cultural anthropologist.

Eurocentric: Focused on Europe.

Exoarchaeology: A subfield of archaeology focusing on the physical remains of human space exploration.

Exogamous: Marrying someone from outside one's own group.

Experimental archaeology: Conducting experiments to replicate past conditions and events, and using the results to interpret archaeological remains.

Fabric: Also known as the ceramic body, fabric refers to the composition of the clay.

Faunal remains: Animal remains, including bones, teeth, shells, horns, antlers, fur, hair, nails, claws, talons, and soft tissue.

Faunalturbation: Disturbance of archaeological sites by animals.

Feature A non-portable object that shows evidence of being manufactured, modified, or used by people, or an arrangement of material remains in which patterning is significant.

Flake tools: Stone tools that are made from a flake originally removed from a cobble.

Flintknapping: Manufacturing stone tools by chipping or flaking.

Floralturbation: Disturbance of archaeological sites by plants, including trees.

Fluorine, uranium, nitrogen dating: A relative dating technique based on the premise that after the death of an animal, the relative amounts of fluorine and uranium in bone will increase and the amount of nitrogen will decrease.

Foramen magnum: The hole at the base of the skull through which the spinal cord passes to connect to the brain.

Forensic archaeology: Archaeology done in the context of criminal investigations, including the search for evidence using archaeological methods and the identification of human remains.

Frequency seriation: An archaeological dating technique based on the relative frequency of certain artifact types; based on the premise that artifact types go through a period of acceptance, after which they flourish and then decline.

Frescoe: Decorative painting on a plastered surface.

Garbology: The study of fresh household trash and contemporary landfills.

General theory: Focuses on explaining the significant events of the human past and the nature of culture; also known as grand theory and high-level theory.

Generalized forager: A person who employs a subsistence strategy based on collecting a wide variety of wild food resources, with no primary dependence on one kind.

Geoarchaeology: Archaeology focusing on sediments from sites and the reconstruction of abiotic environments, including natural landscapes.

Geographic Information Systems (GIS): Computer software that allows layering of various types of data to produce complex maps; useful for predicting site location and for representing the analysis of collected data within sites and across regions.

Grand theory: Focuses on explaining the significant events of the human past and the nature of culture; also known as general theory and high-level research.

Grave goods: Items, usually artifacts and food, included with a human burial.

Gray literature: Archaeological reports with limited distribution.

Green movement: A social movement focusing on environmental sustainability and conservation. Also known as environmentalism and conservationism.

Head Man: One kind of village leader in tribal societies, with no real power or authority. Also called Big Man.

Heritage industry: A growth industry involving the promotion, preservation, documentation, assessment, interpretation, and presentation of heritage. In North America, some view cultural resource management to be equivalent to the heritage industry, while others view it to be only a component of the industry.

Heuristic theory: A theoretical framework that guides research; also known as conceptual framework, paradigm, research strategy, research approach, general theory, and grand theory.

Hieroglyphics: The pictorial form of writing used by ancient Egyptians.

High-level research: Archaeological studies that focus on explaining significant events in the human past and the nature of culture in general; also known as grand theory and general theory.

Historic archaeology: Focuses on a time period in an area for which written records exist. Also known as historical archaeology.

Historical particularism: The conceptual framework that suggests the evolutionary course of every culture is unique, disregarding any general laws of cultural evolution.

Holistic: The recognition that all components of a culture are interrelated.

Hominidae: The biological family to which modern humans belong and which appears to have originated several million years ago. Includes the genera *Ardipithecus*, *Australopithecus*, and *Homo*.

Homo: The biological genus to which modern humans belong and which appears to have originated about 2.5 million years ago.

Horizon: A descriptive unit reflecting cultural continuity over a broad area, typically from several hundred to a few thousand years.

Horticulture: A subsistence strategy based on plant cultivation with hand tools only.

Household archaeology: Focuses on individual houses, including the physical characteristics, construction methods, and social uses.

Human waste: Biological waste of humans, including coprolites and cess.

Iconography Forms of art and writing that are thought to symbolically represent ideology.

Ideal data: Data that archaeologists desire to test an hypothesis.

Ideal methods: The preferred methods to obtain data, both in the field and the laboratory.

Indian industry: All the work revolving around the assertions of aboriginal rights, especially in Canada, and specifically regarding the activities of lawyers, historians, sociologists, anthropologists, and archaeologists involved with First Nations claims.

Indigenous archaeology: Archaeology done by, with, or for indigenous peoples; most often associated with the Aborigines of Australia, Native Americans of the United States, and First Nations of Canada.

Industrial archaeology: A subfield focusing on sites and objects of heavy industry such as mining, logging, and power generation.

Inka: Also known as the Inca. The Inka civilization was centered in Peru but developed into an empire that dominated many other groups in western South America for about a century until the conquest by the Spanish in the early 1500s.

In situ: In its original context, undisturbed; literally meaning "in place."

Judgmental sampling: A sampling strategy based on an archaeologist's judgment or opinion of where to look for sites or excavate; also known as non-probabilistic sampling.

Law of superposition: In undeformed sequences of sedimentary rock, each bed is older than the one above it. It is recognized that deformation can fold or overturn sedimentary layers, placing them out of sequence, and that rock can also form from rising magma, making deep layers younger than those above.

Level bags: Bags used by excavators to collect material remains (usually excluding artifacts, which are collected separately) while excavating a particular level in an archaeological site.

Lithic: In archaeology, it usually means stone tool or the waste from stone tool manufacture.

Lithic debitage: Waste from the manufacture of stone tools.

Lithic scatter: A scattering of lithic waste flakes (debitage or detritus) created during the manufacture of stone tools.

Living museums: Museums where people dress in period costume and often reenact the the time being portrayed, such as acting as shopkeepers and blacksmiths.

Low-level research: This generally refers to archaeological field and laboratory work.

Material culture: The physical aspect of culture, such as things that can be touched; distinct from behavior and ideology.

Material remains: The physical remains of human activities and ecofacts.

Matrix: The sediments surrounding the artifacts, features, and ecofacts.

Megalith: A large stone, often in association with others and forming an alignment or monument, such as at Stonehenge and Carnac.

Mesoamerica: Central America, including Mexico.

Mesolithic: The time period from about 11,000 to 9,000 years ago; not commonly used outside of Europe.

Microdebitage: Very small, often microscopic pieces of waste created during the manufacture of artifacts, usually stone.

Microwear: Wear on tools from use by people, usually only seen under magnification.

Midden: A large, discrete accumulation of refuse.

Middle-level research: Refers to research that links field and laboratory work with the grand theories. It focuses on interpreting patterning in archaeological sites, primarily through ethnoarchaeology, experimental archaeology, and studies of taphonomy; also known as middle-range research and middle-range theory.

Middle-range research: See middle-level research.

Middle-range theory: See middle-level research.

Minimum number of individuals: On a broad level, it means the minimum number of individuals of any category of material remains represented by an assemblage of bone. In practice however, it usually refers to the minimum number of individuals of a particular species.

MNI: An acronym for minimum number of individuals.

Monumental architecture: Large-scale construction of buildings, earthworks, and other large features.

Mummy: Well-preserved animal remains (usually human and including soft tissue) that result from drying, including those intentionally dried and those dried through fortuitous circumstances.

Munsell system: The standard system of measuring color in archaeology, based on hue, chroma, and value.

Natural formation processes: The natural processes that bring sediments into archaeological sites, such as through water and air. Also known as non-cultural formation processes.

Neolithic: The time period from about 9,000 to 5,000 years ago; not commonly used outside of Europe.

New archaeology: Also known as processual archaeology, it emerged in the 1960s and focused on using explicit scientific method, attempting to explain (rather than merely describe) culture change. Although common in the 1960s and 1970s, the phrase *new archaeology* is rarely used in the early twenty-first century.

New World: The Americas.

NISP: Acronym for number of identified specimens.

Non-cultural disturbance processes: Natural processes that affect the original patterning of archaeological remains; also known as natural disturbance processes and N-transforms.

Non-cultural formation processes: Processes associated with wind and water that bring natural sediments into archaeological sites; also know as natural formation processes.

Non-probabilistic sampling: A sampling strategy based on an archaeologist's judgment or opinion of where to look for or excavate sites. Also known as judgmental sampling.

N-Transforms: Natural processes that affect the original patterning of archaeological remains; also known as natural disturbance processes and non-cultural disturbance processes. Although common in the 1970s and 1980s, the term *n-transforms* is used rarely in the early twenty-first century.

Obsidian: A fine-grained volcanic stone, classified as a glass. Because of its excellent quality for stone tool manufacture, it was traded widely in prehistory.

Obsidian hydration: A calibrated-relative dating technique, based on the knowledge that freshly exposed surfaces of obsidian adsorb moisture from the surrounding environments in measurable layers.

Ochre: A naturally occurring mineral pigment, usually red and often used in ritual and for color in paints or dyes.

Ofuro: A Japanese bathhouse, constructed with a large hearth made from brick or stone, on top of which was placed a tub with a metal bottom and wooden sides. A building surrounded the tub.

Old World: Africa, Asia, and Europe.

Osteology: The study of the human skeleton.

Palaeoanthropology: The study of early human biology and culture.

Palaeolithic: The time period from about 2.5 million to about 11,000 years ago; commonly referred to as the "Old Stone Age" and subdivided into the Lower, Middle, and Upper Palaeolithic.

Papyri: The writing material produced from plants in ancient Egypt.

Paradigm: A theoretical framework that guides research; also known as conceptual framework, research strategy, research approach, heuristic theory, general theory, and grand theory.

Participant observation: A technique of ethnographic research in which researchers immerse themselves in a culture as both participants and observers.

Pastoralism: A subsistence strategy based on the herding of animals.

Pedological: Having to do with the study of soils. Pedology is also known as soil science.

Petroglyphs: Designs carved or pecked into large boulders, bedrock, or the walls of cliffs, caves, and rock shelters.

pH: A measure of acidity. Archaeologists measure the pH of sediments.

Phase: A descriptive unit reflecting cultural continuity in a region or subregion for a relatively short period (i.e., usually less than 2,000 years).

Phytoliths: Small particles of silica from the cells of plants.

Pictographs: Paintings on large, immovable boulders or bedrock, or the walls of cliffs, caves, and rock shelters.

Piltdown Man: Skeletal remains discovered in Piltdown, England in the early twentieth century, purported to be a "missing link"; eventually revealed as a hoax through the application of fluorine, uranium, nitrogen dating.

Pithouse: Semi-subterranean dwelling, consisting of a large depression in the ground covered with an above-ground roof. The roof is usually supported by a log and pole framework and the roof itself is often comprised of bark and other forms of vegetation overlain with a layer of earth. Entrance may be through the side or top via a ladder.

Population pressure: The condition where human population is at or exceeds the carrying capacity of the environment.

Porcelain: A category of ceramics based on the type of clay and its porosity, and requiring a firing temperature between 1,300 and 1,450 degrees.

Post-colonial archaeology: Archaeology focusing on areas once under European colonial rule and in the time period since independence.

Post-depositional disturbance process Any process, cultural or natural, that affects an archaeological deposit after it was initially created.

Postmodernism: A conceptual framework, generally considered anti-scientific in nature, focusing on the subjectivity of interpretation.

Post-processual archaeology: An umbrella phrase for archaeology done since the 1980s in scholarly, but non-traditional ways, often focusing on topics of ideology, gender, and ethnicity, and explicitly recognizing bias in the undertaking and exploitation of archaeological research.

Potassium/argon dating: An absolute dating technique based on the known rate at which potassium changes to argon in volcanic sediments. Often abbreviated as K/Ar.

Pothunter: A generic term used to describe a person who loots archaeological sites.

Pothunting: A generic term used to describe the looting of archaeological sites.

Potsherd: A broken piece of pottery.

Pottery: Baked clay containers, such as a bowls, cups, jars, and vases.

Pre-Columbian archaeology: Archaeology focusing on the Americas before the arrival of Christopher Columbus; usually used to describe the archaeology of the large chiefdoms and states of Mesoamerica, such as the Maya and Aztec.

Prehistoric archaeology: Archaeology focusing on a time period prior to which written records exist in a given area.

Prehistory: The time before written records were kept in an area. The prehistoric period ends at different times around the world, distinguished by when the inhabitants invented writing or when people with the knowledge of writing entered the area.

Prestige goods: Items that are more a function of high status than practical utility; also known as luxury items. Prestige goods may also include raw materials in short supply.

Primary refuse: Refuse that was abandoned where it was created or used and left undisturbed until found by archaeologists.

Probabilistic sampling: Sampling not biased by any person's judgment or opinion. Also known as statistical sampling and includes simple random sampling, stratified random sampling, and systematic sampling.

Processual archaeology: Also known as the new archaeology, it emerged in the 1960s and focused on using explicit scientific method, attempting to explain (rather than merely describe) culture change.

Provenience: The precise, three-dimensional location of an artifact.

Pseudoarchaeology: The study of the human past based on material remains, but not following the methods of archaeology.

Radiocarbon dating: An absolute dating technique based on the known rate of decay of carbon 14 in organisms after death. Also known as C 14 and carbon 14 dating.

Refuse: An umbrella term used to refer to discarded items, including trash (dry items) and garbage (wet or organic items such as food waste).

Register of Professional Archaeologists (RPA): An international list of archaeologists who meet minimum standards of qualification and agree to abide by a strict code of ethics.

Relative dating: Determining the relative antiquity of sites and objects by putting them in sequential order, but not assigning specific dates.

Religious ritual: Formalized, repetitive acts associated with religious beliefs.

Sacred site: Site with presumed religious or spiritual significance.

Science: A method of inquiry based on the collection of empirical data as well as the formulation, testing, and continual reevaluation of hypotheses.

Seasonal round: Where people will be and what they will be doing within their traditional territory at various times of the year, following a schedule.

Seasonality studies: Determining the time of year a site was occupied.

Secondary refuse: Refuse that was moved from where it was initially created.

Sedentary: Settling permanently.

Segmentary society: A type of society characterized by slight social inequality, subsistence usually based on pastoralism and/or horticulture, and populations ranging from a few hundred to a few thousand spread among many villages. Also known as a tribe.

Semi-sedentary: Semi-permanent settlement pattern.

Seriation: Placing objects in chronological order based on their style (stylistic seriation) or relative frequency (frequency seriation).

Shaman: An individual with a perceived connection to the supernatural world.

Shell midden: An accumulation of refuse with a substantial amount of shell.

Shovelbum: A term applied to itinerant archaeological fieldworkers, who often go from project to project working for various employers in the CRM industry.

Site catchment analysis: Determining the source location of all material remains found in a site.

Site exploitation territory: The area habitually used by a group throughout the year; also known as traditional territory.

Site formation processes: The variety of cultural and natural processes leading to the creation of archaeological sites.

State: A type of society characterized by all or most of the following: large populations, cities, bureaucracies, monumental architecture, writing, and armies.

Stelae: An upright stone, often inscribed; common in both Egypt and Mesoamerica.

Stoneware: A category of ceramics based on the type of clay and its porosity, and requiring a firing temperature between 1,200 and 1,350 degrees.

Stratification: A system of social inequality involving classes, such as lower, middle, or upper class.

Stratigraphic dating: A relative dating technique based on the knowledge that layers of sediments are normally laid on top of each other through time; based on the geological law of superposition.

Stratigraphy: The description or study of the observable layers of sediments.

Stylistic seriation: A relative dating technique based on changing artifact styles through time.

Subsistence looting: The practice of looting sites, usually by local peoples, to provide the basic necessities of life.

Synchronic change: Change over space.

Tangible heritage: The material aspect of heritage, such as artifacts and sites; compared to intangible heritage, which includes such things as folklore and traditions.

Taphonomy: The study of what happens to organic remains after death.

Tell: A term used to describe mounds that have been created by successive settlements in the Middle East, western Asia, and northern Africa.

terminus ante quem: A relative dating technique in which the presence of an object of known age is used to infer that all other finds must be at least as old as that object. Often abbreviated as TAQ.

terminus post quem: A relative dating technique in which the presence of an object of known age is used to infer that all other finds must be no older than that object. Often abbreviated as TPQ.

terminus quem: Relative dating based on finding an object of known age and then inferring that other objects must be either older or more recent than that object.

Terra cotta: A category of ceramics based on specific types of reddish clay and its porosity, and requiring a firing temperature less than 1,000 degrees.

Textiles: Fabrics manufactured by spinning or weaving plant or animal fibers.

Thermoluminescence: An absolute dating technique based on the premise that energy becomes trapped in objects when they are heated to very high temperatures. Reheating the objects releases stored energy in the form of light in a way that can determine the length of time since the object was originally heated. Most commonly used for dating ceramics, but stone tools have also been dated with this technique.

Three-age system: Conceptualizing the past through the Stone, Bronze, and Iron Ages.

Total station: An electronic device that can measure distances, angles, and elevations from a fixed point. It runs on software that allows the data to be downloaded and used to create maps.

Trace-element analysis: Subjecting materials to analysis to determine their composition.

Tradition: A descriptive unit reflecting a pattern of cultural continuity over a broad area for at least a few thousand years.

Traditional territory: The area habitually used by a group throughout the year. Also known as site exploitation territory.

Transegalitarian: A term used to describe societies transitioning between egalitarianism and distinct social inequality.

Trepanation: Removing a piece of bone from the skull of a living person; also known as trephination.

Trephination: Removing a piece of bone from the skull of a living person; also known as trepanation.

Tribe: A intermediate category of society falling between egalitarian foragers and ranked or fully stratified societies, with the beginnings of formal leadership and subsistence usually based on horticulture and/or pastoralism. Exhibits populations between a few hundred and a few thousand, spread among many villages.

Type: A category of artifact based on typology; types may be descriptive and/or functional.

Typology: A system of artifact classification based on physical attributes and/or presumed function.

Underwater archaeology: Archaeology that focuses on sites and objects underwater, including shipwrecks.

Uniface: A stone tool that has been modified on one side only.

Uniformitarianism: A geological principle often articulated as "the present is the key to past," meaning that the geological processes in operation today are the same as those that operated in the past. The implication is that since most geological processes are relatively slow, the earth must be very old.

Unilinear theory of cultural evolution: A theory developed in the nineteenth century that proposed cultural evolution was on a singular course and people in various stages of that course could be classified as either savages, barbarians, or civilized.

Venus figurines: Small (about 4 1/2 inches or 11 centimeters on average) figures made from stone, clay, and antler, usually depicting women. Found in Europe and dating to between 20,000 and 30,000 years ago.

World Heritage Sites: Sites receiving designation from the United Nations Educational, Scientific, and Cultural Organization (UNESCO) in recognition of their high significance.

Zooarchaeology: The study of animal remains from archaeological sites.

Bibliography

This bibliography provides complete information on all the articles and books cited within or at the end of chapters, as well as some other important sources for students interested in expanding their knowledge of archaeology. It also includes some of the principal sources the author consulted but that are not cited in the text. In addition to those sources listed here, readers are encouraged to peruse the periodicals listed in Table 3.1 (page 47) and use Internet search engines for scholarly research, such as scholar.google.com.

Allison, Penelope M. (ed). 1999. *The Archaeology of Household Activities.* New York: Routledge.

Ames, Kenneth M., Doria F. Raetz, Stephen Hamilton, and Christine McAfee. 1992. Household Archaeology of a Southern Northwest Coast Plank House. *Journal of Field Archaeology* 19: 275–90.

Association Research Inc. 2005. Salary Survey Conducted for the Society for American Archaeology in Cooperation with the Society for Historical Archaeology. Rockville, Maryland.

Aufderheide, Arthur C. 2003. *The Scientific Study of Mummies.* New York: University of Cambridge Press.

——. 2000. *Archaeology: A Very Short Introduction.* Oxford: Oxford University Press.

Bahn, Paul. 1989. *Bluff Your Way in Archaeology.* London: Ravette.

Bahn, Paul (ed). 2001. *The Penguin Archaeology Guide.* New York: Penguin Putnam.

Banning, E.B. 2000. *The Archaeologist's Laboratory: The Analysis of Archaeological Data.* New York: Kluwer.

Bass, William M. 1971. *Human Osteology: A Laboratory and Field Manual of the Human Skeleton.* Columbia, MI: Missouri Archaeological Society.

Baumann, Timothy. 2004. African American Ethnicity. *SAA Archaeological Record* 4: 16–20.

Baxter, Jane Eva. 2005. *The Archaeology of Childhood.* Walnut Creek, CA: Altamira.

Bayman, James M. and Miriam T. Stark (eds). 2000. *Exploring the Past: Readings in Archaeology.* Durham, NC: Carolina Academic Press.

Beattie, Owen and John Geiger. 1988. *Frozen in Time: The Fate of the Franklin Expedition.* Saskatoon: Western Producer Prairie Books.

Belk, Russell W. 1995. *Collecting in a Consumer Society.* New York: Routledge.

Bell, Martin. 2004. Archaeology and Green Issues. In *A Companion to Archaeology*, edited by John Bintliff, pp. 509–31. Oxford, UK: Blackwell.

Berman, Judith C. 1999. Bad Hair Days in the Paleolithic: Modern (Re)Constructions of the Cave Man. *American Anthropologist* 101: 288–304.

Bintliff, John (ed). 2004. *A Companion to Archaeology*. Oxford, UK: Blackwell.

Bintliff, J.L. and C.F. Gaffney (eds). 1986. Archaeology at the Interface: Studies in Archaeology's Relationships with History, Geography, Biology and Physical Science. *British Archaeological Reports, International Series* 300.

Black, Stephen L. and Kevin Jolly. 2003. *Archaeology by Design*. Walnut Creek, CA: Altamira.

Bocek, Barbara. 1992. The Jasper Ridge Reexcavation Experiment: Rates of Artifact Mixing by Rodents. *American Antiquity* 57(2): 261–69

Bradley, Bruce and Dennis Stanford. 2004. The North Atlantic Ice-Edge Corridor: A Possible Palaeolithic Route to the New World. *World Archaeology* 36: 459–79.

Brodie, Neil, Jennifer Doole, and Colin Renfrew (eds). 2001. *Trade in Illicit Antiquities: The Destruction of the World's Archaeological Heritage*. Cambridge, UK: McDonald Institute for Archaeological Research.

Brodie, Neil and Colin Renfrew. 2005. Looting and the World's Heritage: The Inadequate Response. *Annual Reviews in Anthropology* 34: 343–61.

Brodie, Neil and Kathryn Walker Tubb (eds). 2002. *Illicit Antiquities: The Theft of Culture and the Extinction of Archaeology*. New York: Routledge.

Brothwell, D.R. and A.M. Pollard (eds). 2001. *Handbook of Archaeological Sciences*. New York: Wiley.

Burke, Heather and Claire Smith. 2004. *The Archaeologist's Field Handbook*. Crows Nest, Australia: Allen & Unwin.

Canti, M.G. 2003. Earthworm Activity and Archaeological Stratigraphy: A Review of Products and Processes. *Journal of Archaeological Science* 30: 135–48.

Carman, John. 2002. *Archaeology and Heritage: An Introduction*. New York: Continuum.

Carman, John (ed). 1997. *Material Harm: Archaeological Studies of War and Violence*. Glasgow: Cruithne Press.

Chamberlain, Andrew T. and Michael Parker Pearson. 2001. *Earthly Remains: The History and Science of Preserved Human Bodies*. New York: Oxford University Press.

Chapman, John. 1994. Destruction of a Common Heritage: The Archaeology of War in Croatia, Bosnia, and Hercegovina. *Antiquity* 68: 120–26.

Chisholm, Brian S., D. Erle Nelson, and Henry P. Schwarcz. 1983. Marine and Terrestrial Protein in Prehistoric Diets on the British Columbia Coast. *Current Anthropology* 24: 396–98.

Clark, Geoffrey A. 2003. American Archaeology's Uncertain Future. In *Archeology Is Anthropology: Archeological Papers of the American Anthropological Association* vol. 13, no. 1, edited by Susan D. Gillespie and Deborah L. Nichols, pp. 51–67. Arlington, VA: American Anthropological Association.

Cleere, Henry (ed). 1989. *Archaeological Heritage Management in the Modern World*. London: Unwin Hyman.

Coates, Karen J. 2005. Plain of Jars: The Explosive Implications of Archaeology at Laos' Most Puzzling Site. *Archaeology* 58(4): 30–35.

Coles, John. 1973. *Archaeology by Experiment.* New York: Scribner.

Coningham, Robin and Ruth Young. 1999. The Archaeological Visibility of Caste: An Introduction. In *Case Studies in Archaeology and World Religion*, edited by Timothy Insoll, pp. 84–93. Oxford, UK: Archaeopress.

Cooper, Malcolm A., Antony Firth, John Carman, and David Wheatley (eds). 1995. *Managing Archaeology.* New York: Routledge.

Corbey, Raymond, Robert Layton, and Jeremy Tanner. 2004. Archaeology and Art. In *A Companion to Archaeology*, edited by John Bintliff, pp. 357–79. Oxford, UK: Blackwell.

Crass, Barbara A. 1999. Gender in Inuit Burial Practices. In *Reading the Body: Representations and Remains in the Archaeological Record*, edited by Alison E. Rautman, pp. 68–76. Philadelphia: University of Pennsylvania Press.

Cunliffe, Barry, Wendy Davies, and Colin Renfrew (eds). 2002. *Archaeology: The Widening Debate.* New York: Oxford University Press.

Daniel, Glyn. 1981. *A Short History of Archaeology.* London: Thames and Hudson.

Dark, K.R. 1995. *Theoretical Archaeology.* Ithaca, NY: Cornell University Press.

David, Nicholas and Carol Kramer. 2001. *Ethnoarchaeology in Action.* New York: Cambridge University Press.

Deetz, James. 1967. *Invitation to Archaeology.* Garden City, NY: The Natural History Press.

De Laet, S.J., A.H. Dani, J.L. Lorenzo, and R.B. Nunoo. 1994. *History of Humanity: Vol. 1, Prehistory and the Beginnings of Civilization.* New York: UNESCO and Routledge.

Delgado, James P. (ed). 1997. *Encyclopedia of Underwater and Maritime Archaeology.* London: British Museum Press.

Derry, Linda and Maureen Malloy (eds). 2003. *Archaeologists and Local Communities: Partners in Exploring the Past.* Washington, DC: Society for American Archaeology.

Deur, Douglas and Nancy J. Turner (eds). 2005. *Keeping It Living: Traditions of Plant Use and Cultivation on the Northwest Coast of North America.* Vancouver: UBC Press.

Diamond, Jared. 2005. *Collapse: How Societies Choose to Fail or Succeed.* New York: Viking.

——. 1987. The Worst Mistake in the History of the Human Race. *Discover*, May 1987.

Dickson, D. Bruce and David L. Carlson. 2002. *Ancient Preludes, 2e.* Peosta, Iowa: Eddie Bowers Publishing.

Dickson, James H., Klaus Oeggl, and Linda L. Handley. 2003. The Iceman Reconsidered. *Scientific American*, May: 114–23.

Dincauze, D.F. 2000. *Environmental Archaeology: Principles and Practice.* New York: Cambridge University Press.

Ebert, David 2004. Applications of Archaeological GIS. *Canadian Journal of Archaeology* 28: 319–41.

Evans, Susan Toby. 2004. *Ancient Mexico and Central America: Archaeology and Culture History.* New York: Thames and Hudson.

Fagan, Brian M. 2006. *Archaeology: A Brief Introduction, 9e.* Upper Saddle River, NJ: Pearson.

——. 2005. *A Brief History of Archaeology: Classical Times to the Twenty-first Century.* Upper Saddle River, NJ: Pearson.

——. 2004. *Ancient Lives: An Introduction to Archaeology and Prehistory, 2e.* Upper Saddle River, NJ: Pearson.

Fagan, Brian M. (ed). 1996. *The Oxford Companion to Archaeology.* New York: Oxford.

Feder, Kenneth L. 2006. *Frauds, Myths, and Mysteries: Science and Pseudoscience in Archaeology, 5e.* New York: McGraw-Hill.

——. 2004. *Linking to the Past: A Brief Introduction to Archaeology.* New York: Oxford University Press.

Ferris, Neal. 2003. Between Colonial and Indigenous Archaeologies: Legal and Extra-Legal Ownership of the Archaeological Past in North America. *Canadian Journal of Archaeology* 27: 154–90.

Gallivan, Martin D. 2002. Measuring Sedentariness and Settlement Population: Accumulations Research in the Middle Atlantic Region. *American Antiquity* 67(2): 535–57.

Gathercole, Peter and David Lowenthal (eds). 1994. *The Politics of the Past.* New York: Routledge.

Gero, Joan and Delores Root. 1994. Public Presentations and Private Concerns: Archaeology in the pages of National Geographic. In *The Politics of the Past,* edited by Peter Gathercole and David Lowenthal, pp. 19–37. New York: Routledge.

Gillespie, Susan D. and Deborah L. Nichols (eds). 2003. *Archeology Is Anthropology.* Archeological Papers of the American Anthropological Association, no. 13. Arlington, VA: American Anthropological Association.

Grant, Jim, Sam Gorin, and Neil Fleming. 2002. *The Archaeology Coursebook.* New York: Routledge.

Hackett, Abigail and Robin Dennell. 2003. Neanderthals As Fiction in Archaeological Narrative. *Antiquity* 77: 816–27.

Harris, Charles H. III, and Louis R. Sadler. 2003. *The Archaeologist Was a Spy: Sylvanus G. Morley and the Office of Naval Intelligence.* Albuquerque: University of New Mexico Press.

Hassan, Fekri. 1978. Demographic Archaeology. In *Advances in Archaeological Method and Theory, vol. 1,* edited by Michael B. Schiffer, pp. 49–103. New York: Academic Press.

Hayden, Brian. 2003. Were Luxury Foods the First Domesticates? Ethnoarchaeological Perspectives from Southeast Asia. *World Archaeology* 34: 458–69.

——. 1997. *The Pithouses of Keatley Creek: Complex Hunter-Gatherers of the Northwest Plateau.* New York: Harcourt Brace.

Hayden, Brian and Aubrey Cannon. 1983. Where the Garbage Goes: Refuse Disposal in the Maya Highlands. *Journal of Anthropological Archaeology* 2: 117–63.

Hegmon, Michelle. 2003. Setting Theoretical Egos Aside: Issues and Theory in North American Archaeology. *American Antiquity* 68: 213–43.

Hester, Thomas R., Harry J. Shafer, and Kenneth L. Feder. 1997. *Field Methods in Archaeology, 7e.* New York: McGraw-Hill.

Hilton, M.R. 2003. Quantifying Postdepositional Redistribution of the Archaeological Record Produced by Freeze-Thaw and Other Mechanisms: An Experimental Approach. *Journal of Archaeological Method and Theory* 10: 165–202.

Hodder, Ian. 2003. *Archaeology Beyond Dialogue.* Salt Lake City: University of Utah Press.

Holtorf, Cornelius. 2005. *From Stonehenge to Las Vegas: Archaeology as Popular Culture.* Walnut Creek, CA: Altamira.

James, S.R. 1997. Methodological Issues Concerning Screen Size Recovery Rates and Their Effects on Archaeofaunal Interpretation. *Journal of Archaeological Science* 24 (5): 385–97.

Jameson, John H. Jr., John E. Ehrenhard, and Christine A. Finn (eds). 2003. *Ancient Muses: Archaeology and the Arts.* Tuscaloosa: University of Alabama Press.

Johnson, Matthew. 1999. *Archaeological Theory: An Introduction.* Oxford, UK: Blackwell.

Jones, Sian. 1997. *The Archaeology of Ethnicity: Constructing Identities in the Past and Present.* New York: Routledge.

Keely, Lawrence H. and Nicholas Toth. 1981. Microwear Polishes on Early Stone Tools from Koobi Fora, Kenya. *Nature* 293: 464–65.

Kehoe, Alice Beck. 1998. *The Land of Prehistory: A Critical History of American Archaeology.* New York: Routledge.

Kelly, Jane H. and Ronald F. Williamson. 1996. The Positioning of Archaeology within Anthropology: A Canadian Historical Perspective. *American Antiquity* 61: 5–20.

King, Thomas F. 2005. *Doing Archaeology: A Cultural Resource Management Perspective.* Walnut Creek, CA: Left Coast Press.

Kohl, Philip L. 1998. Nationalism and Archaeology: On the Constructions of Nations and the Reconstructions of the Remote Past. *Annual Reviews in Anthropology* 27: 223–46.

Kohl, Philip L. and Clare Fawcett (eds). 1995. *Nationalism, Politics, and the Practice of Archaeology.* New York: Cambridge University Press.

Konefes, John L. and Michael K. McGee. Old Cemeteries, Arsenic, And Health Safety. [http://waterindustry.org/arsenic-3.htm]. Accessed February 28, 2003.

Larsen, Clark Spencer. 1997. *Bioarchaeology: Interpreting Human Behavior from the Human Skeleton.* New York: Cambridge University Press.

Leone, Mark P., Cheryl Janifer LaRoche, and Jennifer J. Babiarz. 2005. The Archaeology of Black Americans in Recent Times. *Annual Reviews in Anthropology* 34: 575–98.

Little, Barbara J. (ed). 2002. *Public Benefits of Archaeology.* Gainesville: University of Florida Press.

Loy, Thomas H. and E. James Dixon. 1998. Blood Residues on Fluted Points from Eastern Beringia. *American Antiquity* 63(1): 21–46.

Lyman, R. Lee. 1994. Quantitative Units and Terminology in Zooarchaeology. *American Antiquity* 59(1): 36–71

Macinnes, Lesley and C.R. Wickham-Jones (eds). 1992. *All Natural Things: Archaeology and the Green Debate.* Oxford, UK: Oxbow.

Maschner, Herbert D.G. and Christopher Chippendale (eds). 2005 *Handbook of Archaeological Methods, vols. 1 and 2.* New York: Altamira Press.

——. 2004. Between Racism and Romanticism, Scientism and Spiritualism: The Dilemmas of New World Archaeology. In *Archaeology on the Edge: New Perspectives from the Northern Plains*, edited by Brian Kooyman and Jane Kelley, pp. 13–22. Calgary: University of Calgary Press.

McGhee, Robert. 1989. Who Owns Prehistory? The Bering Land Bridge Dilemma. *Canadian Journal of Archaeology* 13: 59–70.

McIntosh, Jane. 1999. *The Practical Archaeologist, 2e.* New York: Checkmark Books.

Meltzer, David J. 2003. Peopling of North America. *Developments in Quaternary Science* 1: 539–63.

Monks, Gregory G. 1981. Seasonality Studies. In *Advances in Archaeological Method and Theory, vol. 4*, edited by Michael B. Schiffer, pp. 177–240. New York: Academic Press.

Moore, Lawrence E. 2005. A Forecast for American Archaeology. *The SAA Archaeological Record* 5(4): 13–16.

Morwood, M.J., R.P. Soejono, R.G. Roberts, T. Sutikna, C.S.M. Turney, K.E. Westaway, W.J. Rink, J. Zhao, G.D. van den Bergh, Rokus Awe Due, D.R. Hobbs, M.W. Moore, M.I. Bird, and L.K. Fifield. 2004. Archaeology and Age of a New Hominin from Flores in Eastern Indonesia. *Nature* 43: 1087–91.

——. 2004. Archaeology of Nikkei Logging Camps in North Vancouver. *Nikkei Images* 9(4): 1–3.

Muckle, Robert. 1994. Differential Recovery of Mollusk Shell from Archaeological Sites. *Journal of Field Archaeology* 21: 129–31.

Murray, Tim (ed). 1999. *Time and Archaeology.* New York: Routledge.

Nelson, Sarah Milledge. 1997. *Gender in Archaeology: Analyzing Power and Prestige.* Walnut Creek, CA: Altamira.

Nicholas, George and Thomas D. Andrews (eds). 1997. *At a Crossroads: Archaeology and First Peoples in Canada.* Burnaby, BC: Arch Press.

Nicholas, George and Kelly P. Bannister. 2004. Copyrighting the Past? Emerging Intellectual Property Rights and Issues in Archaeology. *Current Anthropology* 45: 327–50.

O'Brien, Michael, R. Lee Lyman, and Michael Brian Schiffer. 2005. *Archaeology as Process: Processualism and Its Progeny.* Salt Lake City: University of Utah Press.

Odell, George H. 2004. *Lithic Analysis.* New York: Kluwer.

O'Neil, Dennis H. 1993. Excavation Sample Size: A Cautionary Tale. *American Antiquity* 58(3): 523–29.

Ortner, Donald J. 2003. *Identification of Pathological Conditions in Human Skeletal Remains, 2e.* New York: Academic Press.

Orton, Clive. 2000. *Sampling in Archaeology.* New York: Cambridge University Press.

Orton, Clive, Paul Tyers, and Alan Vince. 1993. *Pottery in Archaeology.* New York Cambridge University Press.

Patrick, Linda E. 1985. Is There An Archaeological Record? In *Advances in Archaeological Method and Theory, vol. 8*, edited by M.B. Schiffer, pp. 27–62. New York: Academic Press.

Patterson, Thomas C. 1999. The Political Economy of Archaeology in the United States. *Annual Reviews in Anthropology* 28: 155–74.

Pearson, James L. 2002. *Shamanism and the Ancient Mind: A Cognitive Approach to Archaeology.* Walnut Creek, CA: Altamira.

Peregrine, Peter N. 2001a. *Archaeological Research: A Brief Introduction.* Upper Saddle River, NJ: Pearson Prentice Hall.

——. 2001b. Introduction. In *Outline of Archaeological Traditions*, compiled by Peter Peregrine. New Haven, CT: HRAF Press.

Peregrine, Peter N. and Melvin Ember (eds). 2001. *Encyclopedia of Prehistory* (9 vols.). New York: Kluwer.

Poirier, David A. and Kenneth L. Feder. 2001. *Dangerous Places: Health, Safety, and Archaeology.* Westport, CT: Bergin and Garvey.

Price, T. Douglas and Gary M. Feinman. 2001. *Images of the Past, 3e.* Mountain View, CA: Mayfield.

Pringle, Heather. 2006. *The Master Plan: Himmler's Scholars and the Holocaust.* New York: Hyperion.

Pyburn, K. Anne (ed). 2004. *Ungendering Civilization.* New York: Routledge.

Quinlan, Angus R. and Alanah Woody. 2003. Marks of Distinction: Rock Art and Ethnic Identification in the Great Basin. *American Antiquity* 68(2): 372–90.

Rapp, George Jr. and Christopher L. Hill. 1998. *Geoarchaeology: The Earth Science Approach to Archaeological Interpretation.* New Haven, CT: Yale University Press.

Rathje, W.L. 2002. Garbology: The Archaeology of Fresh Garbage. In *Public Benefits of Archaeology*, edited by Barbara J. Little, pp. 85–100. Gainesville: University of Florida Press.

Rathje, W.L., W.W. Hughes, D.C. Wilson, M.K. Tani, G.H. Archer, R.G. Hunt, and T.W. Jones. 1992. The Archaeology of Contemporary Landfills. *American Antiquity* 57: 437–47.

Rathje, W.L. and C. Murphy. 1992. *Rubbish! The Archaeology of Garbage.* New York: Harper.

Rautman, Alison E. (ed). 2000. *Reading the Body: Representations and Remains in the Archaeological Record.* Philadelphia: University of Pennsylvania Press.

Reinhard, Karl J. and Vaughn M. Bryant, Jr. 1992. Coprolite Analysis: A Biological Perspective on Archaeology. In *Archaeological Method and Theory*, edited by Michael B. Schiffer, pp. 245–88. Tucson: University of Arizona Press.

Renfrew, Colin. 2000. *Loot, Legitimacy, and Ownership: The Ethical Crisis in Archaeology.* London: Duckworth.

——. 1994. *The Archaeology of Religion.* In *The Ancient Mind: Elements of Cognitive Archaeology*, edited by Colin Renfrew and Ezra B.W. Zubrow, pp. 47–54. New York: Cambridge University Press.

Renfrew, Colin and Paul Bahn. 2004. *Archaeology: Theories, Methods, and Practice, 4e.* London, UK: Thames and Hudson.

Renfrew, Colin and Paul Bahn (eds). 2005. *Archaeology: The Key Concepts.* New York: Routledge.

Renfrew, Colin and Ezra B.W. Zubrow (eds). 1994. *The Ancient Mind: Elements of Cognitive Archaeology.* New York: Cambridge University Press.

Rice, Prudence M. 1987. *Pottery Analysis: A Sourcebook.* Chicago: University of Chicago Press.

Richards, Thomas H. and Michael K. Rousseau. 1987. *Late Prehistoric Cultural Horizons on the Canadian Plateau.* Burnaby, BC: Simon Fraser University Archaeology Press.

Roper, D.C. 1979. The Method and Theory of Site Catchment Analysis: A Review. In *Advances in Archaeological Method and Theory, vol. 2*, edited by Michael B. Schiffer, pp. 119–40. New York: Academic Press.

Roskams, Steve. 2001. *Excavation.* New York: Cambridge University Press.

Rowan, Yorke and Uzi Baram (eds). 2004. *Marketing Heritage: Archaeology and the Consumption of the Past.* Walnut Creek, CA: Altamira.

Russell, Miles (ed). 2002. *Digging Holes in Popular Culture: Archaeology and Science Fiction.* Oxford, UK: Oxbow Books.

Salzman, Philip Carl. 2004. Thinking Theoretically. In *Thinking Anthropologically: A Practical Guide for Students*, edited by Philip Carl Salzman and Patricia C. Rice, pp. 29–38. Upper Saddle River, New Jersey: Pearson Prentice Hall.

Scarre, Chris. 1990. The Western World View in Archaeological Atlases. In *The Politics of the Past*, edited by Peter Gathercole and David Lowenthal, pp. 11–17. London: Unwin Hyman.

Schiffer, Michael B. 1987. *Formation Processes of the Archaeological Record.* Albuquerque: University of New Mexico Press.

Schiffer, Michael B. (ed). 1978–87. *Advances in Archaeological Method and Theory, vol. 1–11.* New York: Academic Press.

Schnapp, Alain. 1996. *The Discovery of the Past.* London: British Museum Press.

Scholfield, John, William Gray Johnson, and Colleen M. Beck (eds). 2002. *Materiel Culture: The Archaeology of Twentieth-Century Conflict.* New York: Routledge.

Shackley, Myra L. (1975). *Archaeological Sediments: A Survey of Analytical Methods.* New York: Wiley.

Shanks, Michael. 1992. *Experiencing the Past: On the Character of Archaeology.* New York: Routledge.

Shanks, Michael and Randall H. McGuire. 1996. The Craft of Archaeology. *American Antiquity* 61: 75–88.

Sharer, Robert J. and Wendy Ashmore. 2003. *Discovering Our Past, 3e.* New York: McGraw-Hill.

Shennan, Stephen J. (ed). 1989. *Archaeological Approaches to Cultural Identity.* London: Unwin Hyman.

Sinopoli, Carla M. 1991. *Approaches to Archaeological Ceramics.* New York. Plenum.

Smith, Claire. 2004. On Intellectual Property Rights and Archaeology. *Current Anthropology* 45: 527.

Smith, Laurajane. 2004. *Archaeological Theory and the Politics of Cultural Heritage.* New York: Routledge.

Sobolik, Kristin D. 2003. *Archaeobiology.* Walnut Creek, CA: Altamira.

Spindler, Konrad. 1994. *The Man in the Ice.* Toronto: Doubleday.

Stacey, Rebecca and Matthew Collins. 2000. Detecting Milk Proteins in Ancient Pots. *Nature* 408: 312.

Stein, Julie K. 1983. Earthworm Activity: A Source of Potential Disturbance of Archaeological Sediments. *American Antiquity* 48: 277–89.

Stein, Julie K., Jennie N. Deo, and Laura S. Phillips. 2003. Big Sites–Short Time: Accumulation Rates in Archaeological Sites. *Journal of Archaeological Science* 30: 297–316.

Stiebing, William H. Jr. 1993. *Uncovering the Past: A History of Archaeology*. Buffalo: Prometheus.

Stockton, Eugene D. 1973. Shaw's Creek Shelter: Human Displacement of Artefacts and Its Significance. *Mankind* 9: 112–17.

Stone, Peter G. and Phillipe G. Planel (eds). 1999. *The Constructed Past: Experimental Archaeology, Education, and the Public*. New York: Routledge.

Stringer, Chris and Peter Andrews. 2005. *The Complete World of Human Evolution*. New York: Thames and Hudson.

Sutton, Mark Q. and Robert M. Yohe II. 2003. *Archaeology: The Science of the Human Past*. New York: Pearson.

Tainter, Joseph A. 2004. Persistent Dilemmas in American Cultural Resource Management. In *A Companion to Archaeology*, edited by John Bintliff. Oxford, UK: Blackwell.

Thomas, David Hurst and Robert L. Kelly. 2006. *Archaeology, 4e*. Belmont, CA: Wadsworth.

Trigger, Bruce. 1989. *A History of Archaeological Thought*. New York: Cambridge University Press.

Tudge, Colin. 1996. *The Time Before History: Five Million Years of Human Impact*. New York: Scribner.

VanPool, Christine S. and Todd L. VanPool. 1999. The Scientific Nature of Postprocessualism. *American Antiquity* 64: 33–53.

Waters, Michael R. and David D. Kuehn. 1996. The Geoarchaeology of Place: The Effect of Geological Processes on the Preservation and Interpretation of the Archaeological Record. *American Antiquity* 61(3): 483–97.

Watkins, Joe. 2005. Through Wary Eyes: Indigenous Perspectives on Archaeology. *Annual Reviews in Anthropology* 34: 429–49.

——. 2003. Beyond the Margin: American Indians, First Nations, and Archaeology in North America. *American Antiquity* 68: 273–85.

——. 2001. *Indigenous Archaeologies: American Indian Values and Scientific Practice*. Walnut Creek, CA: Altamira.

Watson, Patty Jo. 1973. The Future of Archaeology in Anthropology: Culture History and Social Science. In *Research and Theory in Current Archaeology*, edited by Charles L. Redman, pp. 113-24. New York: Wiley.

Wenke, Robert J. 1999. *Patterns in Prehistory: Humankind's First Three Million Years, 4e*. New York: Oxford University Press.

White, Tim D. and Pieter Arend Folkens. 2000. *Human Osteology, 2e*. New York: Academic Press.

Whitley, David S. (ed). 1998. *Reader in Archaeological Theory: Post-Processual and Cognitive Approaches*. New York: Routledge.

Wiber, Melanie. 1997. *Erect Men/Undulating Women: The Visual Imagery of Gender, "Race" and Progress in Reconstructive Illustrations of Human Evolution*. Waterloo, Ontario: Wilfrid Laurier University Press.

Wilk, Richard R. 1985. The Ancient Maya and the Political Present. *Journal of Anthropological Research* 41: 307–26.

Willey, G.R. and J.A. Sabloff. 1993. *A History of American Archaeology*. New York: Freeman.

Wood, W. Raymond and Donald Lee Johnson. 1978. A Survey of Disturbance Processes in Archaeological Site Formation. In *Advances in Archaeological Method and Theory, vol. 1*, edited by M.B. Schiffer, pp. 315–81. New York: Academic Press.

Wright, Ronald. 2004. *A Short History of Progress.* Toronto: Anansi Press.

Wylie, Alison. 2002. *Thinking from Things: Essays in the Philosophy of Archaeology.* Berkeley, CA: University of California Press.

Yalouri, Eleana. 2001. *The Acropolis: Global Fame, Local Claim.* New York: Berg.

Yoffee, Norman and George L. Cowgill (eds). 2001. *The Collapse of Ancient States and Civilizations.* Tucson: University of Arizona Press.

Zangger, Eberhard. 2001. *The Future of the Past: Archaeology in the 21st Century.* Translated from the German edition by Storm Dunlop. London, UK: Weidenfeld and Nicholson.

Zimmerman, Larry J., Karen D. Vitelli, and Julie Hollowell-Zimmer (ed). 2003. *Ethical Issues in Archaeology.* Walnut Creek, CA: Altamira.

Sources

Figures 1.1 "The Parthenon on the Acropolis of Athens," 4.1 "Carnac, France,", and 4.2 "Pictographs from Kakadu, Australia" reproduced by permission of Gillian Crowther.

Figure 1.2 "Machu Picchu, Peru" reproduced by permission of Graham Giles.

Figure 1.3 "Mystery Park, Switzerland." Mystery Park Image #21. Copyright © by Mystery Park, [www.mysterypark.ch]. Reproduced by permission.

Figure 1.4 "Angkor, Cambodia" reproduced by permission of Alexa Love.

Figure 2.1"The Rosetta Stone." Copyright © The Trustees of The British Museum. Reproduced by permission.

Figure 2.2 "Carter No: 255; Handlist description: Third (innermost) coffin of gold; Burton photograph: p0770." Copyright © Griffith Institute, Oxford. Reproduced by permission.

Figure 2.3 "A Statue of Louis Leakey" and Figure 3.3 "Mesa Verde, the Cliff Palace, general view." *Images of Anthropology* (CD). Copyright © Barry D. Kass/Images of Anthropology. Reproduced by permission of the photographer.

Figure 2.4 "Terra Cotta Warriors" reproduced by permission of Vickie Pavlovick.

Figure 4.3 "Chilkoot Trail" reproduced by permission of Casey McLaughlin.

Figures 4.4 "Pompeii" and 9.3 "Roman Coliseum" reproduced by permission of Carmen White.

Figure 4.5 "Man in Ice" reproduced by permission of Owen Beattie.

Figures 5.5 "Large-scale excavations in Peru," 9.1 "Burial with grave goods," and 10.2 "Tikal, Guatemala" reproduced by permission of Suzanne Villeneuve.

Figures 6.3 "Projectile point" and 7.2 "Hominid skulls" reproduced by permission of June Hunter.

Figure 7.1 "Profile of Flores Island site."Morwood, Mike, et al. "Figure 4: Stratigraphic section of the Sector VII excavation at Liang Bua, showing the location of the hominin skeleton." "Archaeology and age of a new hominin from Flores in eastern Indonesia." Reprinted by permission from Macmillan Publishers Ltd.

Figure 9.2 "Castle in France" reproduced by permission of James Morfopoulos

Figure 10.3 "Hummingbird glyph on the Nasca Desert." Aerial View of Nazca Hummingbird Geoglyph (created ca.200 B.C-600A.D.). CJ005830 (RM). Photographer: Charles Lenars, ca. July 1977. Copyright © Charles & Josette Lenars/CORBIS. Reproduced by permission.

The publisher has endeavored to contact rights holders of all copyright material and would appreciate receiving any information as to errors or omissions.

Index